The Altered I

Memoir of Holocaust Survivor

Joseph Kempler

Joseph Kempler

As Told to April Voytko Kempler

April Voytko Kempler

The author attempted to recreate events, locales and conversations from the information provided by Holocaust survivor, Joseph Kempler as accurately as possible. In order to maintain anonymity, in some instances, she has changed some identifying characteristics and details such as physical properties, occupations and places of residence.

For information or additional copies, contact LeRue Press (LRP), 280 Greg Street, Suite 10, Reno, NV 89502

Cover art created by LeRue Press
www.lrpnv.com

Cover photo Mauthausen, Austria: Paul Kempler
Cover photo of Joseph Kempler's eye: Eden Rose Photography
Photo of April Kempler, back cover: Paul Kempler

Library of Congress Cataloging-in-Publication Data

Kempler, April Voytko
       The Altered I: Memoir of Holocaust Survivor, Joseph
       Kempler/April Voytko Kempler
       p. c.m
       ISBN 978-1-938814-01-3
       I. Title

2013954057
CIP

First Edition, November, 2013
10 9 8 7 6 5 4 3 2 1

Printed on FSC paper, responsibly sourced

Dedication

This book is dedicated to a number of people without whom it would not be possible.

To Joseph Kempler: Without you, Joe, there wouldn't be a story.

To my husband, Paul, who encouraged me to write his father's story and supported me energetically throughout this endeavor.

To my parents, Tom and Sally, who gave me a love of books and reading.

And to those thousands of individuals who stood firm in their faith, your shining example continues to inspire me.

Acknowledgements

Joe is an amazing storyteller. His open and honest opinions surprised, pleased, and sometimes shocked me. In addition to his excellent memory, his grasp of historical details proved faultless. Although I have taken the liberty of reconstructing some of the conversations and dialogue, all events are how Joe described them. Joe had a photographic memory. He need only read something once and it was locked into his memory forever. This ability is certainly a bonus when compiling information for a life story.

Special thanks go foremost to Joseph Kempler. He put up with my persistent questions, phone calls and interruptions for an interview. Despite not feeling well some days, he allowed me entrance to his home and kindly sat and talked with me for hours. He opened his life to my scrutiny. For that I am grateful.

Thanks to my husband Paul. He called me a writer before I ever put a word on paper.

Thanks to my mother, Sally Voytko, who after reading an early draft called in tears to say how much she loved it and believed it would be published someday.

Thanks to all my family and dear friends who expressed interest and often cheered me on. Jim Copple, your enthusiasm shored me up when my confidence was low. Your endless requests for a signed first edition always brought a smile to my face and gave me the push I needed to sit in front of the keyboard one more day!

I could not have completed this task without the expert guidance of others. To those people who offered their professional opinions, especially in the early days of writing, a big thanks to: Dani Greer for taking the time to explain how to search for the "nut" of the story. Thanks to my editor Melanie Peck. Thanks to my editor at LeRue Press, Janice Hermsen and her team. This book became as much your baby as mine, Jan. Thanks also go to Joel Engardio, J. B. Kaufman at the Walt Disney Family Museum, Viktoria Hertling, and Jolene Chu. Thanks to my dear friend Danny Mewes for help with the German.

April Voytko Kempler

Table of Contents

Part II: The Camps

"The eye altering, alters all."
-William Blake

Prologue

Growing up in a poor, Jewish household in Poland during the late 1920s and early 1930s, I had very few toys. Only three building blocks were completely mine, but I wished with all my heart for a toy train. Mamusia, my mother, owned a sewing machine; it was perfect, black and gleaming. I saw it as my very own toy train. I could only use the "train" when Mamusia wasn't around, otherwise she would slap me and tell me not to go near it.

When Mamusia sewed garments or pretty things for the home, I stared with longing at the sewing machine. The bobbin on top, combined with the big wheel and handle, looked just like the locomotive engine of a train. Mamusia worked the pedals underneath which caused the needle to speed up, while at the same time she pushed the cloth across the table. The sound of the needle as it pierced the fabric in an even up-down motion, stitching the pieces of material together only increased my desire to be the conductor of my own train.

Unknown to Mamusia, I viewed her sewing machine as my precious possession and secret plaything. Each time Mamusia wasn't looking or went out shopping, I played with it as much as I could, knowing I wouldn't get away with it for long. When I pushed on the pedals, my "train" came to life. I worked the pedals chanting chug-chug over and over, and increased the speed of my feet until my "train" reached top speed. As I approached a scheduled stop, I slowed my feet and made a hissing noise as the "train" came to a halt. Of course, Mamusia always found out I had been touching it and once, she discovered I had broken a clip off the belt. On seeing that, she would become upset and slap me to emphasize the sewing machine was hers and not my "train" to play with. Then she huffed around the apartment complaining about the time and money it would take to fix it.

My fascination and love of trains began when I was little. I loved to hear the sound of the big, black steam engines hissing and screaming down the tracks. As the trains chugged into the station, stopping with a final hiss of steam, I stared, transfixed.

In addition to their imposing size, I was mesmerized by the hectic rush of the crowd. In a steady stream passengers carrying parcels stepped down from the train and new passengers boarded. From the platform, I watched how the passengers maneuvered themselves and their hand-held luggage inside the coach while they made room for other passengers pressing in for space. Eventually, they settled down and waited for departure. After a short while, the train disappeared in the same manner it had arrived, chugging, screeching, and clacking away.

I knew how to read before I started school so I memorized the train schedule. I knew the distance in kilometers to each town along its way. I especially loved the idea of traveling over mountain ranges. Whenever I saw a mountain I always longed to know what was on the other side. I daydreamed about traveling by train to some place far away. A favorite game of mine was pretending to be a train, careening around corners of crowded streets, pumping my arms in a circular motion as I passed pedestrians in the way, chanting chug-chug-chug-chug-chug-chug-chug. I only slowed down to turn the corners. I loved the train game so much that this became my normal way of acting when on the busy streets.

In my early boyhood fantasies, I never realized the future significance of trains in my life. How they would ultimately carry me to ghastly places no child should ever know: destinations so diabolic I could only perceive them as wide-awake nightmares from which I never woke.

In these places, the ghettos and concentration camps of Poland and Austria, I was an eyewitness to unspeakable tortures inflicted upon innocent people: brutal beatings with leather-wrapped, metal horse whips for the slightest infraction; hard labor in the worst weather conditions— freezing cold or sweltering heat; sleepless days and nights, our bodies crawling with lice and encrusted with our own filth; lack of food and water, let alone any comfort or security. Our masters were hardened, cold -hearted murderers.

The tortures never stopped unless the victim died. Those who did survive the torture did so only in the physical sense. Mentally and emotionally they became half dead, lost to the very fact that they were once human beings. All memory of emotion and a sense of having a conscience were arrested. These people became the living dead.

Even though a train carried me to the concentration camp known as Melk, a nightmare camp, it was here where a flickering hope began to develop within me. I became an eyewitness to a different type of people also imprisoned by the Nazis. These people meant no harm to anyone; they were people I could trust not to hurt me. Although I didn't know it at the time, they stood as an example of what I could be.

From one end to the other I have identified with various forms of spirituality. I was a Jew, then a God-hater. I was an atheist, then a Christian, for which I was called a traitor.

Part I

The Early Years

"When I was a child, I used to speak as a child, to think as a child, to reason as a child. —1 Corinthians 13:11

1923-1928
The Nazi Party was banned between 1923 and 1928 and Hitler was arrested and imprisoned.

1928-1933
The Wall Street Crash in the U.S. October, 1929

history4c.pbworks.com/f/rise_hitler2.ppt
The Treaty of Versailles, 1919 unified Polish speaking regions of Europe under a new government. The borders were fixed in 1922.
www.historyorb.com

May 7th 1934
Part of Khabarovsk (Russia) becomes a Jewish Autonomous Region

Apr 6th 1934
418 Lutheran ministers arrested in Germany

www.historyorb.com

1928 – 1934
Birth to 6 years old

Krakow was my hometown, my country, and in many ways the beginning of my death.

Chapter 1

Krakow was my hometown, my country, and in many ways the beginning of my death.

As a precocious Jewish boy, growing up in Krakow's Jewish Quarter, I had before me numerous opportunities and advantages. I was an indulged younger son, educated in a private Hebrew school. I dreamed of one day attending university and becoming an engineer. Because of World War II, Hitler, and the concentration camps, what I became instead was a shattered young man without hope for my future, without trust of fellowman, a self-declared god-hater.

I was strongly attached to Mamusia, and was two and a half years old when first separated from her. I sat waiting with Aunt Hanka in the *fiakier, a* horse-drawn carriage, outside the hospital waiting for Tatus to come out with Mamusia so we could finally go home. Evening fell and still we waited.

Earlier, Mamusia had gone to the hospital to give birth to her third child. There was a lot of commotion at first. Aunt Hanka, Uncles Szaj, Icek and Shmil, were hurrying about, rushing in and out of our apartment. But now everyone was calm, quiet, yet sad.

My parents were hardworking people. My father was more religious than my mother, yet she was the stoic one. Their names were Malka and Max Kempler. Malka was Max's second wife. His first wife died, leaving him two children to raise: Dolek and Dziunka (Jun-ka). Mother, who I affectionately called Mamusia, was an attractive curly headed brunette. She had even features, soft, full lips that seldom curved into a smile and high cheekbones. Tatus, the Polish word for Father, was a handsome, mustachioed man of medium height and build. He had a high forehead, and dark hair.

Dolek (Abraham) was eleven years older than me. He had a lean face and a dark olive complexion. Dziunka, a forward thinking, stylish, young lady, was seventeen years older than me. She had won a local beauty pageant and had enjoyed boasting about her crown. Their relationship with Mamusia was a fond one. Dziunka often said she felt more love and affection for Mamusia than she did her biological mother. We lived together in the Old Town Jewish district called the Kazimierz.

"When do we bring Mamusia and the baby home, Tatus?" I ask my father.

He says, "We can't; She won't be coming home to us." This is all he says, but I overhear my older sister, Dziunka say something about a stillborn girl.

Another girl had been born before me. They called her Rozia, which means Rose. My parents said she was one and a half years old when she began reciting her own poetry, which was merely her own childish speech, but she cleverly made the words rhyme. She was a delight to my mother, I often heard.

I was told Rozia succumbed to Scarlet Fever, a common illness in Poland. At the first sign of the disease she had to be hospitalized. Tragically, Rozia never returned home.

Because it was getting dark, Tatus had to take me with him to the hospital. He had another reason too. Calling me by my family pet name he said, "Joziu will cheer her up." We couldn't all fit in one *fiakier (cabby),* so I was placed in Aunt Hanka's care while Tatus rode in another carriage ahead of us.

I miss Mamusia and sit impatiently waiting to see her. When she is directed toward me there is no light in her eyes; I see her pale, expressionless face. She sits beside me very quiet and still. I try to get her attention, but it is impossible—she doesn't notice me. It's as if I am invisible. Dziunka explains to me that Mamusia is in a catatonic state, but I don't know what that means. I only know she ignores me and she is sad.

Since then, she was unable to care for me properly. I was often left in the care of my grandfather, Mamusia's father. There was something strange about Grandfather. Babcia, Mamusia's mother on the other hand, was a remarkable woman for her time. She was serious-faced, wore her dark hair parted on the side and slicked back in a bun. Her mouth carried a slight downward expression. Although not worldly wise, she had an innate wisdom. She divorced grandfather that same year.

"That is unheard of!" her friends said. "What is she thinking to do this sort of thing?" They didn't understand. Jewish women stayed with their husbands. Family members, who knew what had happened, said that Babcia and Grandfather's relationship developed a very deep problem. He had done something unspeakable. They never said what it was, but deep down, I knew he had done something to me. I don't remember what, but I felt a heavy burden in my little chest; one I couldn't share with anyone.

There were always secrets in our apartment it seemed, because when Tatus or Mamusia didn't want me to hear what they were talking about, they spoke in Yiddish. I came to despise this language, not only because I couldn't understand what they said but also, in my mind, it meant there was important family information kept from me. I didn't want secrets. Their secret language separated me from Mamusia.

Mamusia would gradually come out of her catatonic state, but not until I was closer to seven or eight years old. It would be a long time before she became more interested in household affairs, or me. In the meantime she kept a straight face, always appeared calm and never showed her true feelings.

She had lost two children already and didn't want to lose me so she kept me close to her. Whatever she did and wherever she went, I was always nearby and seldom left alone, our relationship became close.

I was a sickly, skinny child. One cold followed closely on the heels of another. Neighbors and acquaintances called me "*zielony,*" Polish for "green." Like most parents, mine were concerned for my welfare and worried about my frequent illnesses. Taking me by the hand, Mamusia and I walked to a famous polish meat store known for a true Polish ham, where she always bought me a sandwich, loaded with the delicious ham. Eating pork was against our Jewish beliefs—this was not kosher. Encouraging me, Mamusia said, "Please, eat it now. Don't tell your father!"

On another occasion, Tatus took me by the hand and together we marched into the same store. He bought me the same kind of sandwich and begged, "Please don't tell your mother!" Their secret was safe with me. The ham sandwich was one of my favorite treats and I ate it with great delight.

Although they would never break with tradition and eat non-kosher food themselves, they compromised their beliefs for what they considered to be my well-being, putting me first.

When I was about six years old, I was told that the doctor wanted to remove my tonsils. Mamusia was afraid to put me through an operation because she knew the procedure would be a painful one. She tried to keep it a secret from me for as long as she could. One day she said, "Joziu, we have to go to the doctor. He has to check your tonsils."

I didn't know what tonsils were or why they needed checking, but if she wanted me to do something, I wanted something in return; this was my opportunity.

"I'll do it," I said. "But, I want an electric train."

"Okay Joziu, after we see the doctor." She hustled me out the door, but rather than see a doctor we arrived at a furniture store. A furniture store holds all kinds of amusements for a small child. I had a good time bouncing on, crawling under and hiding in all the furniture. The next time we went out, she took me into a building that I mistook for another furniture store. I looked forward to the fun I would have. Stepping inside this building, I realized it wasn't at all similar to the furniture store we had gone to earlier. There was a strange atmosphere where people gathered in small groups and spoke in hushed tones. I didn't feel good about being there.

I was told the doctor would like to see me. This announcement struck me with fear. Earlier, I had seen a piano in the room. I ran and hid under it. A man came toward me wearing a white coat. He tried to pick me up, but I was so frightened; I grabbed hold of the piano leg. The white-coated man tried to lift me, but as he did I bit his hand. Ultimately, I had to go with him, but I was angry, scared, kicking and screaming.

Mamusia had tricked me. I felt betrayed. They carried me to a room and put me on a bed. A dark mask was put over my face and everything went dark. After the operation my throat was too sore for food. Mamusia gave me ice cream, which felt cool on my throat. Later, when I had recovered, I asked for my electric train, but Mamusia said, "No, we can't afford a train." I viewed this as a betrayal.

Although not wealthy, my parents were able to afford a maid. They couldn't pay her much but she was eager to earn a little income. People in those days were eager for any kind of work that brought in the smallest amount of money for their own families. Her name was Marysia. she was a great help to my mother and I liked her. She had a great affection for the family and I especially felt very close to her. We lived comfortably in an apartment building located at number 12 Brzozowa Street. The building was nothing remarkable: four stories with an attic and a basement, brick and cement block walls on the outside, cream-colored paint coated the interior.

A long, winding staircase; old, gray wooden steps and an embellished wrought iron railing lead the way upstairs. A space in the attic was allocated to each family in the building. We kept our personal storage items here, such as our large laundry bucket and Passover dishes. Deep in the basement was a similar division of space for storing potatoes and coal. In Europe, the first floor is usually one level up from the ground floor, where the caretaker lives. We lived on the first floor just above the caretaker's residence.

If you continued down a long corridor, there were rooms to the left and the right. The first room on the right was what I refer to as the mystery room. This was originally a bathroom with a tub; however, the tub no longer worked and the room was sealed off. No bath would ever be taken in that room. Continuing just past the mystery room was the room for the toilet. The next doorway opened up to the kitchen.

Heading down the left side of the hallway was a room kept separate from our living area. The occupant of that room had his own lock and key but used our front door. This tenant was a stranger to our family and I was warned not to disturb him by playing near his door or to pester him with noise. Down the left side of the corridor was my parents' room where I slept in a crib beside them for several years.

The main source of heat came from a tile stove called *piec kaflowy* (pea-etz ka-flovy). The tiles ran from floor to ceiling much like a chimney but inside the building. Placed at the bottom was a small hearth and grate where we burned coal. As the heat rose up the tile chimney it radiated off the tiles and was distributed into the room. Mamusia lit the *piec kaflowy* only on special occasions, such as Friday nights when the family gathered for dinner.

The room across the hall, on the right side of the corridor was a long and narrow dining room. In addition to the dining room table and chairs, there was a small bed for Dziunka and a sofa where Dolek slept.

At night, we cuddled up in our thick feather beds and coverings. Mamusia warmed up the sheets with a hot brick, wrapped up in other bedding or clothing to keep it from burning the sheets. She placed the brick at the bottom of the bed near our feet, keeping us toasty all night.

Marysia, our Polish maid, was a great help to Mamusia, assisting her in chores that often were a two-person job, such as the laundry. I loved Marysia. Each day she read to me out of the cheap children's books Mamusia brought home. I never tired of hearing them. "Read another Marysia," I begged. I listened to them over and over again until I knew them by heart. Gradually, I learned how to read them myself.

Our apartment was usually filled with the aromas of Jewish cooking and baking. Mamusia, while not overly religious, observed the Jewish traditions in our home, ensuring we had a kosher home. Any meat for the meal was soaked overnight in a basin of salt water to make sure all the blood was out of it. She was conscientious about not breaking the laws, even while preparing the meal, as in the case of a knife accidentally coming into contact with any dairy product. If that should happen, the knife was to be thrust into the ground, blade first, buried to the hilt, and left for seven days.

Friday family meals were often exciting, yet stressful if Uncle Shmil (Yiddish for Samuel) had been invited to have dinner with the family. He was one of mother's three brothers and my favorite uncle. He had thick black hair, brushed straight back exposing his widow's peak, and a square jaw. He always made me laugh. His eccentric behavior caused Tatus to be frustrated and cross with him, especially when Uncle Shmil was expected for Friday night family dinner and failed to show up.

The Sabbath dinner ceremony is an important Jewish special occasion, and according to my father's wishes, had an important place in our household. Mamusia lead in the Sabbath dinner by first lighting the candles. She then waved her hands over the flames, closed her eyes, covered her face with both hands, and said the prayer.

Before any of this could begin, we had to wait for Uncle Shmil. As we sat there waiting and waiting, Tatus grew angrier and angrier. When he couldn't hold back his frustration any longer, he shouted out in German, "*Zusammenleben!*" This was an expression meaning "living together." In this case, it meant living together as a family. When Shmil went absent from our dinner arrangement without any explanation, it bothered and hurt Tatus very much. To Tatus, it was as if Shmil was disrespecting the family arrangement of closeness.

Tatus would slam his fist down on the table in one angry gesture, breaking his dish into pieces. The table shook from the powerful blow causing the dishes and glasses to rattle in their places. However, Mamusia had developed a technique for protecting her good dishes. She bought old dishes and put one of those at Tatus' place each Friday. She may have been flustered, but she remained calm. She never reprimanded him by saying, "Don't break the dish." Instead she remained silent and gave him a special dish to break. Until the dish was broken it was as if everyone at the dining room table was sitting on ice. Once Tatus had broken the dish, everyone relaxed and we could get on with the meal in peace.

Often there was the familiar argument between Tatus and Dolek. Tatus wanted to make sure Dolek was on the right career path. Dolek was bright and talented—he wanted to become an artist. Tatus scoffed at that idea. Tatus was a businessman and practical; he didn't understand art. Finally, to satisfy Tatus, Dolek became an apprentice to a tailor in a workshop where he worked his way up from the bottom tier. He swept the floors, ran errands and heated the irons. He did everything other than tailor garments. Eventually he learned the skill of a tailor and quickly rose to master tailor. His garments were beautifully designed, which I attributed to his artist nature. He never took shortcuts with his work.

While not an outwardly affectionate father, Tatus cared for his family deeply. Mamusia could anticipate a happy mood if she heard him singing *"Dlugie wlosy krotki rozum maja,"* which means, "long hair, short on reason" prompting a smile from her.

Tatus owned a bar, called a *szynk*, located on Sebastiana Street, about two blocks from where we lived. Uncle Shmil worked there and helped out with the cleaning and storing of supplies. This was a very good spot in the Old Town, right at the edge of the park, called the Planty, and the Wawel Castle. There were plenty of tourists meandering through the Planty who wanted a drink at the end of their scenic tour. Tatus' *szynk* was the only one for some distance. At the *szynk*, Polish fast food was the fare of the day. Tatus took great pride in ownership, and poured his resources and energy into it.

Before I was born, Tatus had a partnership in a hotel, regarded as one of the top hotels in Krakow. The hotel was situated in the number one location, maximizing on the spectacular view of Wawel Castle. Unfortunately, the business went bankrupt. Besides the loss of money it was a big disappointment for Tatus. He tried out various jobs before coming to own the *szynk*.

Tatus worked long, hard hours in order to succeed and Mamusia helped him in the business. Mamusia prepared all the kosher food and desserts that Tatus served to the customers, so when I entered the *szynk* I was met by the familiar cooking smells of our apartment.

At the front of the *szynk* was a counter where beer, wine and other alcoholic drinks were served. Also displayed were the kosher goodies and snacks Mamusia had brought over on a tray from our apartment: chopped herring salad, smoked herring, herring in cream, eggs with mustard and horseradish. Mamusia specialized in a Jewish dish called *galareta*; it consisted of a gelatin made from the marrow of beef bones. Considered to be an excellent treat by some, the *galareta* was not to my liking. The restaurant also catered to non-Jews, which was reflected in the pork kielbasa served with sauerkraut and mustard, a pub favorite.

An additional room was furnished with tables and chairs and a billiard table. Downstairs was the basement where supplies and foodstuffs were stored, along with kegs of beer and bottles of wine.

Inside the *szynk* the atmosphere was full of cheer and friendly gossip, complete with enough local characters to make it a fun place. The local *fiakier* drivers would line up their carriages near the *szynk* and wait for the tourists to exit the Wawel Castle. While waiting for the park and castle to close, the drivers came in for a special "pure alcoholic" drink called *Spiritus*. The 190 proof beverage came in a mini-bottle (similar to what is served on an airplane) and sealed with a cork. The drivers held the bottle up in the air, just in front of them, and with a quick, firm slap they hit the bottle square on the bottom. This caused the cork to fly right out of the bottle and shoot across the room. Placing the bottle to their mouths, they gulped the liquid, right down the gullet; then, they gave a fierce swipe across their lips with the back of their hand.

Meanwhile, the other patrons of the *szynk* played billiards and had me keep score for them as the phonograph played a humorous song about women in the background. The *szynk* patrons liked to hear that song over and over again. I looked at them in puzzlement. Why did they like this song so much? I was too young to understand the subtle nuances about women they found so hilarious.

Tatus didn't eat at the *szynk*, I brought his kosher meals from home. I felt a sense of freedom on those occasions, carrying it along the busy sidewalk, acting like a grown-up with somewhere important to go. Tatus greeted me with zest. Taking my cheek between his forefinger and middle finger he pinched down hard between them. "*Hundsfot!*" he'd exclaim. What he meant was, "miserable cur!" This was just one of his strange pet names for me. Mamusia didn't use pet names; she called me Joziu. Mamusia brought me up in a formal way and taught me to be respectful to my elders. I was taught to address grown-ups as *pan*, mister, or *pani,* missus. Each time I greeted Mamusia, or any woman for that matter,

I took her hand in mine, bowed slightly and gently kissed the top of her hand.

1934 Germany Party Purge 30th June 1934 :
Adolf Hitler orders a purge of his own political party,
assassinating hundreds of Nazis whom he believed had the
potential to become political enemies in the future later known
as the Night of the Long Knives.

http://www.thepeoplehistory.com/june30th.html

Germany 1934 Germany Hitler 2nd Aug. 1934 :
Adolf Hitler, the chancellor of Germany, became the country's
Fuhrer (president and chancellor) today after German
President Paul Von Hindenburg died. Find More 1934

http://www.thepeoplehistory.com/august2nd.html

1935-03-16 - Hitler orders German rearmament, violating
Versailles Treaty
http://www.historyorb.com/countries/germany?p=8

1936 U.S.A. Gone With The Wind 30th June 1936 :
The book Gone with the Wind is Published. In 1939 Gone
With The Wind was made into the Oscar Winning Film.
http://www.thepeoplehistory.com/june30th.html

1934 – 1936
6 to 8 years old

Because of Tatus' firm religious beliefs
he thought it appropriate I attend a
Jewish school.

Chapter 2

One morning, Mamusia took me to a *cheder*, meaning "room of learning," run by *Chasidim*, a sect of super orthodox Jews. Religious subjects were the only type of subject taught at the *cheder*. I didn't understand this new arrangement; I didn't really want to go to this kind of school.

When we arrived at the school, we were met by a strange looking man. I remember thinking he had so much dark hair, and what a funny looking, bushy beard. I didn't like him or this place. All the boys were sitting in a darkened room rocking back and forth over their books, not reading, but chanting in Hebrew and Yiddish. I didn't understand what anyone was saying.

The bushy-bearded man only addressed Mamusia. They were speaking in Yiddish. What kind of school is this? What are they saying? Why are we here in this dark, strange place? Echoing around me I heard the Yiddish language and I was all the more confused and frightened. The bushy-bearded man turned his black eyes on me. He bent down and reached to take my coat.

"No!" I yelled out. I pulled away and kicked him in the shin. I tried to bite his hand that had grasped my coat. The man became furious and let go.

He took a deep breath then blew it out, attempting to control his temper. Enunciating each word, he spoke in a clear, firm voice, "Please, leave this school."

Mamusia and I were led to the exit, and to my relief we left. I had been rejected from *cheder*. In spite of my father's wishes for me to attend a Hebrew school, Mamusia realized this wasn't a good place for me. She took matters into her own hands, and without discussing it first with Tatus, bustled me to Mizrachi, a private Hebrew school. She left me in kindergarten class and went to discuss the payment arrangements with the school principal.

In order to attend this school my hair had to be cut short and I needed a school uniform, short pants and a plain shirt. Mamusia had always wanted a girl to dress up like a doll. I believe for this reason, with the loss of her two daughters, she dressed me in fancy clothes. For special occasions she dressed me in a silk shirt with pearly buttons. She wouldn't allow anyone to cut my hair. It had grown out in long, blond, curly locks. In later years, I sometimes thought she kept my hair long because it reminded her of those little girls she had lost. She was upset over my required haircut and cried the hardest when it was ultimately cut short.

Mamusia bought my supply of both Hebrew and Polish textbooks before each school year started. I knew how to read before I started kindergarten, so as soon as Mamusia brought the books home, I read the Polish ones through. I read so voraciously that I finished them in a matter of days.

Dziunka also took an active role in my education. I was often sick and stayed home from school a lot during the first grade. One time when I was sick she brought me a book from the library. I read the book that very day. The next day Dziunka brought me another one. I devoured that one too. Dziunka had introduced me to the public library system. She chose the books I would read and left me the catalog index numbers. When I could go to the library on my own I handed the index number to the librarian who brought me the next book on Dziunka's list. I didn't like her choices in reading material. I borrowed the library catalog and copied the index numbers of the books I wanted to read. My favorite books were about science and new discoveries, animals and nature and especially adventure stories. I was developing the ability to read quickly and to remember everything I read. Finishing a book in one day was very important to me. The library was closed on Saturdays. So as not to go one single day without a book I checked out two books on Friday.

The students sat on long benches in rows in the schoolroom. We each had a short table and a stand for propping up for our books. The mornings were devoted to Hebrew subjects along with religious teachings. At noon, we were allowed to return home to eat our lunch or start the assigned homework. In the afternoons, we learned Polish subjects.

As a student, I had to wear a *yarmulke* (a small, round skull cap) every day to school. One day, I learned a very important lesson from Mr. Dodeles, by far my favorite teacher. He had been employed at this school a long time. He had even taught some of the students' parents. He was an older gentleman, very refined and proper, short and of slight build. One day I came to school without my *yarmulke*; I had forgotten it and left it at home. Mr. Dodeles caught me without it and made me write a hundred times in neat, fine script: *"Porządny uczeń nie zapomina czapeczki."* This meant: "An orderly student doesn't forget his *yarmulke*." I never left my *yarmulke* home again.

Although strict, he won my respect. He treated each of the students fairly and was sincere in his commendation. Unlike the other teachers who were all about business, Mr. Dodeles was like a friend.

On May 4, 1935, Josef Pilsudski, the dictator of Poland and beloved national hero, died. My school prepared a very special presentation ceremony in honor of his memory. Someone wrote a poem and I was chosen to memorize it. I wasn't chosen for my great poetry recitation but, as it was becoming known, I had an outstanding memory.

Another of our teachers—not a favorite among us—who was easy to taunt, and who we referred to as The Guinea Pig, wrote a song that all the kids were instructed to sing. A big, loud bombastic song that went:

"It is not true that you no longer exist.

Even though you are gone from us forever; you are not gone from our hearts.

We will not forget you; you are gone but not from our thoughts."

The kids struggled to reach the low notes. The whole production took on a different mood rather than the somber one it was meant to have. Young children, who were in the audience, burst into giggles but were quickly quieted by their teachers.

Mamusia was often missing from my school performances. This hurt my feelings. Why wasn't she there? Was she so busy that she couldn't take the time for her only son? Maybe she just didn't care for school functions all that much. Maybe they were too frivolous for her, but I never could forget it.

Mr. Dodeles, although firm and strict, was an outstanding teacher. I learned Polish reading and writing from him. During his lecture, we were made to sit on the school bench with our hands behind our backs. We couldn't move our bodies an inch and not so much as wriggle our hands. He taught us to speak Polish correctly and, if some student used a common Polish word, he made them put the equivalent of five cents in a metal box on his desk.

When I originally registered for school, my family name was not known as Kempler but as Knobloch. When Tatus' mother, whose maiden name was Knobloch, married his father, it was in a Jewish ceremony not recognized by the registrar. My father was known as Knobloch not Kempler, and I was known by that name too. It wasn't until I was in the third grade that they had straightened it all out and had determined my legal surname was Kempler. For most of my childhood, I had been an unhealthy, skinny boy, but after my tonsils were removed, I gained weight and began to look healthy and robust. Now that my surname was Kempler, my teachers were confused. One teacher forgot what to call me, and referred to me as "the fat kid in the back."

Dziunka and Dolek only went to synagogue when forced. Usually, I was the only one to go with Tatus to the 14th century synagogue he attended. Tatus, while not orthodox, felt the importance of his traditions and showed it by wearing his good, gray-striped pants when he went to synagogue. Reading the Torah and the Talmud were a joy for me. I believed everything I read and was taught. Tatus was pleased to know he was raising a good Jewish boy. His pride in my accomplishments was encouraging and I wanted to please him. Dziunka liked to tease me, and said, "If you don't quit this, you're going to end up a rabbi."

When I attended synagogue, I dutifully recited all my prayers. These were complicated prayers even for adults to deliver, but as a small boy I came to the quick realization that repeating all the words correctly was paramount. There were optional verses within the prayers, but I said every one of the lines so as not to miss one thing. I wanted to get it right and to be right with God. Besides the prescribed Hebrew prayers, there were optional Hebrew prayers, and personal prayers. Whenever I spoke to God in a private personal prayer I did it in Polish.

One day I ruined a new Bible owned by the school. I spilled ink on the corner of the page. The teacher was angry. "You're going to have to pay for that Bible! Tomorrow you come to school with the money for a new one." I was filled with trepidation, knowing that when I went home I would be in trouble. I knew my parents couldn't afford to pay for a new

Bible and I didn't want to ask them for the money. What could I do? I worried about it all night.

The next morning I prayed to God to help me. Since this wasn't a prescribed prayer, I said it in Polish. But what if God doesn't understand Polish? I translated my short prayer into Hebrew, hoping He would get the message. My prayers went unanswered and Mamusia had to pay for the damaged Bible.

Dziunka met and married Jack Laub, a German Jew. He was a talented musician playing in Henry Rosner's orchestra. Rosner was a famous violinist. Jack played the violin, clarinet and saxophone perfectly. He was from a well-to-do family living in Germany. Rosner's orchestra played in many cities abroad. After Jack and Dziunka were married, Dziunka traveled with the band everywhere they were booked to play. She always returned with little presents for me from their travels together.

Often, Dziunka bought books for me to read. She felt I should broaden my viewpoint from religious theories to include scientific ones. One time when she brought me a book on evolution, I was especially drawn to the illustrations, one in particular, of early man. The first picture showed him as a gorilla, but each subsequent picture showed his development into modern man. This was my first indication that the story about the creation of man from the Bible's viewpoint might not be true.

One evening, my parents invited Dziunka and Jack over for dinner. Soon, the after-dinner conversation turned into talk of religion. I was taught to stay out of the way while the grown-ups talked. However, once the subject turned to religion, I got very excited and chimed right in. Before I gave serious thought to my words, I blurted out, "I have a picture of Adam!" All the adults turned to look at me. Mamusia's eyebrows were raised to her scalp. Tatus made a round 'O' with his mouth and Dziunka and Jack looked perplexed. By the astonished looks on their faces I could tell they forgot I was in the room. After a momentary pause, Tatus said, "You have? Well let's see it then."

I jumped up and ran to get my book. I opened it to the illustration of the rather large, hairy gorilla. Tapping at the page with my finger, I said, "There he is, right there. That's Adam."

There was a stunned silence at the table. Tatus' face turned a rather unnatural and discomforting shade of purple. Between clenched teeth he growled, "Where did you get the idea that that hairy ape was Adam?"

Lacking my earlier conviction, I hesitated to answer, "Well ..." I drew in a big breath, knowing I was about to implicate Dziunka in my folly. Finally, I said, "Dziunka gave it to me."

Tatus swiveled in his chair toward Dziunka. He stared at her a long time before expelling a deep breath. He shrugged his shoulders, looked heavenward and said, "That explains it, then."

His modern-thinking daughter was making a big impact on me. I had naive ideas about religion. I was mixing up the science I was learning in school with my strong faith in God.

Dziunka and Jack had recently returned to Poland from Beirut. The audiences there had been favorable. Now, Jack and his orchestra had a new gig for the summer months playing in Krynica (kri-nee-tsah) at the Patria Hotel. This hotel was renowned as a top resort and spa owned by the famous Polish tenor Jan Kiepura.

Dziunka invited me to Krynica to spend part of the summer with them. I was so excited, not to see Dziunka, but because this was the first time I was allowed to ride the train alone. Mamusia packed my lunch and brought me to the train station. I said my goodbyes, boarded the car and soon the train began to move slowly out of the station. I discovered I liked to stand in the corridor between cars by the open window. I spent the majority of the seven-hour trip standing there. Although the journey was long, I wasn't bored for a second! I had a newfound sense of freedom riding on a real train going somewhere unknown.

Once I arrived in Krynica, Dziunka took over the role of mother.

While walking with Dziunka in town, we met a woman walking hand-in-hand with a little girl. This woman was a distant relative of Jack's. The little girl, whose hand she held so tightly in her own, was introduced to me as "Anita." We instantly became bosom buddies. We found out we had a lot in common. We were similar in age (she was a year younger than me), and she lived in Krakow. We both loved the same author, Karl May and talked about his stories.

Few authors of the time wrote stories with as much gut-clenching excitement as the German author, Karl May. To me, his books were pure magic. He wrote Wild West and Arabian action stories. The common theme running through all his books was brotherly love without prejudice. His characters formed real bonds of unity.

I had a great time with Anita during those weeks in Krynica. When it was time for me to return home, I promised I would find her again.

I learned from Dziunka that Anita and her mother were living in an apartment outside the Kazimierz. They lived together with Anita's aunt, Carolla, and robust uncle, Trauring, a well-to-do German Jew. Now that I knew where Anita lived, I was anxious to find her and resume our summer friendship.

Usually shy and quiet around girls, Anita was the first girl I could talk to comfortably. Although I was a rough-and-tumble boy—dirt and smudges on my face and hands, scraped and scabby knees—I always made sure I was clean before visiting Anita. My family always knew precisely the time I was going to meet her. Dziunka teased me mercilessly, "Oh, oh! His knees are clean. It looks like Joziu is going to see his girlfriend today." She gave a hearty laugh as if she just heard the funniest joke.

Anita and I often went to the movies together. When we walked up and down the street, we held hands. Our favorite thing to do was take the tramway to the end of the line in the countryside before looping back. We walked around a bit, talking about movies and books and then hopped back on for the long trip home. Anita became my best friend, one who would continually be in and out of my life.

May 28, 1937:
Volkswagen is founded

On this day in 1937, the government of Germany--then under the control of Adolf Hitler of the National Socialist (Nazi) Party--forms a new state-owned automobile company, then known as Gesellschaft zur Vorbereitung des Deutschen Volkswagens mbH. Later that year, it was renamed simply Volkswagenwerk, or "The People's Car Company."
http://www.history.com/this-day-in-history/volkswagen-is-founded

November 9, 1938:
On this day in 1938, in an event that would foreshadow the Holocaust, German Nazis launch a campaign of terror against Jewish people and their homes and businesses in Germany and Austria.
http://www.history.com/this-day-in-history/nazis-launch-kristallnacht

Aug 31, 1939:
Germany prepares for invasion of Poland

September 3, 1939:
Hitler invades Poland, Britain and France declare war on Germany, United States makes statement of neutrality
http://www.history.com

1937 – October, 1939
9 to 11 years old

**Mamusia didn't think it was appropriate
for a child my age to read this sort of
thing or look at those kinds of pictures,
but I did it anyway.**

Chapter 3

In 1937 or so, I found a book in the library written by a German man about Hitler's persecution of the Jews, homosexuals, Roma, and Sinti (gypsies), who were incarcerated in the concentration camp of Dachau. By use of photo illustrations, the book emphasized the harsh treatment these groups received. The Nazis forced people to stand with their hands up above their heads for hours on end. They beat them through wet sheets so as not to leave marks on their bodies. Mamusia didn't think it was appropriate for a child my age to read this sort of thing or look at those kinds of pictures, but I did it anyway.

Although I was only nine years old, it seemed I was more knowledgeable about the Jewish situation in Germany than others in my hometown. They didn't want to believe things like this were happening. From their viewpoint, this was a faraway situation; it didn't really affect our lives in the Kazimierz. That was about to change.

During 1938, many Jewish refugees from Germany arrived in Poland. They were forced to leave Germany and were only allowed to take their personal belongings in a small suitcase. They were taken by trains and dropped off at Polish borders, carrying only a little bit of money. These were German Jews, but they were not considered to be of German blood. The German officials and scientists considered them to be Polish Jews who belonged in Poland. Some of these Jewish families lived in Germany since before World War I, but it didn't matter to the German officials.

They thoroughly researched three generations back to prove their origins. We saw a great influx of Jewish immigrants into Krakow. They didn't have a home or means of supporting themselves. They were left at the mercy of the Polish authorities. The Poles didn't know what to do with the refugees, so they were dropped off in Krakow to be handled by the Jewish residents. However, most Jewish homes did not have enough room for them. Some were put up in schools or synagogues, and out of charity, the Polish Jews brought them food and shared what meager belongings they had. The refugees were pitiful to look at, completely abandoned, without home or country.

Jack's parents, the Laub's, were living in Germany, but when the officials found them to be of Polish descent, they were deported to Poland. They were sent to a Jewish high school near our apartment. When Mamusia heard the news, she hurried to her kitchen to make a big pot of thick barley soup, called *pecak*. I was dispatched to bring the soup to them at the school. At the high school, I saw a large tangle of people sitting and lying on the floor. There were no beds—people made do with what they had. Some had blankets; none had pillows. They used their suitcases as pillows, propped up under their heads.

The Laub's were somewhere in this crowd. I located them and picked my way over and around prone bodies, toward them. Reaching my destination, I proudly offered Mamusia's *pecak* to Mrs. Laub. The Laub's were grateful for the kindness and sent me home carrying their appreciative words to Mamusia.

Despite my worldly reading, I gave little thought at first to the political changes occurring in the world. Overall, I felt people in Krakow were tolerant of the Jewish culture; as I was growing and learning, I began to experience certain changes in my own community. Graffiti painted on city walls was blatantly anti-Semitic, with statements such as, "Go to Palestine" becoming more and more prevalent in Jewish neighborhoods. Sometimes the Polish kids taunted me and fellow Jewish kids with insulting songs about Jews with beards. They meant to put us down and make us feel inferior. I realized the problem wasn't who I was, but with whom I was hanging around. If I stayed among kids who looked like me and could blend in to look like Poles, then I wouldn't come up against this sort of abuse.

I learned to avoid those who looked like the super-religious Jew, easily recognizable by their clothing and side curls called *payos* (PAY-us). They wore fur-trimmed hats called *shtreimels* (SHRAY-mls) and long, black coats. Children, too, wore Jewish skullcaps called a *yarmulke* and wore a four-cornered garment, called *tzitzit*, with special tassels hanging from each corner. In my opinion, these Jews drew trouble to themselves merely by how they dressed.

I heard that there were occasional beatings of Jewish men by Poles. One story circulating was about some superstitious Poles who believed that if they saw a Jewish man with a red beard on New Year's Day, they had to beat him up or suffer bad luck the entire year. The German refugees told us stories about the terrible beatings they experienced before coming to Krakow. Their belongings were confiscated, their synagogues burned to the ground and their businesses commandeered. Jews had limited access to universities and other anti-Semitic rules were beginning to come into being, and even law, but I was too young to be affected by them. Sheltered in my home, I felt safe within the confines of my family.

The Polish government knew Germany was militarily aggressive, but they weren't preparing their people for war. Still, people knew something should be done and made their feelings clear with sarcastic rhymes:

> *Jak Hitler Budowal Samoloty*
> *Smigly Rydz Malowal Ploty*
> Hitler is building planes and
> Smigly Rydz (president of Poland) is painting fences white.
> And:
> *Jak Hitler Budowal Tanki*
> *Smigly Rydz chodzil do kohanki*
> Hitler is building tanks and
> Smigly Rydz is going to his lover.

These songs illustrated that, instead of preparing seriously for an all-out attack, the Polish government was wasting time on unimportant matters. It seemed to me when citizens made fun of the government, there was some truth in what they were saying.

In 1938, Dolek had been drafted into the Polish Army and then the Horse Artillery. He wasn't really fit for military life. He was the nervous and anxious type. But, due to his artistic nature, he had developed a beautiful penmanship. As a result, he was granted an office assignment writing letters and other correspondence for his commanding officers.

By then, Hitler was making a big push east toward Poland. By August of 1939, Poland became threatened by Germany. The Polish government now had no choice but to prepare for war. About a week before the German invasion, we began taping X formations in the windows to prevent them from shattering in case of an air raid. In the event they used gas on us, we made cotton masks. People volunteered to dig air raid shelters around the lawns and trees of the Krakow Planty gardens. The shelters were built in a zigzag pattern to avoid massive damage caused by bombs. The whole town was called out to participate in digging these air raid shelters. Frequently, I volunteered to help with the digging, not because I was especially patriotic, but because everyone was pitching in to help in the war effort, I wanted to be a part of the action. However, I didn't take it seriously; it was fun and games to me. This was just another adventure that I would write about in my diary.

On August 31, 1939, I took a walk with Uncle Shmil through town. He pointed out the electric and gas companies and said, "If a bomb drops, this will be one of the first places they'll target." He was teaching me a lesson: "Avoid this place at all costs."

Friday, September 1, 1939, I heard planes in the sky and distant explosions. The aircraft sounded like large planes, unlike Polish planes, which were small and easily recognizable. I was almost happy; I didn't feel afraid. Perhaps the military were getting ready for something big to happen. My family didn't have a radio; we relied on newspapers and gossip from neighbors. We had heard nothing. Nobody seemed to realize this was the actual start of war. As it turned out, this was more than practice. We were being attacked by big German bombers.

After breakfast I walked over to my school friend Reiner's apartment near Wawel Castle. When I got there his father told me, "There's a war on."

My eyes widened. "I thought it was just maneuvers."

"Look up there," he said, "and see for yourself." He pointed across the street and up toward the roof. On the roof was a soldier manning a machine gun. My friend and I were transfixed. A German Stuka fighter flew overhead, strafing the building. The soldier manning the machine gun fired back at the plane. This was exciting; we didn't quite understand the significance, but changes were taking place in our lives. The new school year was scheduled to open on Monday, but with the start of the invasion, all schools had been closed. This was fantastic news, as any student not anxious for the school year to start would feel.

While we listened in on the Riener's radio, propaganda from the government began to pour in. Not only over the radio, but from loudspeakers set up in the streets. Grandiose announcements of all kinds were made to bolster the Poles' spirits. We heard statements such as, "How dare Hitler strike Poland! Don't worry. We're going to beat the Germans soon and have them turn tail for Germany."

The bombings were most severe during the first couple of days. During the initial bombing, my family huddled together in a makeshift air raid shelter in the basement where we kept the coal and potatoes. By day three, there were no bombings, but we heard the planes strafing buildings. After things settled down a bit, Uncle Shmil and I took a walk around town to see what had happened. Surprisingly, there wasn't much damage to be seen. We saw a railway station and a military barracks that had been bombed, but it wasn't as bad as I thought it would be.

On Monday, September 4, 1939, widespread panic spread throughout the town. Polish soldiers were running through town completely disorganized. I walked to the Planty, and saw some Polish soldiers limping back. One soldier, from the cavalry brigade, led his bleeding horse gently by the reins. A crowd gathered around him asking about the current situation. I overheard him say, "The campaign is a lost cause. The troops were brave but the German army was moving too quickly. We had no choice but to retreat." Poland's horse cavalry was no match for Germany's modern motorized army.

Even though the fight was over, dauntless reporters broadcast propaganda nonstop. This kept up for a few days, and then ceased when reality finally sunk in. Loud, frightening sirens blasted throughout the air signaling an attack, and the city was shelled by artillery fire day and night.

We spent the evening of September 5, 1939, in our basement shelter, bags packed, ready for flight, while artillery fire, accompanied by the never-ending sound of bombs, crashed down around us. Uncle Shmil was nowhere to be found. He was a person who seemed to like danger. While we were all huddled downstairs like frightened rabbits, Shmil was sleeping upstairs on the sofa in our apartment.

The local gossip was that sometime during the first few days of the attack, Smigly Rydz and General Władysław Sikorski escaped in a plane to England. It was rumored they knew the war was lost from the very beginning. All the propaganda about beating the Germans was broadcast only to pacify the people. The majority believed the propaganda at first; they thought the Poles could win. Now there was panic. Many people ran back to their homes, packed what belongings they could carry, or put belongings onto horse drawn wagons and headed east, away from the

Germans.

Young Jewish people took off on foot, taking whatever they could carry in their rucksacks. My family wasn't prepared to run east. We had nowhere to go. My parents decided to stay in Krakow and wait to see what would happen.

September 6, 1939 was a surprisingly quiet day as German soldiers entered Krakow. Immediately, they began to organize, converting many of the old and narrow city streets into one-way streets, making it easier for transporting German tanks and equipment. That day, I had gone out on an errand with Tatus, who needed to renew his liquor license for the *szynk*. I was in awe of the rapid changes happening to Krakow. I had never seen anything like this before. We had now entered a peaceful time, it seemed; the shelling and bombing were over. Dziunka had recently sent me a wristwatch. That day during our walk, I had been fiddling with it, and the crown had come loose and had fallen off. All around us there were strange happenings: Tanks rumbled down the street. Trucks loaded with heavy equipment rolled past. However, Tatus was more concerned with business affairs, and I was concerned with one broken wristwatch.

Tatus didn't seem sad or overly worried about the German soldiers; maybe because he had spent time in Germany during his youth. He spoke some German, and he felt comfortable around German people. Perhaps he felt that the Germans coming to Krakow wouldn't make the political situation any worse than Polish rule. "Germany is a civilized nation full of famous philosophers, poets and scientists," he said. "I believe everything will turn out okay."

The next day, in the Kazimierz, I saw German soldiers walking down the streets. A few soldiers had cornered some bearded religious Jews and were making fun of their dress. With the blades of their bayonets they scraped off one side of the Jewish men's beards. Laughing, the soldiers left the Jews with raw and bleeding faces. This was the first time I was exposed to this kind of persecution. We knew how the German soldiers treated the Jews in Germany. We were told they beat people, they burned synagogues, but Tatus didn't seem worried. Tatus didn't have a beard, so I didn't worry either.

Shortly after Krakow was conquered, a large victory celebration was to be held in the *Rynek Glowny*, the Grand Square. Civilian Governor Hans Frank, a Nazi lawyer and one of Hitler's legal advisers, was an honoree. He established himself in offices at the Wawel Castle. Soon after the new government was launched the name of the square was changed from

Rynek Glowny to Adolf Hitler Platz. There once had been a big statue of Adam Mickiewicz, a great Polish poet, but it had been destroyed during the invasion and removed.

The celebration was exclusive for the *Reichdeutschers*, German citizens. No *Volksdeutscher*, a Pole of German background, and certainly no Jew, was permitted to attend. I had a wild notion that I would attend this event and Mamusia didn't object. To the best of her ability, she dressed me up to look like a young German boy. This was an inconsistency in my upbringing. Early in my life she had protected me, tying me to her side. Now, she allowed me to wander right into the lion's den. At any moment I could be discovered, thereby putting my family and myself in grave danger. I've never understood it.

When I arrived at the square, I tried my best to blend in with the German kids. To start, everyone sang the national anthem, thrusting hands high in the "Heil Hitler" salute. Following the anthem were ceremonies and speeches. Afterward, civilian Governor Frank climbed inside his limousine ready to depart. All the kids grouped together at the rear of the car, touching the bumper or trunk as it moved away, singing exuberantly in German. Governor Frank, touched by the demonstration of devotion, spoke to them lovingly in German. At this point in the adventure, I became frightened. I didn't speak German. My *Reichdeutscher* impersonation was going to be discovered, and I would find myself in serious trouble. I made my getaway from the revelers and raced back to the safety of my home.

While the occupation was in force, we had to put up with many changes in our daily lives. We weren't free to live the way we used to. All schools were closed initially, but then only Polish schools were re-opened. All the Jewish schools remained closed indefinitely. Dr. Ohringer was the director of my school. In an attempt to help continue education he arranged a secret school in his home for a select number of students. I was included. This arrangement lasted two or three weeks, but it was difficult to continue it longer because life for Jewish people was becoming further complicated.

Polish money rapidly lost value. Based on my parents' recommendations, whatever money I had managed to save or get from Dziunka, had been deposited directly into a savings account. However, when the war started, all the banks were closed. We had some concern and didn't know if we could retrieve the money. When the bank re-opened it was very difficult to access our money. Outside the bank was a long line of people. I stood waiting in line for what seemed hours. When I did receive my money, it had depreciated greatly and was only a small amount compared to what I had deposited. This would be the least of our worries as the German officers continued to rule in Krakow.

Ration cards were issued for Poles and Jews right away; however, the Jews' ration coupons were meager by comparison. Ration cards became a clever form of forced labor for the Jewish people. Only stamped cards allowed the bearer to receive food. Each Jew from the age of fourteen had a ration card, but in order to receive food, some form of labor had to be completed a certain number of times per month. After the work was performed, the ration card was stamped by a Nazi.

Every day there was a new law or restriction against the Jews. On September 8, 1939, the *Judenrat* was formed. This was a Jewish council set up by the ruling Germans to make sure all the Jews complied with each new restriction or order. The ubiquitous small, round kiosks, which were normally used to announce movies, concerts and various entertainments going on around town, were used in Jewish neighborhoods to post the new orders, laws and restriction, which were produced daily. The Jews had the responsibility to make sure they read the orders and followed them. The laws specifically humiliated and tested Jewish traditions. For example, September 22 was the Jewish holiday Yom Kippur. On this day, it is forbidden by Jewish religious law to work or eat anything. However, a forced labor order was issued for September 22, 1939. The Jews were made to go out and cover the anti-aircraft ditches and replant grass.

A school friend and I had a good laugh standing in front of the kiosk pretending to read the postings, acting as if there were new horrible orders. We exclaimed and lamented loudly enough to attract the attention of some passersby—it didn't take too much to draw the attention of a crowd in those days. Immediately, a large group of people drew in close around us. We scooted to the back of the crowd and watched with mischievous delight all the frantic excitement we had needlessly inspired.

Late in October, Dolek returned home. He had been serving in the Alpine Horse Cavalry. His group, assigned to the western border of Poland, defended it against German attack. They ended up on the far eastern border near Russia. After losing a fierce battle, Dolek's unit had broken up and dispersed into various places. Poland surrendered on October 6, 1939, and Dolek had to make his way home on foot. He was just twenty-two years old. When he finally arrived home, his spirit was badly beaten down and he became very pessimistic.

Jack and Dziunka had arrived in Warsaw on August 31, 1939, but now they returned to Krakow. They told us what happened to them. On September 28, 1939, Warsaw surrendered to the Germans, but not before the city was devastated by tanks and aircraft bombardment. Warsaw was practically leveled. Jack and Dziunka's apartment building had been bombed and burned, but was still standing. They decided to hide in the ruins for a while with the misguided belief that the same house is never bombed twice. However, the apartment was indeed bombed a second time, forcing them to flee for their lives. The stairway was destroyed by a bomb. Jack jumped out of the second story window breaking his nose and leg in the process. Dziunka and Jack returned to Krakow, Jack on crutches and Dziunka dispirited and depressed.

By October 26, 1939, ritual slaughter of kosher animals (mammals or birds that complied with Jewish religious restrictions for food), practiced by some Jews, had been forbidden, and all synagogues had been closed. We could no longer meet for public prayer. In private homes, *minyans*, a group consisting of ten men, were formed.

The better Jewish apartments in Krakow were taken over by Germans. I felt that those prosperous Jews had it worse than my family because they were thrown out of their homes. Nobody, it seemed, wanted to take over our apartment.

The War in France and Flanders
3rd September, 1939, to 9th May, 1940
On the day before war was declared the Royal Air Force flew
to France a small advance party of eighteen officers and thirty-
one other ranks. By the 27th September the Royal Navy with
shipping of the Mercantile Marine under their control had
moved to France, without the loss of a single life…
*http://www.ibiblio.org/hyperwar/UN/UK/UK-NWE-Flanders/UK-
NWE-Flanders-2.html*

U.S. Neutrality and the War in Europe, 1939–1940
The outbreak of war in Europe in September 1939 posed a
serious challenge to U.S. neutrality, since Americans'
sympathies lay overwhelmingly with Great Britain and its allies.
The task of remaining neutral became even more formidable in
mid-1940, when it appeared as though Hitler's Germany might
actually win the war. Public sentiment overwhelmingly favored
staying out of the war, yet at the same time most Americans
believed that a German victory would pose a threat to national
security.
http://edsitement.neh.gov/lesson-plan/us-neutrality-and-war-
europe-1939-1940

Mar 18th, 1940 –
Benito Mussolini joins Hitler in Germany's war against France
& Britain
http://www.historyorb.com/events/date/1940?p=1

October, 1939 – September, 1940
11 to 12 years old

Jews were not considered humans at all; we were called vermin.

Chapter 4

According to the German philosophy, we were learning, there were three categories of people: the Master Race, Poles, and Slavs. People who lived east of Germany were considered subhuman. Jews were not considered humans at all; we were called vermin.

Jews were now restricted from many places. There were signs posted in the front of shop windows that read, "No Jews and dogs allowed."

I took advantage of my blond hair and blue eyes, easily blending in with both Poles and Germans. I accessed many places and modes of transportation restricted to Jews. While it was permissible for Jews to travel during the day for work, overnight or out of town travel by train was forbidden. Jews could not be absent from their homes at night under any circumstances. However, I traveled by trolley car, and became proficient at getting around town, rapidly becoming familiar with the time schedule and all the destinations along the route. Attached to the outside of the trolley car was a metal plate indicating in German and Polish, "For Jews," or, "Not for Jews." Each car had an entrance/exit at the front and back. Jews could only enter and exit at the back, where they also had to ride. I dismissed this rule and took great enjoyment sitting in the front of the car, sometimes standing right behind the trolley engineer, imitating his movements.

One day I learned that *Snow White and the Seven Dwarfs*, a Disney movie, was playing in a Polish movie theater. Mamusia gave me money for the show and I walked into the theater without anyone knowing I was Jewish. The movie made an impression on me. While the evil step-mother didn't scare me, the song "Heigh ho" stuck with me long afterward and I often sang it. Another time, the circus was performing on the outskirts of Krakow. I bought a ticket for the trolley and enjoyed myself.

I pretended to be a *Volksdeutscher* (a Pole of German descent) and borrowed books without fear of being caught. I had discovered a promising business venture: there were other Jews who wanted books, but had no way of borrowing them from the library. I had a month-long check out period, but because I read quickly, it was a longer period than I needed. After reading my books, I rented them out for a small fee. With this little bit of income I bought books I wanted to keep and savor.

The chances I took were foolhardy. German anti-Semitism emboldened Poles to display bigotry. There was suspicion and prejudice all around. I unnecessarily exposed myself to danger. I don't know if Mamusia knew the dangers, but she gave me money and the extraordinary freedom to go out despite the perils that existed for a Jew. Both my parents were preoccupied with the struggles of daily life. While the *szynk* was still in operation, ownership and management was now taken over by a German agency that was set up to take over businesses owned by Jews. A Polish man was now in charge as *treuhander*, a supervisor or manager. Tatus became merely an employee without any status as owner.

On November 20, 1939, bank accounts for Jews were blocked and money could not be withdrawn. Tatus turned his ready cash into trade goods. Bolts of fabric were propped in the corners of the apartment and large quantities of powdered cocoa took up space in the kitchen. These were exchanged for food and other necessities. I don't think the cocoa idea worked out as well as Tatus envisioned; but I personally benefited from it each afternoon when Mamusia prepared a cup of the rich, hot drink just for me.

By December 1, 1939, it was mandatory for all Jews to wear Star of David armbands, a six-pointed star symbolizing Judaism. All Jews over the age of twelve displayed their armband on the left arm, just above the elbow. The armbands were made from a white cloth, about four or five inches wide, with a big, blue Star of David. If the German police couldn't see the blue star, Jews were in trouble, and the result was beatings and arrests. This was wintertime and most people attached the armband over their winter coats, but this became problematic. With the natural movement of the arm the cloth scrunched up, causing the star to disappear from view. The band had to be continually maneuvered and stretched out in order for it to be visible. In time, some enterprising Jews began to produce and sell the Star of David made out of stiff celluloid. While this dispensed with the scrunching problems, most people only had one armband. Going outdoors in an absentminded manner without their band displayed, even just momentarily, incurred severe penalties and many months in prison. At this time I wasn't twelve yet, and it wasn't required that I wear one, furthering my misconception that I could blend in.

December brought heavy snows and chilling wind. Shoveling snow off the streets became the exclusive job of the Krakow Jews. In the beginning, the Gestapo drove several large trucks to one location where the workers were forced to assemble; then everyone was given a snow shovel. Later, some Jews discovered it was possible to buy a ration stamp without performing the actual labor. My brother-in-law, Jack, manipulated the system and gave me five *zlotys*, the basic unit of money in Poland, a day if I completed his work for him. He told me he preferred to play music in nightclubs and didn't want to work in the cold and wind. Because I was eleven years old, I didn't qualify for my own card, but since there wasn't any photo identification, I could substitute for him. Shoveling snow was dangerous work at times. There were reports of shootings, beatings and arrests, but I never witnessed them myself.

Soon we were to experience a *razzia,* raid, in the Kazimierz. On December 4, 1939, soldiers from the *Wehrmacht,* the armed forces of Germany, surrounded the Kazimierz. They were present on every street, ordering us over and over, "Stay in your homes. Don't come outside or look out the window. You will be shot if you disobey this order." They came to each apartment using a brusque search and seizure technique. They confiscated jewels, money, and other belongings.

A woman, who lived across from us, was shot and killed while returning to her apartment. When Tatus took a peek out the window, a shot was fired by a soldier standing below. The bullet went through our window and embedded itself in the ceiling of our apartment.

Mamusia, Tatus and I were sitting quietly waiting our turn for the inspection. Although our emotions were running high, we tried to remain calm. We could hear the soldiers tramping up and down the stairway, doors opening and slamming shut. I could only imagine what was going on in the other apartments. Perhaps the soldiers were scouring every drawer, searching for items of value and then, when finding what they came for, leaving the apartment in complete disarray. We lived simply and had few possessions of value. We resigned ourselves to our fate, hoping they would leave us unharmed.

The sudden knock at the door startled us. The officer in charge was formal; speaking politely to Tatus in German, he asked for certain items, money and jewelry. Then, he and his soldiers began looking around for anything they could find. We waited patiently until they were finished. They managed to confiscate a few things, but Tatus told the man in charge, "We're a simple working family with little in the way of luxuries." When they were satisfied with their search, they left our apartment. We hoped they wouldn't come back.

Early in January, 1940, all radios owned by Jews were to be handed over to the authorities. People were scared. With only sketchy rumors to go by, they didn't know where to turn for real answers. Dziunka and her young friends turned to the spirit world to get some of their questions answered. The number one question on everybody's mind was: When will the war end? To find out, Dziunka took me to one of her séances. They were usually held at someone's house. The whole procedure had to be carried out in a specific way. Even the table they sat around had to be made a specific way: glued or doweled together; nails couldn't be used. Everyone placed their hands on the table top, palms down, fingers splayed, touching the fingers of the person sitting next to them. Somebody asked a question. After a short pause the table moved! It shook and moved first one way for "yes," and then it shook and moved the other way for "no." I couldn't believe what was happening; I was skeptical, yet I wanted to believe. The answer received, after all was said and done, was that the war would be over by July, 1940. This was good news. Hearing this made everybody happy and relieved. Dziunka and I went home. I told our parents, "The Germans will be defeated and the war is going to be over soon. We only have to wait until the coming summer."

By February 1940, Jews had to declare all the property they owned. On March 7, 1940, Polish hospitals were not allowed to admit Jewish persons. Jewish hospitals were available to them, but Jews could only buy very simple medications such as aspirin.

Krakow was turning into a city of kidnappers. Jews were grabbed off the streets and shuttled away to forced labor camps. Some escaped and returned, but others did not. People simply disappeared. It was called *lapanki* (wa-Pan-ka). One day, Jack was kidnapped. He didn't come home and no one knew what had happened to him. Jack's family had long since moved from the high school to live in a town called Tarnow, about 50 miles east of Krakow. One day, they received a letter from Jack. He explained as much as he could about his kidnapping. He had been sent to the Postkow labor camp, located even further east than Tarnow. He wrote that the living conditions were difficult, and he was planning an escape. A few weeks later he escaped and returned to his family. Now, Dziunka and Jack were living in Tarnow.

As our lives in Krakow became more desperate, there was a shift in my responsibilities. One day, Mamusia dispatched me to go by train to Tarnow on an errand. This was forbidden and exceedingly dangerous if caught. People tried to smuggle black market luxury items on the trains; as a result, the Gestapo or Polish police made random searches. Apparently, Mamusia had confidence that I would make it to Tarnow without incident. I wasn't afraid of being caught by Germans. There were ways of fooling them, but, if a Pole caught me, I would land in big trouble. A Pole could spot a Jew better than any German. They always could tell the difference. And some of them were willing associates to the Gestapo, lending a hand to the search for any Jew in the wrong place.

In April, 1940, I turned twelve. Now that it was spring, Anita and I could take walks outdoors together. Anita had the same coloring as I: blond, curly hair; blue eyes; fair complexion. She could blend in easily to look Polish. We went to the movies even though Polish movie theaters were declared off limits to Jews. We went to the Planty, but even that was forbidden. We weren't, by law, allowed to sit on any bench, but we took advantage of every opportunity we could, deceiving the world into thinking we were Polish.

In May, 1940, we learned a ghetto, a restricted quarter in which some Jews were required to live, was going to be built. All Jews not permitted to live in the ghetto were ordered to leave the city by August 15, 1940. There was a lot of confusion regarding the ghetto. Nobody knew which, or how many, Jews were going to live there.

When July came and went, despite the prediction from the spirit realm, it became evident that the war would not be ending soon. The German army was victorious in Holland, Belgium and France. Each victory was a painful reminder of the false hope we carried in our hearts.

In September, 1940, we had to let our house servant, Marysia, go. By law, non-Jews could not work for Jews. Marysia, saddened to leave her "family," left in tears.

1940-1941
World War II Fronts and Campaigns

World War II Fronts and Campaigns
Greek-Italian War
Greek gains were small during the winter, but repeated Italian attacks failed. Greece was still on the offensive when Germany entered the fighting on April 6, 1941.

Balkan Campaign
Hitler's moves in the Balkans were motivated more by a desire to protect his flank for the invasion of the Soviet Union than by any wish to aid Mussolini

The Middle East
Great Britain had gained nothing in the attempt to aid Greece, and the withdrawal of troops from North Africa had resulted in a defeat there. Efforts to secure the Middle East proved more successful.

In April, 1941, a group of pro-Axis politicians and army officers seized control of the government of Iraq and asked for German aid.

The Russian Campaign
Hitler considered the conquest of the Soviet Union to be a critical part of his plan to create a German empire.

The War at Sea
Sinking of the Bismarck
U.S. Destroyers for Britain
Mediterranean Action
http://history.howstuffworks.com/world-war-ii/world-war-ii-fronts-and-campaigns-1940-19415.htm

1940 – 1941
12 to 13 years old

> My parents... and I, were not qualified
> to move into the ghetto; so, we were
> forced to move out of Krakow entirely.

Chapter 5

The ghetto was erected in Krakow in the Podgorze section, located in the northern end of Krakow. 15,000 "qualified" Jews (who had some professional service the German military needed or could exploit) were to be allowed to move to the thirty designated streets. Unlike our family, Uncle Shmil was permitted to live in the ghetto. His job had something to do with shoelaces, which were considered important to the German military.

My parents, Babcia, another Uncle called Icek, Dolek and I were not qualified to move into the ghetto; so, we were forced to move out of Krakow entirely.

Because of chaos and confusion, the move-out date had been changed many times but the final date for vacating the city entirely was March, 1941. The goal was to make the town *Judenfrei*, free of the Jews with all essential Jews living in the ghetto. It didn't matter where we went but we could not stay in Krakow any longer. We were simply ordered, "Go away, go anywhere, as long as you go."

From the moment we found out we had to leave Krakow, there was unrest in our household. Where would we go? Once there, how would we live? Every day, Mamusia, Babcia, and Tatus asked themselves these essential questions. Babcia was sent to Nieznanowice, a small village in the countryside, to seek out a place for all of us to live. Babcia had lived there some time ago and was well known. She still had some close friends who were willing to help her. She came back with the news that we had an agreement with a Polish family who were willing to give us a room in exchange for rent money.

Soon, we received orders from the German officials saying we could take what we could carry or put on a wagon. The rest of our belongings were sold in a flea market-type atmosphere, but there was no bargaining. Police looked the other way while our belongings and heirlooms were bartered for food. Polish people came from distant villages by the hundreds in dilapidated horse drawn wagons or carts. They bought up everything in sight at less than bargain-basement prices.

While in the village, Babcia made arrangements for the use of a wagon. We wouldn't attract any unnecessary attention from the Polish police because there were many wagons traveling to and from the various villages surrounding Krakow and the police generally acknowledged that it was Poles buying up Jewish goods and bringing them back to their villages.

Although I wasn't supposed to, I rode with the driver on a few of the trips back to the village. The wagon was primitive with old iron-banded wooden wheels. Once outside the city limits, the road turned into mud. It was tough going, especially for the horse. When we came to the rolling hills interspersed between stretches of flatland along the way, we had to get off and walk alongside the horse or behind the wagon, pushing it uphill.

As we were getting out of town on one of these trips, a police officer stopped us. Eying the heavy load in the wagon he asked, "What's this?"

"Some Jew's stuff," the driver said. Gesturing to me, he added, "He knows."

"Yeah, this is some Jew's stuff we bought." I said.

The police officer continued hammering us with questions until the driver gave him some money to shut him up.

Finally, we arrived at a small hut in the village. *This was where we were to live?* I couldn't see how all of us would fit inside. There were only two rooms in this tiny wooden structure: a kitchen and one bedroom.

It was an isolated place; the nearest homes were a few hundred feet away. The other huts were not uniformly dispersed and varied in size and structure. By comparison, living here made our apartment in Krakow appear spacious and elegant.

We unloaded the wagon and carried our load to the stable. Inside was a cow munching contentedly on some hay. Nearby the stable I saw a big pit. I was told all the refuse from the farm was dumped into it. What came out of it was used as fertilizer on the farmland. Near the pit was an outhouse with a hole at the bottom allowing excrement and urine to be disposed into the stinking cavity.

This was going to be a different kind of life than the one I was used to. I looked forward to getting back to Krakow and its modern living. I turned my attention to the prospect of an exciting journey home.

In early March, 1941, Dolek, Tatus, Mamusia and I left the Kazimierz forever. The day was cold, and there were patches of old snow on the ground. The horse plodded slowly through the muddy street, pulling our creaking wagon behind. As we rocked and bounced along, I thought of all the things I would miss in Krakow: movies, the library, the Planty. I loved sitting on the park bench watching the swans float on the lake. I would especially miss Anita and all the tram rides we took together. Her family had moved to the Tarnow ghetto where the Laubs, including Jack and Dziunka, were living. It made me sad to leave our home, friends, and family. I couldn't help but wonder when I would see them again.

1941

Feb 9th Nazi collaborators destroy pro-Jewish café Alcazar Amsterdam (Alcazar refused to hang "No Entry for Jews" signs in front of cafe)

Apr 17th - British troop land in Iraq/Yugoslavia; surrender to Nazis

May 6th - Joseph Stalin became premier of Russia

May 6th - At California's March Field, Bob Hope performs his first USO show.

http://www.historyorb.com/events/date/1941?p=2

United States
Hitler and Mussolini announce they are at war with America who retaliates with its own declaration of war.
http://www.thepeoplehistory.com/1941.html

1941

13 years old

Inside, to the left of the doorway, was a ladder leading up to a loft where hay was stored...

"This is where we sleep at night."

Chapter 6

The village was called Nieznanowice, literally, "A Place Nobody Knows." It was like stepping back in time to the 14th century. Here, the villagers led a simple farming life. They dressed in plain peasant clothing and carried out their tasks exactly as they always had done countless centuries before. The land was flat, but in the distance, there were rolling hills and a forest. The day we arrived, the entire landscape was covered in a snowy, white blanket. Except for the evergreens, all the trees were bare.

Rolling up to the hut in our creaking wagon, I was struck again by how unbelievably small it was. We were going to live with the Biernat family, a man named Roman and his wife, Maria, and their boy, Janek. There would be seven of us living here all together.

We were met at the door by *Pan* Biernat. He was an old, grumpy man with bony, stooped shoulders. He opened the door, and we found ourselves directly in the kitchen. There was a table, chairs, an oven, and two beds. On the walls were many holy pictures of Christ and his saints. The hut was primitive, completely behind the times in every modern convenience such as indoor plumbing and electricity. I discovered that although rudimentary, there was ample storage space. In the kitchen area was a pantry where cheese, milk, and butter were kept. These, I learned, didn't come from the market, but from the cow that resided in the stable (that was also where we kept a straw basket filled with clothing and other items we brought from Krakow).

Inside, to the left of the doorway, was a ladder leading up to a loft where hay was stored. Fat, clucking chickens and geese were roosting on each of the rungs of the ladder. *Pan* Roman Biernat explained, "This is where we sleep at night." Slinking around the legs of the kitchen chairs was a pretty, white cat. I was drawn to her and wanted to pet her.

Seated at the kitchen table were *Pani* Maria Biernat, a plain looking, youngish woman. Seated next to her wearing old, patched farm clothing was Janek, about 13. He had straight, brown hair; a dull looking face; and dark, disinterested eyes.

Pan Biernat led us to the next room where we would be staying. Sparsely furnished, there were two beds, a small table, and a another collection of holy pictures decorating the walls. After settling in the room, we rejoined the Biernats in the kitchen. They seemed friendly and happy to have us there—or maybe just happy to have paying renters. We hoped our time in the village would be temporary. For now, there was much adjusting to do.

Janek and I fell into an amiable relationship. I envied that he went to school since I wasn't allowed. I was relegated to creating my own school projects. I had been translating a famous Hebrew book entitled, *The Wise Men of Chelm* into Polish.

One day, Janek had an assignment to write an essay about a plum. I told him I would do it for him. I wrote it in a style that Janek wouldn't know how to do. I was more interested in showing off my own skill at writing than helping him get a good grade. Later that day, Janek came back with a corrected paper from the teacher; the words scrawled in the margin were, "You did not write this." This was funny to me. I couldn't pretend to write in any other style than my own.

Over the last few days of winter, Janek and I were often thrown together. Although we were friendly with each other, we were never really friends. We were from different worlds but gradually, I was adjusting to farm living. I probably had it the easiest of all my family. Working on the farm was fun, always a new adventure. Mamusia and Dolek were busy with sewing projects. A few villagers learned there was a tailor at the Biernats' hut. Dolek made one or two garments out of whatever material was available, sometimes even using old horse blankets. But soon, villagers began flocking to him with their garments for alterations.

Dolek developed a good reputation for quality work. He never did anything uncomplicated, and he never took shortcuts. He didn't change his standards just because he now lived in a peasant village. In this way Dolek and I were similar.

Mamusia chopped wood for the fire that kept the coals for Dolek's iron hot. Tatus helped sometimes, but he preferred to smoke a cigarette in private, or visit the few Jewish neighbors in the village. Gradually, Tatus managed to do as little as possible; he suffered from a stomach ailment and I often noticed Mamusia had to take care of him. I was still a carefree boy and didn't understand Tatus' weaknesses.

Mamusia allowed me to bring my books from Krakow to the village. This was a big concession, as space in the wagon had been limited. I kept them in a large basket under the bed in our room. Some of the books I saved and didn't read right away. Once I read any book, I had also committed it to memory and no longer needed it. I liked to savor the book and make sure it lasted so I would have something to look forward to. Because there weren't any books like these found in the village, I treasured mine and kept them set apart to be cherished later.

Sometimes, instead of reading from my "saved" book pile, I found the *Farmer's Almanac* and read it front to back. I learned about herbs, fruit, and the weather. I learned that tea could be made from certain leaves. I learned that nettles, when cooked, were like spinach; cooking destroyed the toxins that caused the itching.

The Nieznanowice peasants weren't particularly given to the kind of books I liked to read, and it became a challenge to find interesting reading material. I befriended the village schoolteacher, the one who recognized Janek hadn't written his own paper. She had many books and allowed me to borrow them, but they were more of an adult nature, not like Karl May adventure stories. One day I was alone in the hut when I found the family Bible, a tome with all the Biernat names written on the first page. This was the first time I had ever seen a Catholic Bible.

Ordinarily, no Jew would read the New Testament. As a result, I had never seen the Bible as a whole with the New Testament included. This Bible was a surprise to me, and I wanted to read it, even though reading the Christian Greek part was frowned upon. I began reading from the beginning in the book of Matthew where all the Jewish prophets, such as Isaiah and others, were quoted. Because I recognized many Jewish names, I was dumbstruck. With the many familiar names and places that I had been taught in my early Hebrew studies included in the Bible, I realized this was a book about the Jews. All the apostles were Jewish; Jesus was Jewish. I was completely stunned by this new knowledge.

Catholics and Jews didn't see eye-to-eye on many different issues, not just religion. There was a total misunderstanding of what they believed and what we believed. In secret I read the Biernat family Bible day after day for months and through my reading found much in common with the Jewish beliefs.

The Altered I

1941-1942

United Kingdom
Churchill launches the "V for Victory" campaign across Europe

United States
Attack on Pearl Harbor, Dec 7, 1941

Russia
Germany Begins the Siege of Leningrad which lasts until 1944
http://www.thepeoplehistory.com/1941.html

1942
Following the US entering the war, the mobilization of war efforts were quick and effective with car makers and other manufacturers changing to production of weapons of war .

Canada interns Japanese:
In early 1942, Canada interned the nearly 23,000 Japanese Canadians who lived in British Columbia -- about three quarters of whom were citizens -- in 10 camps scattered throughout the nation.

January 29
German and Italian troops occupy Benghazi.
Peru and Ecuador sign Protocol of Rio (boundary determination).
http://worldtimeline.info/wor1942.htm

1941 – 1942
13 to 14 years old

...they were staunch Catholics, seldom missing Sunday Mass or services. I felt we couldn't carry out a Jewish ceremony in front of them.

Chapter 7

In April, I was going to turn thirteen. This meant I was going to be subject to a Bar Mitzvah. This is a Hebrew word meaning in essence, "I am subject to the Law." According to the Jewish calendar, I was born on the seventh day during the eight-day Passover holiday.

My Bar Mitzvah was a serious matter, and Tatus did not want it overlooked. However, complications arose. Ordinarily the Bar Mitzvah would be held in a synagogue. We didn't have a suitable venue. There was no choice; it would have to take place in a private Jewish home.

The Biernat's initial warm welcome had been gradually cooling as the reality of living in such close quarters was settling in. Also, we were learning they were staunch Catholics, seldom missing Sunday Mass or services. We couldn't carry out a Jewish ceremony in front of them. In addition to not having a suitable location, we needed ten Jewish men to form a *minyan*. Where would we find them? Besides Tatus, Dolek, and Uncle Icek, there were only about three other Jewish men in the entire village. They were hiding from the Gestapo like we were. Still, we needed four more brave men, who would be willing to face a curfew and run the risk of traveling to our village dressed in the typical paraphernalia for the ceremony. Without them, I couldn't have my Bar Mitzvah.

Tatus and Babcia put their heads together and discussed how to find more Jews. Even though this probably caused added stress, they felt strongly about seeing this through. They set out to neighboring villages and located some men who were willing to come to the village on my birthday. Everything was in place. The Bar Mitzvah was a primitive affair, held secretly in a mill owned by the one Jewish family in the village. In attendance were a few guests from the village. Afterward, instead of a big happy celebration, as would have been the custom, with a banquet feast, we offered a few simply prepared food items. Then everyone rushed out to their huts and neighboring villages hoping they wouldn't get caught out after curfew. While it was sweet, it was over too quickly.

Summer

I was sent on the errand of retrieving mail from the post office located in a village called Niegowic (Nay-go-vitz). We regularly received updates from Dziunka. In one recent letter, she described how she accidentally left her armband on her coat and went outside without it. She only went out for a few minutes, but in that short time she was caught and sentenced to three months in prison. She was free now but it was a warning to us not to take any unnecessary chances.

In addition to picking up our mail, I was sent out to Niegowic to get the flour rations. When Mamusia was given a live chicken in exchange for tailoring, I went to the little village of Gdow, where the kosher butcher lived to have the chicken butchered.

Walking to these places allowed me to meet interesting people along the way. There was a family of two sisters and a brother from Krakow. They were *intelligentsia* and had escaped to Niegowic right after the war started. The first people arrested by the Gestapo were *intelligentsia*— the educated and intellectual elite, college professors and people otherwise considered to be enemies of the state. I became sociable with this family. They knew things, wrote about things, and thought about things. They often let me borrow books and allowed me to listen while they discussed various issues.

They had a Polish poem of special interest to me. A long, ancient prophecy, in the style of Nostradamus, called "The Prophecy of Wernyhora." Some claimed it was 900 years old. I was so impressed by its sayings that it became fixed solidly in my mind. What made it so extraordinary was its accuracy. In a very loose translation it said, "And once more the world will become red with blood when black eagle flies east, but it will return with broken wing." A black eagle was Germany's symbol. At this time, the Germans hadn't attacked "the East" which, I felt, was Russia. This was something not even known about. Another verse read, "Once more the world will become bloody when the East turns its attention to the North." I took it to mean a forthcoming war between some unknown country in the East against a country in the North. We wanted the prophecy to be true. The idea of believing anything positive, no matter its origins, was something in which we placed our hope. When the family of *intelligentsia* discussed the verses' meaning, I was a captive audience.

Almost in fulfillment of prophecy, starting in May 1941, we witnessed a tremendous number of German military trucks moving east. Spring rains had turned the dirt roads into a quagmire of mud. The soldiers were heading toward a village to spend the night. Because their trucks were stuck in the mud, they had little choice but to bivouac wherever they could.

Tatus, a smoker, knew the German soldiers had cigarettes. He sent me to trade eggs for cigarettes. They were a group of friendly, nice guys and I spoke enough German to be able to communicate with them and arrange the trading. Usually a group of soldiers stayed for a night then left the next day, only to be replaced by a new batch. I traded with group after group of German soldiers passing through the village. This aroused the jealousy of the other Polish kids in the village. They wanted to trade with the German soldiers too; however, they couldn't speak a word of German. I taught them a few phrases, but when they approached the soldiers, eggs held tremulously in their hands, the soldiers simply handed them cigarettes without any words having to be said.

On one occasion, I brought a German officer back to the hut to meet Tatus. They spoke to each other in German for some time and then Tatus offered him some schnapps. Although Tatus didn't drink it himself, he kept a private stash as a bargaining tool. They sat talking amiably together about daily life, steering clear of the subject of how the war was going. The German officer wouldn't have sat down with a Jewish man, so he must have believed Tatus was a Polish villager. To me, it seemed, Tatus enjoyed having friendly conversation with the soldier. I was surprised to see a polite, affable German. I could see the Biernat's marveling to each other, and I imagined them saying, "Max communicates with a German officer?"

On a lazy day in June, Janek and I were lying in a grassy meadow when I heard the sound of distant explosions. I bolted upright but I couldn't hear the blasts anymore. I lay back down in the grass and pressed my ear close to the ground: there was the sound again, muffled. I whispered to Janek, "Listen! Put your ear down on the ground. Do you hear it?" He nodded.

The Russian border was more than 200 miles away, but we could hear the explosions through the ground, Janek and I marveled. Janek ran to his parents and told them what we had heard. The next day the explosions were louder, but by the third day they were fading. I had to lie on the ground with my ear pressed close in order to hear better. On the fourth day, the sound of the explosions was completely gone. The rumor spread throughout the village that the explosions were the start of Germany's attack on Russia, which turned out to be true. It was generally thought the German military had made a big mistake attacking Russia. People in the village believed the war would be ending soon with Russia the victor.

The Biernats usually treated me with respect because I worked alongside them on the farm, but my parents, who concerned themselves with their own business and didn't do much farm work, were treated with barely concealed disdain. Thinking the war would end shortly with the Russians as victors, they suddenly began treating my family with more courtesy.

Autumn

During the fall of 1941, I was sent to the Tarnow ghetto to deliver a blanket to Dziunka and Jack. Dziunka had written Mamusia mentioning that when they were forced to leave Krakow, they left in such a hurry they hardly brought anything with them. It would be winter soon, and Mamusia thought they should have one of our blankets. We were able to bring many things out of Krakow and were able to spare a blanket. When folded up, it fit compactly inside the rucksack I wore on my back. Wearing my new *jopka,* a varicolored jacket Dolek made for me out of an old blanket, I was ready for my journey.

Traveling by train was especially dangerous, as inspections had increased. However, there was another option. Since the war with Russia started, there was a continuous flow of German trucks traveling both directions on the road. I found it more convenient to catch a ride in the open back of one these pickup trucks, than deal with trains and tickets and the potential of being discovered. The trouble was getting a truck to stop. Some of the drivers were friendly and stopped for people who hailed them down, while others just kept on driving. Sometimes trucks didn't pass by for long stretches of time. I waited awhile before a truck stopped. I told the driver where I wanted to get dropped off, hopped in the open back, and we were on our way.

Once deposited in Tarnow, I now faced the dilemma of finding the ghetto. I couldn't just go up and ask someone the location of the ghetto. They might ask themselves, "Why would a Polish kid want to go to the Jewish ghetto?" Then they would realize I wasn't Polish, and they would probably report me to the police. I began purposely looking for people who wore Star of David armbands. I found someone. I followed one man, but it soon became clear he wasn't headed toward the ghetto. Finally, I found a small group heading in what seemed to be the right direction. When I arrived in the ghetto, I saw that it wasn't strictly guarded. People were freely walking in and out. I walked right in and began wondering what my next step would be.

Dziunka had no idea I was making the trip to Tarnow, and therefore, she wasn't expecting me. I knew she worked in a soup kitchen, so I asked someone on the street where the kitchen was. I found it with little difficulty, went inside and asked for my sister by name.

"She's not here. She went home," A woman said.

"Where does she live?" I asked. They gave me some directions, and I found my way to her apartment.

When she saw me she exclaimed, "Joziu, what are you doing here?" She grabbed me by the shoulders and hugged me close. "I'm so happy to see you! Come in."

I entered her sparsely furnished apartment. I saw she wasn't alone but I didn't recognize the people. Apparently they lived in the apartment as well. I opened the rucksack and handed her the blanket. She asked, "What have you got there? You brought a blanket for me? How nice, it'll be perfect for this coming winter." Holding it close to her, she said, "Make sure you give my thanks and love to Mamusia."

Soon Jack came home. He worked outside the ghetto teaching violin to some Polish kids. We sat up late talking. I told them about life in the village and working on a farm, and they told me what was happening in their life in the ghetto.

I asked about Anita, but Dziunka told me she and her family had been moved back to the Krakow ghetto: "Her Uncle does some kind of work for the Germans. He has an important situation with them. Don't worry about your little girlfriend, Joziu. Her uncle provides her with a much better life than what we have in this ghetto!"

I stayed the night; but because of the other families living there it was uncomfortable and there was no privacy. When it was time for bed, the people put some bedding down and slept on the floor. And once the beds were made, it was difficult to walk around without stepping on someone.

Everywhere I looked things were shabby and worn out. There was hardly any furniture or the typical trappings that would make the place habitable. It was just walls and floor and poor people. It was discouraging to me, but the attitude of the people was hopeful. They were living like this just to survive to the next day, and each day brought them closer to the end of the war. As long as things were quiet, and they weren't bothered by anyone, they suffered the hard living conditions with dignity.

In the morning, all the people rolled up their bedding, ate whatever they had and rushed to work. Jack and Dziunka left for work also and would be gone all day. I couldn't go with them. They decided I should stay at Jack's parents' apartment. After depositing me with the Laubs, Dziunka gave me a piece of bread and left me alone with them.

There wasn't much for me to do here. I had no friends, and it was very quiet with everyone away at work. I spied a thick Polish dictionary and began to read. Starting at the beginning I worked through the alphabet, spending the whole day reading. It was like a drug for me, and I only came back to reality late in the afternoon when Dziunka arrived for me. After eating a meager dinner, we spent more time talking, but in all our conversations we avoided talking about the future.

"Joziu, I feel bad about the apartment," Dziunka said. "There's no room for you here and you're not comfortable."

I shrugged, and remained silent, but she was right. I had been living in the Biernat's tiny hut for several months. While the hut was cramped, at least we had our own room.

"I've made arrangements with some friends of mine, the Novak's," she continued. "They're Poles, but they are friendly with us and want to help. I told them I'd bring you over tonight."

After we talked, Dziunka took me to meet the Novak's. They lived about two miles away outside the ghetto in a small apartment. Dziunka introduced me, and then rushed back to her own apartment before curfew. *Pani* Novak showed me a place to sleep, and we all went to bed.

The next day, I went back to Jack's parents' place in the ghetto. I scrounged around for a while looking for things to do, but I didn't find anything. I resigned myself to read the dictionary again until Dziunka came for me.

When I left the ghetto the streets were empty, quiet and dark.

Without warning two Polish policemen stepped out in front of me. One policeman grabbed me roughly by the front of my *jopka* and ripped the buttonhole. That made me angry. It was my only jacket, and I didn't want anything to happen to it. But, right now I had worse trouble than a torn *jopka*.

The policeman gripping the lapels of my coat snarled, "What's your name?"

"B-Bialik," I stammered.

"Where's your *ausweis*?" he demanded.

A Pole wouldn't know about an *ausweis*. "What is *isweiss*?" I mispronounced.

He wasn't fooled and continued grilling me, "Where are you going?"

"I'm visiting some friends, and I'm on my way to the family called Novak," I said. "I'm staying with them."

My answers didn't seem to satisfy them. The other policeman asked, "Who's your father? What does he do?"

"He's a translator. He translates from German to Polish." Tonight, I was ready with an answer for everything. I put on a false front. If they thought my father did important work for the Germans, perhaps they would leave me alone. Instead they searched me. In my pocket they found a little notebook calendar with some addresses in it, one Jack had given me a long time ago.

The officer thumbing through the pages said, "These are all Jewish names."

"My brother-in-law gave me the book. He's a musician and he travels all over the world meeting people. These are the names of people he met in his travels."

They kept asking questions until one of them, tiring of the interview, said to the other, "Go over there," he pointed to a dimly lit entranceway. "Pull his pants down and see if he's Jewish or not." He dragged me over to a little alcove. He pinned me to the wall with one hand and with the other fumbled for his flashlight.

This is it for me: I'm dead. They're gonna see I'm a Jew. And I'm not wearing the armband: They'll take me away! Frantically, I looked for a way out, but there was none. *What am I going to do? What can I do? If they get me they will eventually find my parents. What have I done?*

Even though my parents were living in the village legally, living with the Biernat's was not quite right. I felt guilty for my foolhardy ways, and putting everyone at risk. If they were caught it would be my fault.

Just then, a woman, apparently a prostitute, sauntered past. The policemen became more interested in her than me. They decided they had enough of me. "Go!" one of them ordered, and abruptly pushed me away. I didn't hesitate for a minute and took off running down the sidewalk. Saved by a prostitute! It was a miracle. When I ran a safe distance away I threw the notebook in the garbage.

The next day I confessed the whole thing to Dziunka. She was terrified for me, "Joziu, you could have been killed! You can't stay here; you need to go back to Nieznanowice." Although she was scared for my life, I was calm about the matter. I was developing the ability to lock my emotions away in the deep recesses of my psyche. I was more irritated by the policeman's roughness, resulting in a torn *jopka*.

I had safely delivered the comforter; now my job was done. Since I didn't have a full rucksack, I decided to take the train home. No Jewish person had a train schedule, so to my disappointment, I learned that I had just missed the train to Krakow and had to stay one more day at the Novak's. The next day, I boarded the train without incident.

When I arrived back at the village, Mamusia asked how everything went in Tarnow. I left out the altercation with the two Polish policemen. I was scared that if she found out, she would never let me go again. I determined never again to carry anything incriminating, such as the address book Jack had given me. Babcia had a Polish friend who gave me a small, oval, holy medal of an unknown saint to wear around my neck. To ensure I passed as a religious Pole whenever I went out, I always had it with me.

Winter

The Biernats' were of the mind that the war couldn't last long. In the meantime, they thought they could put up with certain discomforts, as long as they were temporary. None of us knew how the war was progressing. Some asked, "Were the Russians winning? Were the Germans winning? Would the war end soon?" But there were no answers.

With winter approaching, we felt keenly aware that our living conditions were going to get a lot worse. All of us were lodged in the hut during the snowy days and nights. There was nowhere to go to get away from each other. Maria Biernat was becoming more and more unpleasant to be around. She wanted her old room back. She had had enough of sleeping in her own kitchen. We were now relegated to the kitchen area.

Sleeping in the kitchen was even more primitive than the bedroom. I didn't mind the new arrangement; however, it must have been hard on Mamusia, who treasured her privacy. Tatus, because of his stomach issues, didn't feel well a lot of the time, but nobody dared to make a complaint.

Unless it was bread-making day, the kitchen was cold. It was a busy thoroughfare during the day, as peasants frequently dropped in for a visit or card game. As long as there were visitors in the kitchen, we couldn't go to sleep. Finally, when the guests left and the Biernats went to the bedroom, we were able to sleep. Because we had no electricity, we used kerosene hurricane lamps. Kerosene was expensive and used sparingly. I learned how to make carbide gas lamps out of a carved-out turnip. The lamps were cheaper and brighter than kerosene, lighting up our little hut quite well.

Village women came over and told scary stories to each other. I found them to be a very superstitious bunch. As the story unfolded, the listening women huddled in closer together, some making the sign of the cross. One time, one of the peasant women had visited Krakow. She related some of the outstanding miracles she saw, "The houses are four stories tall," she said. "Inside the rooms there is light coming down from the ceiling. Then, in another room I saw water coming out of the wall—there was no well that I could see, just water coming out of the wall!" Everyone "oohed" in amazement; some sat with their hands covering their mouths, eyes big and round, shaking their heads back and forth in disbelief. I laughed to myself. Krakow was only 20 miles away from the village, but apparently, only this one woman had been there and seen modern conveniences, which she misunderstood as magic.

These women enjoyed gossiping and sharing stories. Sometimes I had a little fun at their expense. One time I decided I would read their palms and pretend to tell their fortunes. Often, they handed me a piece of bread for the service. I was observant and took advantage of their superstitious nature. If I saw a young, single woman I told her, "You are going to marry a very kind man." Or, if I saw a woman who squinted a lot I would say, "You have problems with your eyes." She would look at me in amazement and agree, "Oh yes, I do." I took their hands in mine and studied the lines in their palms. I would say, "You have a very long life line." If she was married, I always told her things pertaining to marriage. I said, "You have a good husband, a man who cares for you. I see by your line here that you will have a very nice, long marriage." This seemed to make them happy. I gained their respect and hoped they would bring an extra piece of bread or cheese the next time they visited.

Winter was a tough time. Getting the water from the well in the village was a hard job. We slipped and skidded our way across the icy path to the well. After we filled our buckets we walked carefully back, trying to keep our balance and not spill the water.

Trudging through hip-deep snow to the outhouse was another inconvenience. We didn't have proper winter shoes; often we just did our business out the door. Just to urinate was easy. I had special fun trying to write my name in the snow. Maria, who never wore underpants, lifted her skirt, stuck her rear end out the door and proceeded with gusto. Mamusia and Tatus tried to maintain their dignity and chose to struggle through the deep snow.

By December 1941, all mail going in or out of the Krakow ghetto was stopped. We no longer had any communication with Uncle Shmil. The Tarnow ghetto was still open, and we frequently got updates from Dziunka regarding the situation of the Jews.

The Altered I

1942

January
62 German submarines sunk this month (327,000 tons).

February 24
Voice of America shortwave radio service (propaganda tool) begins broadcasting (in German).

April 27
Belgium Jews are forced to wear stars.
Tornado destroys Pryor, Oklahoma, USA killing 100, injuring 300.

May 12
Extermination of Jews begins at Auschwitz.
David Ben-Gurion leaves Jewish state in Palestine.
German submarine sinks American cargo ship at mouth of Mississippi River.

Soviet forces occupy Crackow.
http://worldtimeline.info/wor1942.htm

April to July 1942
14 years old

It was decreed that when a Jewish boy reaches age fourteen, he has to leave and join a work force somewhere.

Chapter 8

Beginning in April 1942, orders came from the authorities that all Jewish men 16 years and older had to report to Lapanow (wa'panuf) to register. None of the Jewish men from our village wanted to register, but they had no choice; they had to obey the orders. Dolek now 25 years old, tried to be clever and devised an excuse why he and Uncle Icek couldn't go. Dolek reported to the authorities that they couldn't report because they didn't have travel passes, and they didn't want to get in trouble traveling without permission. It didn't work. The authorities sent travel passes to them, and shortly after, they all had to register. After a few weeks, we received a postcard from Dolek telling us that they were in a labor camp at the Krakow airport called Rakowice (rako'vitzay) run by German civilians.

Every village had an elder, called a *wojt* (pronounced voyt) in charge of the village. One day, the *wojt* came to our hut with disturbing news. It had been brought to his attention that I was now fourteen years of age. It was decreed that when a Jewish boy reaches age fourteen, he has to leave and join a work force somewhere. The *wojt* received orders saying I had to leave the village and report to a work commander in another town. I didn't want to leave. Mamusia talked to the *wojt* and somehow, I don't know how, the matter was forgotten and dropped.

We missed Dolek. Without him, there were no exchanges made

for tailoring work. As a result, we didn't get much food. We paid the Biernats for everything we needed, but Polish money had little value. Mamusia began trading our clothing or whatever possessions of value we had for bread and vegetables.

Twelve miles away from our village was a town called Wieliczka (vi' litzka), famous for its ancient salt mine. Salt was in short supply. I was dispatched several times to Wieliczka to get salt in order to trade with the peasants for food. I lugged back heavy bags, each weighing approximately 25 pounds. Together Mamusia and I transferred the salt into smaller containers we had made out of newspapers. Then we went around to the villages trading for bread and vegetables.

Besides trading the salt, we loaded up baskets with our clothing. Together we walked around Nieznanowice, as well as to a number of other villages in the area, hoping people would give us food in exchange for our personal items. The day was hot, and the ground burned and blistered the soles of our bare feet. We were completely at the villagers' mercy, depending on what they needed. Some Poles were friendly with us, but others saw in us the reason for all of their problems. Mamusia begged them, "We have this blouse, could you give us bread or potatoes?" The villager would come up with something small, such as a piece of bread or a few small potatoes. Sometimes we were given a handful of grain to make bread.

Soon, we received worse news. There was an order given that within four or five days, our entire family had to leave the village and report to the town of Bochnia for "resettlement" inside the ghetto. The Germans called it resettlement, but we were well aware of what was happening to people when they were "resettled." Dziunka sent us coded messages to warn us about resettlement and what we should do in case we received such an order. When she wrote, "Uncle Abraham got sick and died," we knew that meant Jews were being killed. She warned us to do anything possible to avoid being taken, "Hide yourselves. Change your names. Do anything, but do not go!"

Now we were terrified. Yet, we weren't frozen in fear. We were desperate to do anything to escape this fate.

Tatus wanted to hide some of his valuables. He had some jewelry, an old watch, and a few other things. We packed all of it in a box, put some old clothes around it to make it waterproof, and then wrapped it again in another layer of cloth. We buried it in a secret spot in the stable. I felt certain no one would find it.

Mamusia heard some Jews were hiding their children with Polish families, passing them off as Polish. She knew some Poles who were friendly toward us, and she tried to persuade them to take me in for the duration of the war. Perhaps if I had been a girl it would have been easier, but no one wanted to take a chance with me.

I felt hopeless. I began to imagine we were going to be taken away and shot. As Mamusia and I were walking one day, I attempted to comfort her. With resignation in my voice I said, "When they shoot us, we won't feel a thing. We will die together, holding hands. We'll be okay. There won't be any pain."

July 1942

World War II Timeline: July 9-July 23

July 9:
Teenaged diarist Anne Frank goes into hiding along with her family and friends as the Nazis begin to purge Amsterdam of its Jewish population.

July 15:
In the first deportation of Holland's Jews, some 2,000 are sent to Auschwitz under the guise of being relocated to a Nazi German labor camp.

July 22:
The Nazis open the Treblinka death camp outside of Warsaw, Poland. Like Belzec, Treblinka's mandate is exclusively extermination, not confinement and labor.

http://history.howstuffworks.com/world-war-ii/axis-conquers
-philippines16.htm

July 1942
14 years old

I didn't ask her where she was going, but I could tell by the way she was dressed it was somewhere important.

Chapter 9

In a nearby town lived a young policeman, well known for his womanizing. He was a big man who had been given power and authority. Because of that power, he was troublesome. This man was ordered to be our watchdog, ensuring we wouldn't escape before reporting to Bochnia. There were two days yet before we would be forced to leave Nieznanowice.

Tatus invited him inside the hut for a drink of schnapps. He had hopes of making some kind of an arrangement with the young policeman. After some congenial conversation, the officer started to write a note indicating a way out for us. As he slid it across the table towards Mamusia, I caught a glimpse of it. The police officer wrote, "Let M. Kempler come and visit me tomorrow at 1 p.m. We will work something out."

That was very strange. I wondered whom he was speaking to in his note. In Polish, *Pan* is used as an honorable title, such as Mr., or *Pani* for missus. He didn't finish the title by writing "*Pan* M. Kempler." He only wrote M. Both my parents' names began with the letter M. Which one was it, Max or Malka? Was it *Pan* or *Pani*? I wasn't entirely sure what to make of it. I was still very innocent. I had no knowledge of any kind of motivation a man might have to allow a woman and her family to escape a Nazi order. I was about to speak up when the officer scraped back his chair and abruptly left the hut. I kept quiet and decided to see what the outcome would be. In two days' time, a horse and wagon would pick us up at the hut and take us away for resettlement. We were allowed to take up to 44 pounds of belongings in a suitcase.

The next morning dawned a perfect and beautiful day. If my mood hadn't been so somber, I would have thought this was a good day to be alive. That morning, I walked to my favorite spot in a meadow nearby the hut. Sometime later, I saw Mamusia walking down a pathway near where I lay in the meadow. She didn't look at me; she didn't so much as say, "Hello," or, "I'll be back later, Joziu." I didn't ask her where she was going, but I could tell by the way she was dressed it was somewhere important.

In the village the women typically dressed in old work clothing: drab and shapeless. That late morning, Mamusia looked her best in the dress she wore for special occasions. It was a fashionable, navy blue dress with white polka dots. She looked quite pretty in it. I could tell she had combed out her hair and applied lipstick. In that moment, I knew something wasn't right about her going to the policeman, I was confused. I had mixed emotions—I wanted her to be successful and save us, but I didn't want her to go to the policeman for help.

I lay there drinking in the beautiful sunshine, the beautiful, tall grass. I remained a long time listening to the peaceful sounds all around me: the birds singing, the cows mooing, and somewhere in the distance I heard a rooster crow. There were some kids playing nearby and I heard their peals of laughter. My senses were intensified. There was the faint perfume of flowers all around me. I watched as the breeze played along the leaves of the trees, making them tremble, and caused the flowers to sway gently. I heard the drone of insects nearby. This was a delightful day—a good day to be alive, but the thought drumming through my mind was, "Tomorrow I am going to die." A terrible feeling overcame me. I was taking my last look at the life I could have had in the village. I was saying good-bye to life. We were all going to Bochnia to die. There was no way out, no escape for us, and this perfect, bright day with plenty of sunshine was truly a dark, black day.

Yet, there was a conflict inside me, hopelessness fighting against the hope that Mamusia could do something to change our fate. I got up and went back to the hut. I walked inside and found Tatus slumped over the table, his head lowered in the crook of his arms. We didn't talk to each other or acknowledge each other's presence. I lost respect for him at that moment. How could he let Mamusia go to the policeman? What was wrong with him? I turned around and went back out to the meadow.

Later in the day when I saw Mamusia coming back down the path, she avoided my gaze, and as she passed by, I averted my eyes from her. Deep down I knew she had given herself to the policeman. She had done it to save us, but I felt she had somehow betrayed me. I was angry at her now. She had no right to do anything like this to me; she was my Mamusia.

Something inside me snapped. I stayed in the meadow until the dusky time of day, the sky purple and hazy. When I got up, I felt I had changed into a completely different person, someone remote and uncaring. I felt no love for Mamusia anymore. When I came back inside the hut, no one was talking. Mamusia was crying quietly, packing a suitcase.

This was the first time I ever saw her cry. She kept her face averted from Tatus, and neither of us talked to her. Her only words were to tell me what to pack and to dress in layers. I wished I could take my books, but there was no room for them. I remembered the Biernat's family Bible. So far, I had read up to the book of The Acts of Apostles; regretfully, I wouldn't finish it.

Babcia came with her suitcase, and we were ready to leave. I didn't know where we were going to go. I only knew we had to leave.

On this quiet Saturday night the policeman failed to arrive for guard duty, and we made our escape into the night.

July 1942

Germany Initiates the Battle of Stalingrad, USSR (July, 1942):

A German offensive in an attempt to capture Stalingrad, beginning July 17, 1942. By its completion in 1943, it would become the deadliest battle in human history. The Nazi army penetrated inside the city, engaging in urban warfare with the Soviets.

July 23:

Judenrat president Adam Czerniakow, who is charged by the Nazis with delivering 6,000 Jews a day for "resettlement" from the Warsaw Ghetto on penalty of the death of his wife and some 100 other Jewish hostages, takes his own life. A day earlier, he was unable to convince the Nazis to spare the ghetto orphans from being sent to Treblinka as part of a mass deportation of Jewish children.

http://history.howstuffworks.com/world-war-ii/axis-conquers
-philippines17.htm

July 1942
14 years old

I couldn't imagine how Tatus, Mamusia, and Babcia would handle the arduous walk into the forest.

Chapter 10

Beyond the village was a ravine with a flowing river. North of the ravine stood a densely wooded forest. The abundant undergrowth provided a safe haven for many small animals. We hoped it would provide sanctuary for us too.

The Biernats' nearest neighbors offered to help us escape. In hushed tones, Mamusia made our arrangements. The grown son of the family offered to lead us to the river where we would cross the bridge to the edge of the forest.

I couldn't imagine how Tatus, Mamusia, and Babcia would handle the arduous walk into the forest. At this time Mamusia was 44, Tatus was 59 or so, but not healthy or strong. Babcia was elderly and frail. Despite their limitations they were desperate to escape, only I didn't know how we could manage the trip, especially with a sick man and an old woman; I just went along with it.

"Wait until it gets dark," Stepinski instructed. "When the moon sets, you can go without being seen." We waited with nervous anticipation until the prescribed time. True to his word, Stepinski came over in the evening. We took our suitcases and followed him through the back roads, avoiding the villagers relaxing in their huts and their dogs who could send out a warning bark.

Stepinski left us at the bridge, but because we didn't want to be seen from the road, we trekked through the river, which was shallow at this time of year.

Stepping onto dry land on the other side, we started climbing uphill through pine and oak trees, but it was hard to carry all our suitcases, and it was especially hard for Babcia and Tatus. They slipped on the dead, dry leaves and pine needles lying on the forest floor. The leaves were deep and every step we took rustled the leaves and made a crunching racket. Small twigs snapped beneath our feet. We whirled around at each sound, and looked behind, fearful and breathless. I thought that someone had certainly heard our racket and we would be caught.

My parents were confused and didn't know which way to run or where to hide.

I took over the command of our little troop, "We can't continue like this. We're making too much noise. It's too dangerous! We have to find a dense spot and stay there until morning." Everyone nodded numbly. Mamusia trusted me to lead the family. Tatus and Babcia didn't know what to do or where to go. The forest was so dark we couldn't see where we were or if the place was safe enough, or deep enough into the woods.

Eventually, we found a place to rest for the night. We barely made it: Babcia and Tatus were huffing and struggling to stand. When we found the spot, we landed in a big, exhausted heap. Using our suitcases as pillows, we lay down and hoped we wouldn't be visible when daylight came. Everyone relaxed, our heavy breathing under control. We were safe … for now.

The next morning was Sunday. We heard voices along the trail not too far away from where we were hidden. There was the sound of happy laughter like that of a group of young people. They must have been going to the church just over the hill. We were afraid to move for fear they would discover us. We didn't dare make a sound. We stayed as still as possible. An hour or two later we heard them coming back down the hill. This time we could hear the boys chasing the squealing girls all through the woods. We were in great danger of being found, but because we were hidden by the trees, away from the path, they didn't see us. As the afternoon wore on, the forest became increasingly quiet. Gradually, we relaxed our stiff positions, but we decided we should move deeper into the woods. My goal was to be so well-hidden no one could stumble upon us by accident. We also needed to find water.

We trudged through the woods carrying our suitcases, Babcia and Tatus trying to keep up as best they could. Tatus seemed to be suffering the most. He walked haltingly, struggling to catch his breath with each step. He needed our help walking, especially when going down a steep hill.

I found another place that seemed quite secluded and ideal for our needs. Once again, we threw ourselves down in complete exhaustion and tried to make ourselves comfortable in the darkening woods. Mamusia doled out bread and I brought water from a nearby brook. We tried to remain very still and quiet, but soon I saw Mamusia and Babcia huddled together, whispering.

"What are you talking about?" I whispered.

"We're going back to the village," Mamusia said. "We want to know what happened to our friends and if they've discovered we didn't report to Bochnia."

"I want to go with you."

"No," Mamusia said firmly. "Joziu, you have to stay here with Tatus. He might need you."

I was puzzled. I thought I had found a good place, far enough away. I couldn't understand them. Why did they need to go back? I couldn't believe Mamusia and Babcia could make it safely back to the village by themselves—or even find us again. Mamusia didn't know where we were; she had no map of any kind; no light to see where she was going, except maybe the light of the moon. But they were determined more than ever to go back to the village.

"What if you can't find us?" I asked

"We will," Mamusia said. "Stay here; we'll be back."

As the night wore on and they didn't return, my thoughts began to torment me. I wondered what had happened to them.

"What do we do if they don't come back?" I asked Tatus. "Do you think they're lost? What if somebody sees them or a dog finds them and barks, waking the villagers?" Questions without answers flew out of my mouth. My anxiety increased with each passing minute. Tatus felt as helpless as me. *They can't make it without me. I should have gone with them.*

Finally, very late into the night, the pair stumbled back to our makeshift campsite. Tatus and I were sitting quietly waiting for them. We didn't betray the nagging worries and inner turmoil that had tormented us during the waiting hours. I had to admit, they were shrewder than I gave them credit for. Not only did they find their way to the river and get to the village without incident, they made it safely back to the river and were able to find our spot in the forest. Mamusia told us they had found their Polish friends and stayed with them for a while. They were given bread to take back to us. They heard many stories.

The Jewish family who owned the village mill where I had my Bar Mitzvah hid in the mill area, but were found. They were rounded up by the Polish police and mercilessly shot. Other Jews were taken away. There was a price on Jews' heads. The police told the villagers, "Whoever finds any Jews, we'll give two kilos of sugar." No one had seen sugar in a long time. We knew the villagers would hunt us down like animals.

We had to find a new hiding place. I couldn't comfort myself. No place was really safe, but it had to be better than our current campsite. If Babcia and Mamusia found us again so easily, who else could stumble upon us? We waited until daylight before moving even deeper into the woods. I found a small section of flat land that abutted a heavily wooded mountainside. The hillside jutted up sharply and there was no trail. The trees formed a canopy overhead that created a cave-like atmosphere. We were invisible to anyone beyond the path. Although I wasn't familiar with the forest, I felt we were deep enough into the woods that we would be safe here. We had plenty of fresh water nearby; the night was warm and the ground dry.

Our first problem was to escape reporting to Bochnia. Mamusia succeeded in solving it with her deal with the policeman. He failed to arrive for guard duty, enabling us to escape into the woods. The next problem became how long to hide and what we could do next? We spent the whole day sitting quietly thinking, but no one came up with any idea or plan. We were dejected and felt that no matter what we decided on, we were in trouble.

The next morning we heard rustling in the woods. A man appeared unexpectedly in our midst. His presence terrified us. I looked at him warily. He was tall and refined looking. I could tell he wasn't a peasant. He was dressed in plain clothes. *Who is this guy? Is he going to report us? What does he want?* We remained silent and let him be the first one to ask the questions.

He smiled in a friendly way and said: "Hello, I'm a forester in these woods. When I was patrolling up on top, I saw a glint of something reflecting off the sun. I came down to investigate, and here I find you."

I looked around at what it could have been that tipped him off to our presence, but couldn't find anything, until I glanced at one of our suitcases. I knew then what had happened. Tatus' suitcase had small metal corners. These were what the forester saw glinting in the sun. Now he realized we were Jews on the run.

He assured us: "Don't worry I'm not going to report you. Just stay right here. You must be hungry—I'll bring you something to eat."

Did he truly want to help us? I couldn't believe it. Just as quietly and suddenly as he had arrived, he left.

After waiting awhile, I became scared.

"What happens if he comes back with the police?" I asked my parents.

Tatus said, "Oh, I believe him. He looked nice. I think he'll bring food." The other two nodded in agreement.

"Yes," Mamusia said, "I think he will help us." At first, I wanted to believe him, too, and wait for him to bring back some food. But my suspicious mind got the better of me.

"What if he's lying, and he doesn't want to help us?" I said to Babcia.

"Trust your parents and me," she said. "We can tell when someone wants to help or not."

At that moment I couldn't trust anyone. Wild thoughts entered my mind. I looked around for a thick branch. I decided when he came back, I would club him with the branch. Of course, that would work if he came back alone, but what if he came with the police? I had to face another tough decision. Do I trust him? Do we stay here and hope he's not lying? Or should we take our chances in the woods and leave this place? Back and forth I went, trying to decide. My parents wanted to stay, they felt good about it, but I felt panicky. I felt strongly within that we had to leave. Finally, my mind made up, I said: "We can't trust him, he's a Pole. What if he brings the police?"

After much debate, I managed to convince my family to leave. Once again, I searched for another place deeper into the woods. We walked for several hours, only stopping for a short time to rest before beginning again. We tried not to leave marks, footprints or broken branches, so if the forester came back he wouldn't find us. After trudging around for what seemed an eternity, I could see Tatus walking in a daze. He was suffering, but he wouldn't stop; it was a struggle every step of the way, but he kept up with us. His steps were uneven and shaky. He wasn't walking with purpose anymore. The suitcases hung heavy on his arms. Babcia was struggling beneath the weight of her suitcase, too. Mamusia, younger and stronger than either of them, volunteered to carry Babcia's and Tatus' suitcases. Fear of discovery and a will to survive pushed us to find sanctuary. After a few hours, we found a place that was hidden from view and seemed safe, and as we did before, we collapsed in an exhausted, breathless heap on the ground. We were near another brook, and Mamusia took care of us, carefully portioning out the food.

That first day in our new hiding spot, we sat quietly but trembled in fear.

I asked my parents: "What if the forester finds us? He knows this forest better than we do."

They shrugged; they didn't know. We would just have to wait and see. After a couple of days of waiting without being discovered we began to feel comfortable with our hiding place. Soon, we became confident that we wouldn't be discovered here. The sun had been shining for several days now. The nights were warm, the forest quiet but for the birds singing. There was peacefulness in the woods that comforted us. Still we didn't know what to do next or where to go from here. We were all thinking about it, but no one said a word. For now, we resigned ourselves to remain here as long as we could. I didn't dare contemplate the next day.

The Altered I

July 1942

In Science:
Radar comes into operational use.

Nobel Prizes in Science
Chemistry: None awarded
Physics: None awarded
Physiology or Medicine: None awarded

In Entertainment:
Casablanca premieres in theaters.
Bing Crosby releases "White Christmas," from the film Holiday Inn. The song goes on to be the all-time, top-selling song from a film

http://www.infoplease.com/year/1942.html

July 1942
14 years old

> My nights were filled with nightmares of getting caught and killed. I spent my days fantasizing about how good life had been in Krakow.

Chapter 11

Although the woods felt peaceful, my mind didn't give me any rest. Over and over, I was plagued with self-doubt. How could I be sure this place was safe? I picked the first place, yet Babcia and Mamusia found Tatus and me easily. Then I found another place, but the forester found us. *How do I know we won't get caught here? What remains of our meager food supply will run out soon. We can't just sit here forever. Where do we go next?* My anxieties were growing.

I felt a mounting sense of responsibility for the safety of the family. When I looked to Mamusia, Tatus and Babcia for the solution, the answers didn't come. They didn't know where to go or what to do. If we had waited for that forester to come back with food, who knows where we would be now? I was the one to tell them what we should do. But, what if I pick the wrong place again, and a policeman comes and shoots my parents and Babcia? How can I bear to see that? The burden weighed heavily upon me, but I kept it to myself. There was a fearful possibility that if I failed in this and we are all caught, we were going to die.

After several days, a number of feelings began to emerge. I realized the burden of responsibility had become too much for me. My nights were filled with nightmares of getting caught and killed. I spent my days fantasizing about how good life had been in Krakow. I began to think of Anita and all the fun things we did together: our tram rides, our storytelling, our card games. Once the thought of going to Krakow entered my mind, I couldn't get rid of it. The daydream was wonderful to me, and all my thoughts focused on the imaginary picture I created in my mind.

I had made two prior trips to the Krakow ghetto since moving to the village. The first was when we had some communication with Uncle Shmil. He was married and was expecting his first child. He and his wife lived with her mother. I went by train, but first had to walk eleven miles to Klaj, the nearest train stop. I was so excited to ride the big train, although the trip was a short ten miles.

The main train terminal, Dworzec Glowny, was in the center of town and very dangerous. Often, people tried to smuggle black market goods and were sometimes caught in random inspections by the Polish police or German officers patrolling the train terminal. To get by the inspections safely, I depended upon my Aryan features, age, and speech patterns. Above all, I tried not to call attention to myself.

I decided it was best to get off at Plaszow (Pwa'shuf) Krakow station, one stop before the main station, and walk to the ghetto. Once there, I could see that it was blocked off and surrounded with walls. Any windows facing out to the Aryan side of the street were completely bricked up because the Germans didn't want Jewish faces to be seen peering from windows. The only entrance, serving also as an exit, had a tall brick and stucco wall with four arches and tall arched gates. The gates were strictly guarded by Polish police, German *Schutzstaffel*—the infamous SS guards—and Jewish police. The Jewish police were known as the Ordinance Police, called *ordnungsdienst* in German, or OD. They were given privileges and authority by the German officers, but the other Jews despised them for it. While some OD tried to be kind and obey the German orders without cruelty, others felt compelled to be tough. Most of them were diligent in their inspections and didn't hold back punishment. They didn't scare me, but maybe they should have.

The ghetto was encircled with barbed wire and walls. At the northern end was a steep hill, called Krzemionki. I knew people were sneaking in because I was told to look for a cut in a section of the barbed wire near Krzemionki. I found the cut in the wire, pulled it apart making a small hole, and squeezed through. After putting the wire back together, I set off to find my uncle.

All three of them, including Shmil's sick mother-in-law, were at home when I found them in their one-room apartment. People were crammed into small living quarters, where one apartment was home to several different families. The Krakow ghetto looked as depressing as the

Tarnow ghetto where Dziunka and Jack lived.

The next morning Shmil and his wife went off to work, leaving me alone in the room with the mother-in-law, who was paralyzed and didn't speak. She lay in bed staring at me. I began to feel self-conscious, so I ignored her. Whenever I felt her gazing at me, I avoided looking at her. I busied myself inspecting the books lined up on a small bookshelf. I found a medical book and pulled it from the shelf. I became absorbed in reading it. After a while, I became bored with the book and decided to see a movie. I left the apartment and headed toward the area of the cut wire. Soon, I slipped out of the ghetto, and bounded toward another adventure.

I didn't have an armband, so going outside the ghetto was even more dangerous than sneaking in, but I took my chances. I rode the tram to the movie house in Krakow where the German film, *Stern von Rio* was playing. Late in the afternoon I risked getting caught again, and returned to the ghetto through the wires, staying another night with Shmil. I spent about three days with Shmil and after the third day I left for the village.

Lying quietly in the forest, reflecting on the good times in Krakow, I was emboldened to pursue my goal of getting back there. They weren't all fond remembrances; there was that bad time in June 1942, when we heard there had been an *Aktion* in the Krakow ghetto. The Germans called it an *Aussiedlung* meaning resettlement, but, by this time we knew people either were killed right there on the spot, or taken away to an unknown destination, where we thought they were taken to work.

Hearing of this *Aktion,* I was sent to Krakow to investigate the situation and make sure Uncle Shmil and his family were all right. This time, rather than go by train, which was far too dangerous now, I went by German truck. Once inside the ghetto, a resident told me that after the *Aktion,* the size of the ghetto had been reduced. This *Aktion* had been a selection based on age, health, and desirability; it was a bloody thing. People began hiding themselves in order to avoid being killed or taken away. Uncle Shmil's apartment was no longer part of the ghetto. When I came to his apartment, nobody was there: no Shmil, no wife, no baby, and no paralyzed mother-in-law. The whole family had disappeared, and none of the people I asked knew where they were. I hoped they were taken to a work camp someplace, but the prevailing worry was they had been killed. Everyone had been afraid for their lives. I was afraid now and hurried to leave and report back to Mamusia.

Now, hiding away in the forest all I did was daydream about going back there. I began to think that I could leave the forest. I had gone to

Krakow by myself those times. I knew the way, and I knew I could make it. I agonized over it for a whole day, and by the next morning, I couldn't resist the strong desire to leave: I had to get away! I wanted to shrug off the heavy responsibility of caring for the family. I couldn't carry the burden any longer.

The very thought of staying in the forest and possibly making a mistake, getting us all killed, motivated me to make my move. How do I go about it? As much as I wanted to speak the truth, I couldn't just announce that I had had enough. I had to proceed carefully and logically.

After building up enough courage, I told Mamusia: "I have to leave. There are too many of us here, and there isn't enough food for all of us."

She knew what I said was just an excuse, and asked me quietly, "Where are you going to go?"

I told her, "More than anything I want to go back to Krakow."

She didn't blink an eye; she looked steadily at me and said, "But, you give us hope."

No matter what she said, I couldn't be persuaded to stay. I no longer wanted the responsibility, although it was disloyal. Ever since the day in the meadow, just before we escaped into the woods, I had changed. The closeness with my mother had disappeared. Since she went to visit the policeman, I had felt numb toward her, and my love had cooled. I felt concern only for myself, and besides, I believed we were going to die. I was young and wanted to live.

"I know how to get to Krakow," I told her. "I can do it, and it will be better for you when I'm gone." I had to lie, and Mamusia knew I was lying. I was overwhelmed by my desire to get to Krakow. Anita was there and she was the vision I needed to motivate me to say I'm leaving.

Mamusia saw the same thing I did: there was no hope in the forest, and she accepted my departure. Immediately, she set about preparing a rucksack for my trip. She rummaged around in our suitcases. Then, she searched through Tatus' suitcase and found his gray-striped trousers. Once they had looked sharp and clean, but now they had a patched knee and dirty smudges. Up to this time, I had only worn short pants. She handed the trousers over to me, "Joziu, put these on; they're yours now."

I felt choked up and nervously played with the medal dangling from a string around my neck. Next, she said, "Hold still." She had Tatus' razor in her hand and began to shave away the blond fuzz that had barely begun growing on my upper lip. I had a head of bushy, curly hair, but she couldn't do anything about that. She filled the rucksack with a large section of a round loaf of bread, a little money, and a change of socks. I pulled layer after layer of shirts over my head, and soon I was ready to go.

I told them my plan: "I'm going to the bridge, but I'll wait in the ravine under the bushes. Then, when there's a good opportunity, I'll cross over and walk to where I can get on a truck traveling to Krakow."

They nodded. Tatus said it sounded like a good plan. But then they surprised me. Mamusia said, "We're going with you. We want to make sure you make it across safely." I didn't like this idea, but they wouldn't back down. I couldn't believe they were going to leave this safe place and go into danger, but they insisted on it. So, together we walked out of the forest.

After leaving the safety of the dense forest, we hiked down well-traveled roads in order to get to the bridge. All the while, I was holding my breath at every noise, hoping we wouldn't be seen. We arrived at the bridge in the evening. We hid in the thick, prickly bushes in the ravine. Some bushes had nettles growing near them, and some bushes had thorns that tore at our clothing as we squirmed underneath them. Sleep was impossible in this inhospitable, damp environment.

The next day I wanted to wait for just the right opportunity to make my move. I kept my eyes peeled for any traffic on the bridge. As soon as traffic died down it was as good a time as any to jump up out of the ravine and go. There were no drawn-out goodbyes or assurances of seeing them again. I didn't expect to see them ever again. I imagined they weren't going to make it. I couldn't even be sure I would survive.

As soon as the bridge was empty, I clambered up, eyes sweeping left to right, but then I focused straight ahead where the danger lay. I didn't look back down at my family. I made the first step across, and with every step away from them, I felt more and more relieved. I felt like I was walking on air; I felt free. Once I had crossed the bridge and was on the village road, I didn't look back.

Peasants journeyed down the village road, going about their business. They were strangers to me, and I paid no attention to them. I walked just over a mile to the main road to Krakow. The walk took close to half an hour, and during that time, I didn't encounter any police or "helpful" citizens looking to do their duty and report a Jew. The danger I faced in the forest was now in the past, and it was as if it had evaporated from my mind. I came to the corner of one of the crossroads and stopped. One way led to Bochnia and the other to Krakow. I remembered then that

Bochnia was the town we had been ordered to report; but, I sought a different destiny. I waited there hoping a truck to Krakow would soon drive by.

At first I stood alone, relatively at ease. I waited for hours without a truck stopping. Eventually, a woman holding a bag came along. She stood next to me, apparently also waiting for a truck. We began to wave at trucks going by, but no one stopped. By the afternoon a man joined us. He waited, too. The sun was going to be setting soon, and with each passing minute it occurred to me that I wasn't going to get a truck this day. I began to formulate my next move. Across the road was a potato field. The leaves were fairly high, making it the ideal place to sleep for the night, and then try again to a get on a truck the next morning.

Just at that moment I saw Janek walking down the road from Nieznanowice, leading a cow. I knew he was headed to another village where they had a bull he was going to mate his cow with. I realized he would, without a doubt, see me. Seeing me, he stopped dead in his tracks, turned on his heels and headed back towards Nieznanowice. I knew Janek wouldn't waste time getting Roman and they would report me. I had about a half an hour before they would arrive from their village hut. Before I could make a decision, I could see Roman Biernat, off in the distance, face beet red, tearing down the road towards me. Janek had dispatched the news of my arrival quickly. Roman looked like he had dressed hastily in his Sunday-best suit, his hat askew on his head. I knew he wasn't going to church. He had purposely dressed up to make a big impression when he reported me to the police in Niegowic. I knew over four pounds of sugar was too tempting a reward.

Miraculously, at that same moment, a German truck came barreling down the road. We made a last effort to hail it down, hoping this time it would stop, and it did. Safely situated in the bed of the truck, I turned around, put my thumb on my nose and wiggled my fingers, making a rude, mocking gesture at Roman Biernat, as if to say, "You can't catch me old man!" I was relieved and pleased with myself. I found a place to sit among the group of people who, like me, were hitching a ride to Krakow.

I sat quietly, listening to the women talk, or just watching the scenery as it blurred past. Along the side of the road there were many shrines and small chapels with the figurine of Mary or some saint on them. The custom of the Catholic Poles was to put food underneath the shrine. Every time we passed one, the women passengers crossed themselves. I learned to keep a lookout for those shrines, so that when I saw one, I would make a big display of crossing myself like they did. As we passed through the town of Wieliczka, I saw long columns of Jewish people, dressed in worn out and dirty clothing. They were carrying bags and shambling very slowly, accompanied by German guards. They looked dejected and lost. I assumed they were going to the Wieliczka train station. I recognized it at once as an *Aktion*. The *Aktion* apparently was not confined to the Bochnia ghetto, but carried out in the whole surrounding area.

One of the women sitting near me began to laugh, "Look," she said. "They are taking the Jews away." Another woman said, "The Germans are taking care of the Jewish problem for us." They enjoyed watching the Jews march away, happy in their own security. I didn't want to make them suspicious of me, so I began to smile and laugh, acting like them, but inside I was horrified and terrified. This was the first time I had seen Jews taken away. In a startling moment, I realized this is what our fate would have been had we reported to Bochnia. I gave those departing Jews a hard look. They were beaten down, shuffling along, spiritless. Had Dziunka not warned us to run away, it might have been us in that crowd. I reflected dismally how Mamusia saved us by giving herself to the policeman.

When we arrived at the edge of Krakow, I could see ahead of us a police cordon across the whole width of the street. They were checking papers and bags. Most of the people coming into town were Polish peasants who carried food for trading, but everybody was checked. I didn't have papers. I could see no way of getting through. I kept hidden behind the large crowd of people waiting to be cleared. I needed to find another way around the cordon. I waited and observed the situation for some kind of opening, and I wasn't disappointed.

Right beyond the cordoned section was a city tramway line. This stop was the end of the line for that particular two-car tram. Once it let off its passengers, it made a loop heading back to town. As it made the loop, I could see that the tram turned between the police line and me. I observed it for a while. The tram came every ten minutes and did the exact same thing: after letting the people off, it stood still for a few minutes then started up, making the loop going back the other direction.

I settled on a plan. The next time the tram made the turn, I would run toward it, hiding between homes and trees on the way. Finally, I was close to the tramway line. When it came to make the turn, I ran like mad and jumped on board.

I waited for someone to notice me, but nothing bad happened.

The tram kept moving forward and nobody questioned me. I paid my fare, sat down and watched for my stop. One block down from the tram loop was a familiar corner: 12 Brzozowa, the building I grew up in. When the tram came to the next stop, I got off and walked to my old apartment.

The Altered I

1942

Aug 4th -
German occupier orders all Dutch homing pigeons killed

Aug 9th -
200 Jews escape Mir Ghetto in Poland

Aug 22nd -
Brazil declares war on Germany, Japan & Italy

Aug 26th -
7,000 Jews are rounded up in Vichy-France

http://www.historyorb.com/events/date/1942?p=3

Summer 1942
14 years old

**Everything looked and smelled exactly
the same way it had when I lived here.**

Chapter 12

Darkness was falling; the curfew was going to be in effect soon. I went to the building, walked up the stairs and knocked on the super's door. Standing there waiting, I recognized the odors of cooked cabbage and meat wafting from someone's kitchen, reminding me how my life used to be. Everything looked and smelled exactly the same way it had when I lived here. A sudden sadness replaced my once happy feeling of freedom. I realized how much my life had changed.

The door opened, interrupting my bitter reverie. Standing before me was the super. He recognized me right away. Although friendly in the past, he was taken aback to see me now. He looked puzzled, and calling me by my Polish name, asked, "Jozef! What are you doing here?"

I began my tale: "I've come to Krakow to find my brother, Dolek. He's in a work camp and I want to find him. It's going to be dark soon. I haven't any place to go." I looked at him with hope, "Can I stay here, please?"

Looking down first one side of the hallway then the other, he said, "Come in; don't stand there for the neighbors to see and hear." After shutting the door behind him, he directed me to sit in a chair. Taking a deep breath he eased himself down in a chair. "Now, tell me, why are you here?"

"I want to get inside the ghetto. I have friends there, but for now I need a place to stay. I won't bother you; I can sleep on the floor."

He was visibly scared, "No, absolutely not. If I get caught with you here, my whole family will be in danger. You don't know how it is now."

I felt dejected. I had no place to go. But he was a kind man, and seeing my worry, he softened a little. After a long pause he said: "I'll tell you what. You go up to the attic. You can sleep there; no one will see you tonight."

I readily accepted and stealthily made my way to the fourth floor. At the entrance to the attic space was a big iron door locked with a padlock. There was a small tile landing just before the door. I couldn't get inside, but I felt safe in the knowledge that no one would come here at night. I lay down on the cold, dusty tiles, and with my rucksack for my pillow, I slept until morning undisturbed.

That morning I had developed a plan. Going down to the super's apartment, I asked if I could leave my rucksack with him for a while so I could take care of some things. I didn't want to be weighed down with it or draw unnecessary attention to myself.

Running a dirty hand through my bushy hair, I realized I hadn't had a hair cut in a long time. I left the apartment building and looked for a barber away from the former old Jewish section. I told the barber I wanted all the curls cut out. Afterward, looking at my reflection, I felt a sense of relief. Now I would be safe walking the streets.

I went back to Brzozowa Street to the library. Jews used to run it, but now some unfamiliar Polish people were in charge. After all the time I had been away in the village, I learned that the rules for borrowing books were still the same: pay a monthly fee, one book per day. My primary reason for going to the library this day wasn't to get a book, but to obtain an I.D. card. I paid the fee and the woman at the desk filled out the pink card. When she asked my name I gave her a fake one, Jozef Kiepa (pronounced Kenpa). It was close enough to my real name, but sounded like a Polish surname. She handed me the folded I.D. card. I checked out a book and went to the Planty. I sat on a bench all day and read. I was not thinking about what I would do next. I was not thinking about my parents or food or where I would sleep. I was totally absorbed in the book and only stopped reading to change benches.

In the late afternoon, people began leaving the park. I decided to leave, too. I went to a favorite movie house called Uciecha (Ush'why-ya:)

Joy Theater. Not until after the movie ended did I think about a place to sleep. It was 7 p.m. and the curfew was about to start. I didn't want to go back to my old apartment building. I remembered our beloved former maid, Marysia. She had family living in Rakowice. One time she had taken me to visit them. They were friendly to me then. Would they still be? With a hopeful attitude that some friendly Poles would keep me for the night, I set off towards Rakowice.

When I arrived at their doorstep, the father didn't recognize me. "I'm Jozef Kempler," I said. "Marysia worked for my family." He was having trouble placing me. "She brought me here once." At last recognition lit up his face.

"Come inside, please," he said. "What are you doing here?"

I told Marysia's family how I wanted to get inside the ghetto to my friends, but needed a place to sleep tonight. Marysia's father looked the same way the super had looked, scared but sorry for me at the same time. "Wait here a moment," he said. He left and I could hear quiet talking in the background. After a short while he came back. He said, "You can stay for one night, but you have to leave very early in the morning when no one will see you." I felt a wash of relief. At least I had a warm place to sleep. In those days, I only thought in terms of moment by moment, never looking ahead.

The family took pity on me. I hadn't eaten all day. They gave me some bread. I was satisfied; I had a little bit of food and a nice, comfortable place to sleep. This was the first time since leaving the village back in July that I had slept inside a house. I finished my book and fell fast asleep.

The next morning, very early, I left Marysia's family. I was developing a pattern. My first stop that morning was at the library, where I returned my book and checked out another. Then I went back to the park and sat reading again all day. Later, clouds came overhead and the sky turned dark and rainy. With book in hand I ambled off to go see a movie.

Movie houses were dangerous places for Jews. Often police officers invaded them, conducting random searches, closely inspecting papers. According to my foolhardy thinking, sitting in a darkened movie theater was worth the danger. After the movie ended, I realized I had nowhere to sleep. Briefly, I wondered what I was going to do. I went back to the old neighborhood on Brzozowa Street. Most of the old Polish homes were built with a common courtyard in the center. I began scoping out some of these courtyards and found one near a carpenter shop. Some of the wooden boxes they made for shipping were left outside in the courtyard. I found one big enough to fit me comfortably. Looking first to the left, then the right, I quickly crawled inside. I couldn't stretch out completely, but I had little trouble falling into a dreamless sleep.

The next morning when I awoke, I realized I had nothing to eat. I had left all my belongings, including the bread Mamusia had given me, in the rucksack with the super. I wasn't hungry and I didn't feel the need to go back for it. I was making up rules as I went; one rule was never return to the same Polish place twice. I feared I would be recognized, and be reported for the reward. I was learning not to trust Poles.

The Altered I

Summer 1942

Joseph Stalin, Winston Churchill and Franklin D Roosevelt
met in Moscow. Western Allies worked with Stalin to battle
Hitler and determine Poland's future.
http://www.pbs.org/behindcloseddoors/episode-2/

August 21, 1942
Nazi-allied French leader Marshal Petain celebrates the German victory over the Allied invasion at Dieppe.

http://www.secondworldwarhistory.com/1942-ww2-events-
timeline.asp

Summer, 1942
14 years old

"I'm a Jew." I announced. "I want to get inside the ghetto. My brother's fiancée, Renata lives there. I'm trying to find her."

Chapter 13

My goal was to get inside the ghetto. I wanted to see Anita, and I thought I could find Dolek and get work in his camp. Once in Dolek's work camp, I would have some food and shelter. I had no expectations beyond those goals.

The number three tram shuttled through the center of the Krakow ghetto. There was a guarded, barbed wire fence at the entrance and exit of the tramway, and once the tram entered the ghetto it was a continuous ride all the way through without any stops. I didn't think the cut wires by Krzemionki were available to me anymore. The ghetto had become more secure, and it was very dangerous to try to sneak inside by that route. If I rode the tram a number of times I hoped I would be able to find out a way to get inside. Each time I rode the tram, I alternated which side of the car I sat on. Looking out the window at the people, I noticed how poorly dressed they were. Most shuffled along. Some were curled up on the sidewalk doing nothing at all. Although I knew children lived there, when I looked for them, I didn't see any.

In particular, I looked for German or Polish police. I saw very few OD (short for Jewish Ghetto Police) ruffians who could be counted upon to carry out German orders. They didn't carry guns, only sturdy batons, which they used to beat Jews into order. The ODs were most despised by the Jews because they were betrayers of their own people. Once inside the ghetto, it appeared to me that it would be safe and I could go undetected by the Polish police. However, at this point just getting into the ghetto was going to be a challenge. There was the issue of obtaining the *kenncarte*, an identification card. A *kenncarte* was mandatory and authorized the bearer to remain in the ghetto.

Dolek had a fiancée who lived in the ghetto. Her name was Renata. She was a very pretty German Jewish girl with a beautiful smiling face and laughing eyes. If I could find her, I knew she would help me. I spent the next six days in Krakow trying to figure out a way to contact her. I started by observing the ghetto from some nearby streets, once in the morning and again toward the evening. These were the times when there was a large movement of people marching to and from work. They were brought to town marching in either large or small groups. Others were brought by German trucks. Once in town they dispersed to their work sites. After work in the evenings, they went back to the ghetto the same way they had arrived.

All of them wore Star of David armbands, but they had no guards. On the sixth day, I walked a short distance behind one of the working groups as they headed out of the ghetto. The group marched some distance into the better section where the Germans lived. Then they broke up into ones and twos. I followed two young women. When they stopped walking, I approached them.

"I'm a Jew." I announced. "I want to get inside the ghetto. My brother's fiancée, Renata lives there. I'm trying to find her." After giving them her name and description, I asked if they knew her or had seen her.

They were apprehensive at first. There was a general distrust of strangers, and especially one who declared he was a Jew. Before they would answer my question, I had to answer many of theirs until their suspicions were allayed.

Finally, one of the young women said: "No, we don't know her, but you can't just saunter inside the ghetto. You need a *kenncarte* and an armband."

"If we can arrange a meeting place, will you bring me these things?" I asked.

"No! We can't help you. Leave us alone." They left me standing there and hurried off to their work assignments.

I had to try to remember where Renata worked. I sat for a long time trying to picture some of the letters Dolek had written to us about her. Finally it came to me. Toward evening, I made my way to where I thought she was working. I waited outside where the group assembled to return to the ghetto. I saw her! I rushed to where she stood. She was startled at first. But recognition dawned across her face. "Joziu!" she exclaimed. "What are you doing here? Where are your parents?"

I explained why I was in Krakow and asked for her help getting inside the ghetto.

"Yes, of course I'll help you," she said. Looking around suspiciously, she continued: "We can't talk here. Meet me tomorrow and I'll think of a plan." We arranged a meeting place and I left. I felt confident, knowing she would get me inside the ghetto.

The next day she came with an armband and told me exactly what to do and when to do it: "You don't have a *kenncarte*, and they check everyone. This is going to be tricky. Are you up for it?"

I nodded mutely. I couldn't turn back now. There was no place for me to go.

"Okay, listen to me carefully," she continued. "Stand outside the gate wearing this armband. When the truck comes in and unloads us, I'll go inside. Once I get inside, I'll get a man's *kenncarte* for you. You sneak around by the barbed wire to the other side of the gate. I'll come around from the ghetto side and hand you the *kenncarte* through the wire. Go then to the front entrance, show the guards your *kenncarte*, act calm, and you should be fine."

After she left, my spirits lifted; but now I realized I was giving up my freedom. I wanted one last escapade before giving myself up to the ghetto life. I decided I would treat myself to a train ride. I would ride it as far as it went. I planned to take trolley number one to the train station, and so as not to miss the earliest trolley, I slept close to the station in the dense hedges. I was so excited I could hardly sleep at all. The next morning, around 6 a.m., I started on my last adventure.

Once at the station, there was long stairway with wide steps. The final stage of my adventure was just before me. Right away, however, I noticed a police line. They stood shoulder to shoulder and checked everybody's papers before allowing them entrance to the stairway and the trains. There was no way of penetrating the cordon of policemen. I grew afraid and backed out of my adventure.

Dejected, I walked to a special section of the Planty called Lazienki, where there was a lovely little lake. Lazienki was a peaceful place and nobody bothered me. I sat and watched the swans glide across the surface of the water. From early childhood I had come here with my parents. I sat on a bench all day with another book, but I was in no mood to lose myself in a book. I was in a deep meditation, trying to work things out in my mind. Privately, I mourned my life. By submitting myself to the ghetto, I was ending a certain kind of freedom, which saddened me.

I left the park just before curfew. I ambled back to Brzozowa Street, looking for someplace to sleep. Becoming adept at this street urchin lifestyle, I searched for a courtyard and another wooden box to sleep in. Several days had passed since I had had anything to eat. Poles had ration cards, but I didn't have a ration card, and the small amount of Polish money Mamusia had given me wasn't enough.. I spent another night with an empty stomach.

The next day, I had to wait until the evening when the workers went back to the ghetto. There would be German police and ODs waiting to check everybody's *kenncarte* before allowing them admittance to the ghetto. Renata's plan felt like something out of a spy story. At the prescribed time, I walked over to the ghetto where I saw people going inside. I stood waiting, concealing myself from view. I still needed a partial view of the entrance. I waited there until I saw her and her signal: a slight move of her hand, to let me know she saw me. I went over to a narrow passage between the wire and a wall. People could go to the barbed wire unobserved here. I saw her on the other side with the *kenncarte*. As she handed it to me through the wire, I trembled, a bit nerve-wracked, but no one saw us. We had done it! I examined the photo in the *kenncarte* and saw it looked nothing like me. Butterflies in my stomach threatened to make me nauseous.

As I watched, the OD was checking *kenncartes*. I walked to the gate as straight and confident as possible. I showed the OD the *kenncarte* and waited for him to discover I was a fraud. He didn't even bother to look at the picture; he simply waved me through. There were so many people coming in from work, he couldn't check that everyone matched their *kenncarte* photo. As easy as that, I was in the ghetto.

Renata was waiting for me around the corner. She was very happy to see I got in without trouble. Now I realized I had nowhere to stay. I knew I couldn't stay with her, wherever she was living. The normal arrangement in the ghetto was for several families to live together in one apartment. Usually a few people slept in one room. The ODs randomly raided apartments to search out any who were living there without the proper papers. The problem was not so much bringing people into the ghetto; it was remaining in the ghetto undetected. If I was allowed to sleep in someone's apartment and was caught during a search without my own *kenncarte*, everybody in the apartment would be punished. The risk was too great for anyone to take.

I was left on my own; Renata gave me a piece of bread and a hug goodbye. I headed out to look for a safe place to sleep. After making some inquiries, I was directed to a courtyard where there were other Jews who had escaped from various labor camps or from other villages and small towns and were hiding out, like me. They had sneaked into the ghetto, but they had no papers and no right to be there. And, like me, they lived on the streets and slept in the courtyard.

The courtyard was huge. People were sleeping in bundles any-where they could find a spot. Considering the crowd, it was a very quiet place, with little conversation. As a rule, people avoided contact with each other. I was warned that the Jewish Ghetto Police conducted sporadic raids in the courtyards, searching for stragglers. If we were caught, they would turn us turn us over to German authorities. Even so, I felt safe here, behind barbed wires, with other Jews. The real danger, in my opinion, was outside the ghetto among Poles and Germans.

Anita never lived in the real world like I had. She was innocent and sheltered. Because of her uncle Trauring's connections to the Ger-mans, the family lived unlike the other Jews in the ghetto. Other Jews lived together with several families crammed into one apartment. Anita, her mother, and aunt and uncle were the only occupants of a two-room apart-ment. Uncle Trauring was a big, fat man. He provided his family with plenty to eat, clean clothing, and a nice apartment. Because he seemingly knew of any *Aktions* that were to take place beforehand, the family felt secure. They were doing better than most in the ghetto; living life like it was before the war.

The first thing I wanted to do once in the ghetto was see Anita. The day I found her she was alone in the apartment. Her Aunt Carolla, Uncle Trauring, and mother were out working. She was stunned to see me at her doorstep. I didn't give much thought to my appearance, but I must have been a sight. The last time I bathed had been six months ago. I must have stunk from living on the streets. Still, she greeted me warmly and invited me inside. The apartment seemed luxurious by comparison to my living standards. I was so intimidated, I could barely speak.

Anita had to talk first: "Tell me, Joziu, why you're here? Where is your family?"

I didn't want to tell her the whole story: the police officer in the village, the forest, or how I had abandoned my family. I resigned myself to the partial truth, saying what I had been telling everyone since arriving in Krakow: "I want to find Dolek and work in a camp. But first I had to see you." She seemed flattered by my confession. There was an awkward silence. After struggling for so long to get inside the ghetto and find the object of all my affections, I didn't know how to resume the friendship.

Soon, we fell into our previous easy camaraderie and began to play all our favorite games. It was as if we were now entering a world of our own creation. We told jokes, played card games, and told each other silly stories. We became so completely involved in what we were doing that we didn't even notice the passage of time visible by the lengthening shadows in the room. Being with Anita, I felt like I had gone back in time. This was what I imagined our reunion to be like. I could believe that everything was all right, that nothing bad had ever happened. We understood the critical circumstances surrounding us. There was so much death and despair, yet we forgot it and played in complete oblivion.

That night, when the grown-ups came home from work, they were surprised to see me; yet, they made me feel welcome and safe under their roof. They let me stay and eat with them, but afterward I had to go back into my world of sleeping in the courtyard.

Once in the courtyard, I found my spot on the ground and fell instantly asleep. Even though I slept deeply, subconsciously I was on the alert for unfamiliar noises. I continued to sleep in the courtyard for several nights. One night a bunch of ODs snuck into the courtyard. I awoke instantly. I peered around, but it was quite dark and I couldn't see anything. There were sounds of scuffling and people being beaten. At one end of the enclosure was a dilapidated structure with a lot of junk piled up high on top of it. It was fairly inaccessible, and therefore, I deemed it a good hiding place. As soon as I heard people crying out, I ran toward the big junk pile. I clambered to the top like a squirrel and scooted as far as I could away from the courtyard. I found a reasonably flat place, covered myself up with some debris and lay down.

I wasn't afraid. I had no prior experience with the ODs. Naively, I thought they couldn't do anything to me. I'm Jewish and they're Jewish. I recognized their authority, but I mocked them; they couldn't catch me. I didn't realize how dangerous they were. I heard people scrambling around, being dragged out of the area. Soon, the courtyard became quiet and people came out from their hiding places as things settled down again. Later, I climbed down from my perch and went back to my spot on the ground. I slept safely with the idea that the ODs weren't going to make another sweep that night. It was over now, and I could relax.

The next day I went to see Anita. While there, Anita's uncle came home with some unexpected news. He gathered the aunt, mother and us children together and announced, "I heard a rumor there may be an *Aktion* tomorrow." Looking at us, he continued, "You children have to be out of the ghetto when it happens."

"What will we do? How do we get them out of the ghetto safely?" Anita's mother asked nervously. She gathered Anita close to her as if someone were coming to take her away at this very moment.

"Not to worry." Uncle Trauring said, "I've arranged to put them both on a truck tomorrow." Then looking directly at me he said: "Joziu, you take care of Anita; you're the older one. Remain in Krakow. Keep her safe. Don't come back here until the truck comes for you. Understood?"

I nodded solemnly.

Each *Aktion* increased in intensity. Each time, new tricks were incorporated to get people to report to the Plac Zgody (Square of Peace) for their selections. There were stamps put onto the *kenncarte* at various times, and each stamp decided the bearer's fate. I learned that the stamps were periodically and selectively given and ranged in color. One day a particular color stamp may mean something entirely different from another day. Often, it was difficult to know which color stamp would be the color that meant the bearer survived a selection. Today, for example, if it was a blue stamp, that could save a life; however, tomorrow the blue stamp would indicate the end of it. No one knew which color stamp was the desirable color to have in one's *kenncarte*. A person caught in the ghetto without a *kenncarte* was in an especially dangerous position—to the SS, this indicated that the person was there illegally and therefore was deported and/or killed.

The next morning, through Uncle Trauring's connections, Anita and I were put on a work truck headed for Krakow. We were both wearing the regulatory armbands, but as soon as the truck let us off in the city, we discreetly tore them off and hid them. Our plan was to blend in and appear as Aryan-looking as possible. My clothing was now quite worn and shabby. I was dirtier than ever from sleeping on the street, but I didn't worry about it while in the ghetto. Those who lived in the ghetto wore rags; nobody really washed, so if someone stank, it was normal. Now, out on the city streets of Krakow, among people who regularly washed, I hoped that no one would notice two scrappy looking kids.

Roving the familiar city streets, we began to feel that Krakow was ours again, like old times when we were allowed freedom to go about our business like everybody else. We were spending the entire day in the city and we needed to find something to occupy our time. Since I was more experienced at roaming the streets, I knew where we had to go to be safe from suspicious eyes. The park had always been a haven for me. I knew that we could remain there without any problems. Anita trusted me to lead and protect her.

I took charge right away and suggested we go to the park. She readily agreed, but said, "What do you think we should do when we're there?"

"We could play games or get books from the library," I suggested.

"I think that would be too hard." She stopped mid-stride, and then said: "I know Joziu, I want to draw something! Let's get some paper and pencils."

"We'll make drawings. Then we can write our own stories!" I announced.

Our plans finalized, we stopped in a store where they sold paper and the necessary things for our project. Where we got the money for our writing project, I can't remember now, Uncle Trauring must have given it to me since I had no money of my own. Those weren't details that stood out in my memory. At the cash register, the sales lady was in the final process of ringing up our order when she smiled at me and politely asked, "Will that be all *Pan*?" I was at once astonished, "Y-yes *Pani*," I stammered. Despite my initial amazement, I was secretly gratified. This was the first time anyone ever called me mister. I felt respectable and grown up.

Once at the park, we became immersed in our games and our secret fantasy world. The reality was that we were Jewish children running free in a city that, by law, was forbidden to us. Every second was dangerous. What do I do if there is an *Aktion* in the ghetto today? What if we can't get back? How do I protect Anita out here? But instantly, I cut off those worries. I was survival-minded and instead pretended we were just two ordinary children playing in the park; we had a right to be there, the same as anybody else.

Ghetto life was oppressed and dangerous every day. But in the park it was a beautiful day. The sun was shining and the ghetto life disappeared from our minds. We lived freely and fully for one day, treating it as a gift of life. This was the very last day of freedom for me. Soon, I would voluntarily resign myself to a labor camp. I kept my secret, not wanting to worry Anita.

In the evening, we turned our attention homeward. Tentatively, Anita asked: "Joziu, do you think there was an *Aktion*? If there was one, will the truck come for us?"

"We'll just have to go back to the drop off and see," I said. "Don't worry. If the truck is there, then we'll know there wasn't an *Aktion*."

Hand in hand, we strode toward the drop off place. When we arrived, to our great relief, we saw the other workers waiting for the truck. We looked around to make sure we weren't seen, then, put our armbands on. The truck arrived; we hopped into it and headed back to the ghetto.

At the ghetto entrance the trucks weren't inspected and the ODs didn't check *kenncartes*. Looking around the ghetto, everything looked the same; depressing as it was, everything seemed "normal."

August, 1942
The Battle of Guadalcanal took place in 1942 when the
US Marines landed on August 7th. The landing at
Guadalcanal was unopposed - but it took the
Americans six months to defeat the Japanese in what
was to turn into a classic battle of attrition.
http://www.historylearningsite.co.uk/
battle_of_guadalcanal.htm

Aug 8, 1942
During World War II, six German saboteurs who
secretly entered the United States on a mission to
attack its civil infrastructure are executed by the United
States for spying.

http://www.history.com/this-day-in-history/german-
saboteurs-executed-in-washington

August, 1942
14 years old

> In the meantime, I hoped I would have
> an opportunity to get a message to
> Dolek.

Chapter 14

I felt a strong need to find Dolek in the work camp and leave the ghetto behind. Sleeping on the streets, constantly looking over my shoulder was making life difficult. I had to devise two important plans: how to leave the ghetto and how to join Dolek in the camp. In the north part of Krakow was Rakowice, a military airport for the German *Luftwaffe*, or air force. German civilians managed building projects for the German military. One was called the Artur Johr Company, and was comprised of about 150 Jews who worked for them on various building projects. I knew Dolek was working as a tailor inside this camp at the airport.

There were work groups living in the ghetto that traveled to and from the Rakowice airport by truck. This was called a *placowka*, or "placement," meaning the same people worked in the same place in one work group. There were many different cells of a *placowka* in the camp of Rakowice. Every morning, I heard the loud rumbling sound of many trucks.

One morning I walked in the direction of the sound, and was lead to the main square, Plac Zgody where the *placowka* gathered for work assignments. When I arrived, I saw hundreds of people. The ODs were screaming at them and hitting them, trying to get them to form lines from which they were loaded onto trucks. This was a place of rushed activity and confusion. I milled among the crowd undetected until I could figure out what was going on and how I could get on a work truck to Rakowice. Because the trucks weren't marked, it was difficult to tell where they were headed. There was a man standing near one of the parked trucks.

I asked him, "Which truck goes to the airport?" He pointed to a truck across the way. I noted the markings of that truck and slipped out of the Plac Zgody. I silenced a deep sigh. It would take several days for me to gather the facts about the inner workings of the airport. Building inside me, too, was the knowledge that one mistake could be deadly.

In the meantime, I hoped I would have an opportunity to get a message to Dolek. Often, people from Artur Johr and the *placowka* from the ghetto crossed paths and had interaction with each other. Sometimes, though, the groups wouldn't meet each other for long spans of time. Still, I was hopeful that I would get a message to Dolek. I managed to locate a worker going to Rakowice and convince him to relay a message to Dolek, if he saw him. "Tell him I'm here, in Krakow. I left our parents, and I want to join the work camp," I said. I waited days without a reply from Dolek. Relentlessly, I questioned if the worker had word from Dolek. He assured me each time that he had delivered the message, but there was no reply from my brother.

Gradually, I gathered enough information about the airport to formulate a plan for sneaking in. The next morning, I went directly to the truck identified to me as the one going to Rakowice. I had to be quick about my business. ODs were running around with batons, wildly beating people into formation. I didn't want to get myself clubbed in the process. Seeing a worker leaning against a truck, I asked, "Can I get on this truck to Rakowice tomorrow?"

"Yeah, kid," the worker said. "But hide yourself. Don't let an OD see you."

"How do I find the Artur Johr people in the camp?"

"Once we are let off the truck at the airport, go toward the right; there will be construction work there. Those workers are the ones you're looking for."

Hurriedly, I left the Plac Zgody. Tomorrow, I would be leaving the ghetto. I said my goodbyes to Renata and Anita. I'd miss Anita the most, but she was protected here; I wasn't. Uncle Trauring gave me some pointers and other information he deemed useful. I said goodbye to the Trauring family and left.

The next morning, I climbed aboard the truck without incident. I hid myself, and when we arrived at the airport, I hopped down from the truck. Just as the worker had told me, after the workers dispersed, I kept to the right until I came upon construction workers. I walked up the path a short distance and soon encountered a building. When I peeked inside, I saw Jewish people busy cleaning and washing the floors and windows.

I walked in and asked the nearest guy, "Is this the Artur Johr group?"

Without taking the time to stop his chore, he nodded, yes. Rather than ask, I announced, "Good. Let me work with you." I didn't want to just sit there and wait; I had to do something. Spotting a broom leaning against the barrack wall, I began sweeping the floor with the other workers. In the afternoon, two of the owners came in to inspect the work. Both looked friendly: one, a big, fat guy with a nice personality, and the other a quiet, skinny guy with a friendly face.

The big, fat guy noticed me first. "Who are you?" he said.

"I'm Jozef Kempler. Dolek Kempler is my brother. He works here as a tailor. I want to work in your company too."

He inspected me closely. "How old are you?" he said.

I risked the truth. Looking him boldly in the eye, I said, "Almost fifteen."

"Okay. You're in the work group." Then he strolled out of the barrack. Since I was underage and not qualified, he could have reported me, but to my relief he didn't. In the evening, after work, we were marched to the camp. I was now a worker in the Artur Johr labor camp.

There were two, small, sleeping barracks. Each barrack had two tiers of wooden platforms spanning its length. In one structure, Uncle Icek and two other men from Nieznanowice slept in the upper corner of one section of the platform. I was directed to sleep there, too. Also, in the camp, were different types of workshops. Dolek, working as a master tailor, made clothing for the Germans working at the airport. He shared a space with a shoemaker who repaired or made new shoes for the German men, their wives and children. Both of them were assigned to sleeping quarters in the basement of one of the workshops. I went out to find Dolek in his workshop. Upon entering the basement, I saw that Dolek's quarters were big, bright and pleasant. This was unlike my sleeping arrangements on the dirty platform, squashed in with all the other workmen. I found Dolek, but he did not seem particularly glad to see me. In fact, he was quite hostile. I wondered why he didn't respond to my messages, but that was just like him to be moody and silent.

"Why are you here, Joziu?" he demanded. "Where are Mamusia

and Tatuś? You need to be with them."

"I had to leave," I explained. "We couldn't survive together. I wanted to be here. Mamusia agreed. She knew this would be better for me."

I believe he felt burdened with the added responsibility of my life in his hands. He only knew me as a little kid who couldn't do anything for himself. "You're going to have to take care of yourself," he said. "Don't expect me to do it for you. I have my own work." Realizing I was here to stay, he grudgingly accepted my presence.

Dolek had little to complain about, in my opinion. He was a privileged worker, spared the hard labor that most of the unskilled men were assigned. He was well known among the Germans, who liked him enough to give him extra food. In contrast, at night I slept beside people I didn't know, and during the day I was assigned whatever construction job they had for me that day: digging ditches, or hauling and mixing cement. This was my first exposure to this kind of life. There was a lot to get used to: the smells, the close living, and the dirty beds.

Even so, I felt protected inside the camp. I had accomplished my three goals: escape the village of Nieznanowice, escape the forest and escape the ghetto and the abominable *Aktions*. I deceived myself into thinking that since I was working for the Germans now, I would be protected somehow from the ghetto authorities.

The Altered I

Dziunka Laub & Jozef

1942
14 years old

> **After a few steps my knees began to wobble. I battled to keep my knees straight, but I collapsed in a heap on the ground, the cement sack tumbling to the ground next to me where it ruptured.**

Chapter 15

On some occasions, after working hard all day, a long, freight train arrived loaded with cement and bricks for Artur Johr. I dreaded such days. After slaving away all day, we were called to come and unload the train. No one was spared in this task, regardless of job assignments; it was all work, no rest.

Someone directed me to haul a cement sack up a hill to the designated storage place. These cement sacks were heavy, weighing 110 pounds. Two people situated in the car placed the cement sack on my back. I took two steps forward. I struggled for a bit, doing my best to stand upright, but I wasn't strong enough. With shaky steps and a hunched back, I managed to get one bag up the hill. I went back for another. After a few steps my knees began to wobble. I battled to keep my knees straight, but I collapsed in a heap on the ground, the cement sack tumbling to the ground next to me where it ruptured. Cement exploded in a puff of gray dust, coating my entire body. More than the discomfort of cement caking my skin, I became afraid for my life. *If I can't work, and I can't carry these heavy loads, what will they do with me?* As I lay there in a dusty heap, one of the workers came over. Kneeling down he said, "Go unload the bricks."

That was it? No one threatened to beat me and nobody reported me to the authorities.

A chain of five workers lined up at the freight car door. The bricks were handed down to the first guy in the line, then tossed over, two bricks at a time, to the next man in line. The last man in the string stacked the bricks neatly. This was something I could handle. I felt confident again. The only drawback was catching bricks two at a time. The edges were rough and uneven, scratching and nicking my young, tender hands until they bled. I considered the wear and tear worth it, as it was a job I could accomplish. Yet, I felt like a fraud. I didn't truly belong here. I feared that if I didn't perform my duty, I would face trouble from the authorities. So, I did whatever they wanted me to do: dig ditches, haul cement sacks, mix cement.

Each day, several freight trains arrived and required unloading. We worked late into the night. Then, before we retired to our barracks, we cleaned the inside of the freight car, readying it for departure and its next heavy load. Though all of us experienced bloody scrapes, I received more than the others because of my inexperience. As a young boy of fourteen, I felt out of my league with seasoned, muscled laborers.

One day a German man, a carpenter by trade, picked me out of a lineup to work for him. He was a tall, silent fellow, who only spoke to hurl gruff orders at me. As I turned the grinding wheel, he sharpened chisels. If he didn't like something I did, he slapped me—a nice, easy slap, but I didn't like it. A kindly slap in the face was the accepted way of handling apprentices if the apprentice didn't do things just right. In context, a slap in the face wasn't so bad. I set out to improve myself, fixing how I did my work and tried to avoid getting slapped.

I worked six days with Sunday off. Sunday was a day to catch up on cleaning clothes, or making some food. I always spent it with Dolek. However, Sunday wasn't a day off for me. The slave of the Germans had his own personal slave. Since I was determined to stay in camp and be a burden to him, Dolek arrived at an arrangement where I tended to his needs before my own. For example, he had been given some potatoes, so it fell to me to scrounge for firewood, build a fire and peel, cook and tend to the potatoes for hours. Also, the clothing had to be washed and hung up to dry. Whatever menial task there was to accomplish became my responsibility.

During the day we seldom saw each other; when we did, neither of us spoke. But, on Sundays, the penalty I paid for wanting to be with him was to do his work.

Built a year and a half before I arrived in Rakowice was a big, two-story Air Force hospital. They had used untreated, wet wood for the beams, which now had begun to deteriorate and collapse. The Artur Johr Company got the contract from the military to put in new floors and beams. I was switched from carpenter's assistant to treating these beams with a toxic preventative for termites and rats. The end of each beam had to be painted with this yellow glop before being inserted into the walls.

In order to accomplish the job, I climbed a ladder to the beam, climbed on top of the beam and while straddling it, balanced a pail of the preventative substance. The beams had to be coated one after the other. Not spilling any of the yellow substance became a particular challenge for me.

As jobs went, I liked this one because it was inside and sheltered. Some of the work the civilians had us do was outside. Rain or shine, the work had to be done. Often, they sent one of two big trucks to pick us up for the tough, outside work. One was a diesel truck, and whenever I smelled the diesel fuel coming in the distance, I knew some very hard labor was involved. In comparison, coating beams indoors was fairly easy to accomplish. Of course, I wasn't a real painter, and my work was sloppy. Not only did I sprinkle the yellow substance everywhere, I managed to sprinkle it all over my face, arms and clothing—and the stuff didn't wash off!

Our overseer, the nice, fat, amiable fellow, didn't want to see us work so hard without a rest. As a kind gesture, he arranged that we could have passes to the Krakow ghetto for some weekends. When the Krakow ghetto *placowka* returned to their homes on a Saturday night, we could get a ride with them. On Monday, when the Krakow *placowka* returned to Rakowice, we rode back with them.

One weekend I got a pass. By this time the feeling that I was a fake in the camp had disappeared. I now had my paperwork to justify my presence and I felt confident I would have little trouble from ODs when I arrived in the ghetto. However, to my surprise, a big Jewish guy grabbed my arm and pulled me over to the side.

"You know you have jaundice?" he growled.

"No," I said "Why do you say that?"

"Your face and hands are all yellow! What's wrong with you?"

I realized what it was he was looking at and laughed, "No, I'm okay. It's just paint." I turned and went on my way.

The first thing I did was go see Renata and let her know I had made it safely into the work camp, and I was doing fine. I knew that Dolek often came to see her, but we seldom crossed paths, and I wasn't sure if he would speak to her about me. Then, I went to see Anita. I felt a little embarrassed by my yellow face and dirty appearance, but she didn't seem to care about that. We spent the day playing bridge. She let me borrow a book, which I devoured that weekend.

My life, although hard, wasn't too bad. The labor camp was tough, but it was not like the situation in the ghetto: German SS guards and ODs constantly shouting orders, keeping everyone on tenterhooks. I didn't experience any persecution or hunger. That is not to say that we had plenty of food. There was never enough food. With a shower only allowed every two or three months, it was impossible to keep clean. My clothing was dirty, smelly and wearing out. I managed as best I could.

The one thing beginning to bother me was my feet. My shoes were wearing out. Dolek made, out of mismatched colored canvas, a new pair of pants for me. Tatus' striped, gray dress pants had fallen apart by then. My new canvas pants fit just right. Partly red and partly gray and as strong as iron, I had a new pair of pants I could be proud of. Now, I was even respectful-looking enough to visit Anita.

Surprisingly, mail service was active in the camps. Of course, everything going in or out was censored. Sending or receiving mail was a small privilege we were allowed. One day, Dolek received a letter from our parents. I hadn't seen or heard from them in several weeks. I hadn't known where they were or if they were alive. I was impatient for Dolek to finish the letter so I could hear their story.

Apparently, after I left them at the bridge, they decided they, too, could no longer hide in the forest. Regardless of the all-out manhunt for Jews, they picked up their bags and walked in plain sight to the nearby town of Bochnia. Nobody attacked them. They eased right into the Bochnia ghetto, no questions asked. They were assigned a place to live and began their life anew.

The sad truth, I learned later, was that during this time in 1942, the German officials selected six cities in southern Poland as an "open house" invitation to flush out all hiding Jews, like my parents, and gather them into one place. They were unharmed on their journey to Bochnia because the German authorities allowed them free passage into the ghetto. When I gave it any consideration, I couldn't help but think how strange an image it must have been to see three Jews, without armbands, passes and with suitcases in hand, strolling down the road, eager to find sanctuary in a ghetto.

Dolek and I knew for a certainty that they were all alive, though I had doubted it for a long time. Mixed emotions of relief and guilt flooded me. I realized they still had no knowledge about where I was. I comforted myself that Mamusia would be happy to know I made it to the camp, and I was now with Dolek.

At the same time, a letter arrived from Dziunka. She didn't know about me or where our parents were. Only Dolek and I shared the knowledge that everyone was safe, for now.

Dolek wrote a letter to each and apprised them of our situation. My worries and doubts were alleviated; Dziunka, Tatus, Babcia, and Mamusia had survived the selections.

Part II

The Camps

September 5, 1942:
The mass deportation known as the "Sperre" began the roundup and removal of more than 15,000 children, elderly and ill Jews in a one-week period from the Lodz Ghetto. This Aktion profoundly shocked the Jews of the ghetto. http://www.yadvashem.org/yv/en/exhibitions/this_month/september/08.asp

24 September 1942:
The Germans conducted a round-up in the ghetto. Able-bodied men unable to produce worker's permits were arrested. A group of 100 men were sent to the Rakowice (Rakowitz) labour camp (near Krakow), a heavily guarded military airfield surrounded by a barbed-wire fence.

http://www.deathcamps.org/occupation/bochnia%20ghetto.html

September, 1942
14 years old

My shoes were in really bad shape now
and rubbed my exposed ankle raw. Soon
a sore developed on a spot near the side
of my heel, but no one slowed down, or
offered to help me.

Chapter 16

I entered Rakowice in the summer of 1942 with just the
clothes on my back. It was the fall and soon it would be turning colder.
I didn't have suitable clothing for the cold months ahead and this concerned me. *How was I going to survive the winter without warm clothes?* This
concerned Dolek and some others, too. We approached our civilian
masters with our concerns. With their approval, those of us who came
from the village Nieznanowice were permitted to return there and retrieve our clothing. There were six of us who made plans to leave the
camp: Dolek, Uncle Icek, me, and three others.

We knew there was enough clothing in the Biernat's barn for
all of us. But, I wondered what the reception would be from that family.

"Dolek, when I left, the Biernat's were about to report me to
the police. What a surprise they'll have when they see me again," I said.

"I just hope they give us our belongings," Dolek said. "They
probably think they own it since we've been gone so long."

"They have to, don't they? We have special permission to be
there. They don't have a right; it's our stuff."

"We'll see," Dolek said. "But, I bet they put up a fight."

In the morning, the six of us set out by foot to Bochnia, 25
miles away. Rather than go directly to Nieznanowice, the group decided

to go to Bochnia first to see Tatus, Babcia, and Mamusia in the ghetto. Although out of the way, we wanted to take advantage of our freedom. Also, we thought our parents would want us to bring them something from the village, too. I looked forward to the happy reunion.

We journeyed all day and night, passing woods and farmlands along the way, but had few interactions with people. The night was especially long. My shoes were in really bad shape now and rubbed my exposed ankle raw. Soon a sore developed on a spot near the side of my heel, but no one slowed down, or offered to help me. We had a deadline to keep and it was up to me to keep up as best I could. I limped along, but suffered each time I took a step. Eventually, the sore festered. All I wanted was some relief from the pain. I found a big leaf and stuffed it between my foot and the shoe. This helped ease the agony, but I was in pain all the way to Bochnia.

In the morning, we arrived at Bochnia. We showed our passes to the Jewish police and were granted access to the ghetto. This particular ghetto had recently experienced an *Aktion*. The authorities took some people to Auschwitz or Belzec, but the majority of the people remained in the ghetto. With the remaining Jews, the German SS divided the ghetto into sections: Ghetto A and Ghetto B. Ghetto A was for Jews considered necessary, those who could work. Ghetto B was designated for the old and the sick, as well as those who could not work. Whenever there was a smaller *Aktion*, the Jewish Police, having a quota to fill, selected people from Ghetto B. When Dolek and our group found Babcia, Mamusia, and Tatus, they were living in Ghetto B.

I never expected to see the three of them again after leaving them in the forest. I felt then with a certainty that they were going to die, but they had proved me wrong. They were delighted to see Dolek and me. All three lived together in a tiny, one-room house. We had a distant cousin (who I call) Mr. G., a Jewish functionary in the Bochnia ghetto. He assisted them in settling into these quarters. I wasn't overly fond of him. I felt he was just like those ODs who only looked out for their own skin and bullied people to get better privileges for themselves. Tatus, Mamusia, and Babcia were satisfied with their situation, and they wouldn't hear me complain about Mr. G.

In my opinion, the small house was primitive, and bereft of most of their furniture, it was hardly suitable. Surveying the room, I saw in one corner a small stove for cooking, its pipe vented through the wall. Next to it stood a little table and some old chairs. My gaze focused on the small table. Placed in the center was a lace doily. I recognized it from our apartment in Krakow. My heart was touched at the reminder of normal life. A big lump formed in my throat; a strong, intense pressure built up inside my chest. I tried my hardest not to cry in front of everyone, but the sharp stinging behind my eyes threatened tears. How strange that this doily caused such turmoil in my emotions. How could I cry over this bit of feminine decoration and not over Mamusia and her sacrifice for the family?

We had a happy, but brief, reunion. Mamusia gave us a list of items she wanted and we readied ourselves for our next stage of the journey. Before leaving for the village, Mamusia tenderly bandaged my sore ankle.

In the early morning hours we arrived in Nieznanowice. Dolek and I separated from Icek and our other three companions and walked to the well-to-do home of the only person we considered a friend in the village. Her surname was Kupiecka. She was the same woman Mamusia and Babcia went to see the night we hid in the forest.

Welcoming us in, *Pani* Kupiecka said: "Come in, sit down. Let me give you some food. You look so tired. Have you been walking all night?"

"Yes." Dolek answered for all of us. "We haven't much time, but we need some of our belongings and warm clothes."

"I hope you get them," she said. "But, the changes that have happened in this village, you won't believe." While she talked, she bustled around the kitchen, first to the pantry, then back to the table, placing some food before us. "People used to help each other," she continued. "Now they watch each other suspiciously, waiting for some opportunity to report someone."

I couldn't pay attention to what she said. I could only drool over the breakfast of bread and eggs. I hadn't seen this kind of delicious food in a long time and didn't know when I would taste it again.

"We have special passes," Dolek assured her. "We'll be okay."

"It's a good thing. I don't know what the other villagers would have done to you. They might have had you arrested." Sitting down to the table she looked around at us ogling the food, "Eat, eat! You must be hungry."

Grateful for the food, we dug in. While currently there was little joy in our life, I could say this was a pleasurable experience. We took full advantage of each opportunity as it came, never knowing when the next good thing would happen.

Afterward, Dolek and I left Icek and headed toward the Biernat's hut. When Roman Biernat saw us, he looked astounded. "What are you doing here?" he demanded.

"We came for some clothes. We have special permission." Dolek said.

Maria Biernat heard her husband and ran over. She yelled, "You can't get any clothes. They're ours. You have no rights." She looked to her husband to agree with her. "Tell them they have no rights," she implored of him. "Tell them if they don't leave, you'll call the police!" She stood facing us with arms akimbo.

We stood our ground. "We're not going anywhere until we get what we came for," Dolek said. He kept trying to convince them we had special passes but they wouldn't listen.

"I'm going to report you to the police. I'm sure they're looking for you," Roman Biernat said. Wagging his finger at us, he added, "You made a mistake coming back here!"

I didn't know what to say or do anymore, but we couldn't continue arguing with them and we couldn't force them to give us the clothes. In the meantime, the old man went to the police.

"What are they going to do to us Dolek? Will they shoot us?" I asked.

"How should I know?" Dolek grumbled. "But we can't go back empty-handed." We sat down to wait and see what would happen.

Soon, two policemen, accompanied by Roman Biernat, arrived at the hut. One looked directly at Dolek and demanded: "What are you doing here? Why aren't you in the ghetto?"

"We don't live in the ghetto; we work at the airport," Dolek explained. "We have permission to get warm clothes for the winter."

"Show me your papers," demanded the policeman. We handed over our papers not knowing if he would accept them or rip them up in front of us. The policeman didn't bother to look at them. "Come on you two. You belong in a jail cell."

In a short while, we were joined in the prison cell by Icek and the rest of our group from Rakowice. Over and over we told them we had special permission: "We have permits! The German Gestapo gave them to us. Look at them!" yelled Icek. His pleas fell on deaf ears; they wouldn't believe us.

"We're going to check this out," one policeman said. He had a malicious gleam in his eyes. "If it doesn't make sense, I'm going to shoot you myself."

I believed he would enjoy it. We waited in that jail cell four or five hours, not knowing what was going to happen to us. We were in the hands of the police and they could do whatever they wanted to us. To our great amazement, they actually called the Gestapo in Bochnia, and the Bochnia authorities checked with the authorities in Rakowice, and the Rakowice authorities confirmed what we had told them. We heard later that our Rakowice boss threatened the village policemen saying, "They're involved in important government work and they need to get back here! Don't delay them further or you'll be the next ones we report to Berlin."

We were released without delay. The police escorted us to the Biernat's hut in order to ensure that we were allowed to take what we had come for. When the Biernat's saw us once again, they couldn't believe their eyes. They were completely flabbergasted.

A policeman told them, "They have permits to take their stuff; you better give it to them."

"What do you say?" Roman Biernat asked. "I should give them my possessions? They're Jews. What do they own?"

"You better do it," the policeman warned. "Or you'll be thrown in jail." The Biernat's looked confused and insulted. I imagined they must have wondered, "How had this situation turned upside down on us?" According to their point of view, Dolek and I should be in jail, but instead they were the ones threatened with imprisonment.

We went to the barn where we had kept our things in a big basket. We rummaged through everything. Roman Biernat stood nearby, supervising. Maria Biernat, standing beside him, fumed in restrained silence. Orders had to be obeyed without question. The policemen weren't on our side and didn't care about our rights or justice, but these orders came from Germans and they couldn't disagree with them.

We took our time sorting through everything. For once, the law was helping us. I found my *jopka* and a small trunk, big enough for my *jopka* and a few other pieces of clothing. Next, Dolek turned his attention to picking out whatever Mamusia had requested. When we finished, we had only what we could carry wrapped up in sheets and pillowcases. Carrying my trunk, I smiled smugly at the Biernat's and nodded a brief "goodbye." Then we began our long journey back to Bochnia and finally Rakowice.

Although we were worked very hard, occasionally arrangements were made for us to have some recreation. There was another Jewish work group at the airfield some distance away. Our bosses wanted to form a soccer match between the two work groups, in order to build up morale.

After heading back to the camp after one such soccer game, a certain Dr. Hilfstein, the only doctor among us, noticed a louse crawling on my jacket. He made a big deal about it. Pointing at me he shouted: "Lice! I see lice on you. You'll spread typhus, and then we'll all die. You need to come to my office immediately!"

At first I ignored him. I wasn't the only one who had lice: everyone did. Why bother with just me? However, the idea of typhus spreading throughout the camp was a great scare. The next day, he called me in to his office and had my head shaved.

Lice crawled on the others in the group but he picked me out of the crowd because I was just a kid. Anybody else would have told him to shove it, but I was a nobody in the camp. I felt so ashamed. I wanted to blend in with the crowd, but, I stood out as different, and everybody knew why. Even when I was permitted to go to the Krakow ghetto, I didn't go. I couldn't take the embarrassment of being seen as a pariah: What would Anita think?

In October, 1942, the *placowka* from the Krakow ghetto didn't arrive in Rakowice. We wondered what had happened to them. After two days, the *placowka* returned as normal to the airport for work.

I saw a man I was acquainted with and asked, "What happened to you yesterday? Where were you?"

"There was another *Aktion*," he said. "We were all ordered to leave our homes and meet in the Plac Zgody."

He went on to describe that for this particular *Aktion*, ODs sat at tables in the square. The people had to line up before them with their *kenncarte* available for inspection. People with a valid *kenncarte* were shoved aside. The others were forced to stand in big groups surrounded by SS and dogs.

"Many people were hiding in their apartments because they had an invalid *kenncarte*," he continued. "But, the SS searched for them and shot some on sight when they found them. Others they dragged to Plac Zgody for resettlement."

I was speechless. He described complete chaos, shooting and killing. Even children were shot on the spot. In some cases, even if people had a perfectly valid *kenncarte*, the SS would not accept it and they were told to stand aside for resettlement. Nobody could be certain who was safe.

Finding my voice, I asked, "What happened to those they took away?"

"Some were taken away to Auschwitz; families were divided, but a lot were rounded up and killed. There was so much killing. The blood flowed in the streets!" Then, leaning close to my ear he said, "That wasn't nearly the worst of it. The German soldiers took the babies by their legs and swung them around, smashing their tiny heads against the wall, right in front of their mothers and other children!"

I was told that a man named Amon Goeth had orchestrated this *Aktion.*

Work groups weren't coming to Rakowice from Krakow any longer. The ghetto had been isolated and was being run by the SS. We weren't allowed to go to Krakow on the weekends any more. I was cut off from Anita and any news about the war came from other sources, mostly by word of mouth. Later I learned the *placowka* was building barracks for a camp outside the Krakow ghetto on land that was an ancient Jewish cemetery. People from the Krakow ghetto were to be relocated to this new camp called Plaszow.

In comparison, Rakowice had extraordinary freedom. The Artur Johr people were in and out of Rakowice, mixing with people from the outside. As a result, we had greater access to German news. Of course, what we heard was mostly propaganda about German victories.

However, on one occasion in the beginning of 1943, the truck runners brought us news about the Battle of Stalingrad. This was a major defeat for the German army. The winter had been hard and the snow and cold made it complicated. The Germans phrased it in their newspaper as a realignment of the strategic lines. Did they want us to believe it was a strategic withdrawal? I considered it a German defeat, and felt it was encouraging news. Even though things were continually getting worse for the Jews, we still had hopes that the war would be over, the Germans would be defeated, and we would survive.

Not just the cities, towns and villages, but now the ghettos were being made *Judenfrei*, clean of Jews. We were hearing rumors about concentration camps and extermination camps in Auschwitz and the mass killings and elimination of ghettos in smaller towns. *Aktions* intensified against the Jews.

In March of 1943, there was a final *Aktion* in the Krakow ghetto, making it *Judenfrei*. Thousands of people went to Plaszow (Pwa'shuf) labor camp, located 6 miles outside the center of Krakow ghetto, to complete the building work. The sick, old, and undesirable went to Auschwitz located 50 miles southwest of Krakow. I didn't know the details of what went on in Auschwitz, but I knew people were killed, even though I had no idea how it was done. As for the approximately 2,000 killed in the Krakow ghetto, they were taken to Plaszow and buried in a mass grave.

The Altered I

Tatus (Max) in front of Szynk

Early Spring 1943
14 to 15 years old

> Mr. G had made these arrangements for Tatus, but it didn't look like a hospital to me. I went in and saw one tiny room, just big enough for the small cot Tatus lay in.

Chapter 17

O ur boss, "The Big, Fat Guy" was head of all business within the Artur Johr Company. He had full control over the workers without interference from the Gestapo, and wasn't required to report to the SS or the military. As such, he was sympathetic toward us.

One job in the company involved running a truck to the Klaj Forest and bringing back lumber for the camp. During the springtime, I had made arrangements with the driver of the truck to ride with his group. I wanted to visit my parents in Bochnia, which was just past the Klaj Forest. The driver conspired with me and asked my boss for extra workers for that day. I was approved for the work.

Just as the driver passed the turnoff and continued on to Bochnia, it came to my attention that one of the workers was planning an escape. He had made plans with an unknown person to pick him up and hide him once he arrived in the village. When the truck slowed to a stop, the escapee turned to me. He shook my hand and said, "Goodbye." I wished him success and hoped he would be okay. Then, he jumped down from the truck, took off running through the woods, and I never saw him again. The truck continued on toward Bochnia and left me off at the ghetto entrance. The driver gave me instructions to be ready when they returned, two or three hours later.

Attached to the left side of my shirt was a metal plate with a photo I.D. and the number 6210. This indicated to the OD that I was working with the Germans and was not to be kept in the ghetto. Once at the gate, I showed the OD my metal nameplate, passed through, and made my way to my see my parents.

When I arrived I found only Mamusia at home. She was very happy to see me, but I was a bit reserved with her. "Tatus is sick," she said. "Our cousin got him a bed in a sort of hospital. It's a bit makeshift, but I'd like you to go see him. I think he'd like it. Joziu, he's not doing well."

"Okay." Then looking around, I asked, "Where's Babcia?"

"She's out for some firewood. I don't know when she'll be back. I hope you see her. She'll be so happy you're here."

We exchanged some news; I told her about my friend who escaped. That interested her.

"Won't there be trouble?"

"I don't know," I said.

Mamusia told me that the ghetto was quiet and she liked it, but she missed me. She was worried about Tatus, who was in bad shape. We talked for a little while, then she said, "Go now Joziu; go see Tatus."

I wasn't especially overjoyed to do this. I still felt resentful toward him, but for her sake I went.

After getting directions, I found the old house, but it was more of a shack than a house. Mr. G had made these arrangements for Tatus, but it didn't look like a hospital to me. I went in and saw one tiny room, just big enough for the small cot Tatus lay in. Across the hall was a room that passed for a kitchen. Tatus was by himself, lying very still and quiet. I didn't say a word to him. There was an estrangement between us, and I couldn't feel respect for him. Tatus had allowed Mamusia to pay the price for our freedom. I was still dealing with those damaging memories, and I found it hard to feel love for him.

When I was small, pleasing and making him proud were all I cared about. Although he never expressed his feelings to me outwardly, his love for me had been evident during the summer of 1939 when I was eleven years old.

Tatus and I had gone on vacation together. We took a train to a place called Kroscienko in the Tatra Mountains. Tatus bought me a fancy walking stick. I walked around tapping it on the ground simulating the way a train sounds rattling down the tracks: Tap-pity tap! Tap-pity tap! Tap-pity tap! I was so excited to be there with him, I wanted to do everything there was to do. There were other vacationers who were going to climb a mountain. Tatus stayed behind because it was too difficult a climb for him, but he let me go along with the group. He expected to see me again around noon; however, he was in for a long wait.

When we got to the top of the mountain, the group decided to climb another summit called the Three Crowns. I didn't want to miss anything, so I climbed it, too. It was a beautiful day; the air was clean and fresh. After reaching the summit, we hiked down to the river Dunajec. It was a fast-flowing mountain river embedded with boulders and thrilling rapids. The local people ran wooden rafts down the river to Kroscienko. The rafts were hastily tied together wooden logs, but we ignored the possible danger for the prospect of a fun adventure. Our raft rushed down the river, spilling over the rapids. At one point, it looked like we were headed straight for a large rock: Everyone screamed with fright. Just at the last second, the skillful rafters swerved, narrowly avoiding a collision with a large rock. Everyone burst out laughing and shouting, "Again, again. Do it another time!"

Around 10 p.m. or 11 p.m., our raft touched the sandy shore of Kroscienko. I never gave it a moment's consideration that Tatus would be worried about me until I saw his pacing silhouette in the darkness. As soon as he saw me, he hugged me close, yelling, crying, and laughing at the same time. He thought I had gotten lost or that something terrible had happened to me. I only thought of the things I wanted to do and forgot that he had expected me back at noon. This was the first time I saw his emotions and loving concern. It touched me to the heart, and I was deeply sorry I had disappointed him.

Now, four years later, I found we had nothing to say to each other. He simply looked at me, and I didn't know how to talk to him. I could see he was in bad shape. He looked very thin and sickly. Of course, being thin wasn't unusual for a Jew living in a ghetto, but he was much thinner than I remembered him.

After staring at each other a few moments, he reached under his pillow and pulled out a cigarette. He said: "Would you light this for me? There's a fire in the kitchen; you can light it there." After lighting the cigarette, I took a quick drag on it before bringing it back to him. After handing the cigarette to him, I walked out of the room, out of the hospital and back to Mamusia's room. I never saw him again.

When I got back I said: "I saw him. Where's Babcia? Is she back, yet?"

"No," Mamusia said. There was a moment of awkward silence between us before she spoke again.

"Can you stay here, Joziu? It would be so nice to have you here with us. Is it possible you could leave the camp, like your friend?"

"No, I can't!"

I could tell my abrupt answer had hurt her feelings. But, I had to be firm. I longed for the familiarity of home. Mamusia looked the same and wore familiar clothing. Trinkets from home now graced this tiny room. All of it reminded me bitterly of my life from the past. Compared with living in the camp, this would be wonderful. I felt a strong temptation to stay. A powerful longing for my old life began to pull at me. Could I get away with it? If I stayed, it would be like home. The moment I thought it, however, I rejected the idea immediately.

"I can't," was all I could reply. She could never know the quarrel within me.

Gone were any feelings of family loyalty. My need to survive was strong. I didn't know what the future held for me. I had no bright prospects, either, but I wasn't going to stay with Mamusia. I knew I was safe in the camp.

"It's very comfortable here; you'd like it," Mamusia said. "We'd be together again as a family." As she said this she reached out, her arms open wide.

"No," I said, "I can't. I'm safe in the camp. Can't you understand? The ghetto is dangerous. I'm not safe here. Please, don't ask me anymore." I turned from her in frustration. "I have to go back; they'll be waiting for me at the gate, and I can't be late."

She was very quiet. There must have been a conflict within her. She wanted me to be with her, I sensed that she was lonely, but she didn't try to persuade me further. She trusted me to make the right decision. We had reached a sad conclusion: She couldn't leave the ghetto, and I realized that if I wanted to live, I couldn't stay with her. Together we walked to the gate. I waited with her behind the gate until the truck came.

As soon as the truck arrived outside the ghetto entrance, the workers waved me over. "Hurry up!" the driver yelled. "Let's go. We're late!"

With a slight wave, I softly said, "Bye." Then jumped on the back of the truck and clambered to the top of the chained-up logs. The truck rumbled off for Rakowice.

Later that evening, the boss called me in to see him. He learned of the escape earlier that day. Initially, he suspected that I was the escapee. "Who was the guy? Where did he go? Do you know?" he asked.

"I don't know," I replied.

The boss didn't make a big fuss about it. He had responsibilities and a job to get done, but somehow he was just anti-Nazi enough to allow people to escape. He was mumbling to himself, and then, realizing I was still in the room, he said, "Get out of here." I flew out of the office and ran back to my barrack.

Soon after visiting Mamusia in Bochnia, Dolek and I received one last communication from Mamusia. Torn from something similar to a paper bag, written in big scrawling letters, was a note of few words: "Tatus has died." The news did not come unexpectedly to me. He had looked very sick the last time I saw him, and I felt then that he was going to die. That day I saw him in the hospital shack, I had blocked my feelings for him and left him in silence.

I knew of some workers in the camp who still held to their religious customs. They gathered early every day before work, every Saturday, and before each holiday to pray. They especially prayed *Kaddish* (the prayer for the dead), which means sanctification. I went to the place these co-workers gathered in order to say *Kaddish* for my father. I felt a sense of duty deep down in my soul to pray for him properly.

By this time it wasn't a question of faith, but of formality. The prayer was prescribed words without any meaning to me, a repetition of words I was expected to follow. Saying the prayer was a way of acknowledging that Tatus was dead. I always tried to do what was right with regard to religion, as far as I was able. However, of late, my faith in God and religion had been lessening.

Rather than feeling grief, I felt depressed. But even that depression was more for Mamusia than for myself. Because Tatus had been sick, I felt that he was more of a burden for Mamusia, and that his passing was for the best. Still, he was her husband and he always took care of her as best he could.

I felt beaten down. On the other hand, Dolek was becoming famous with the German *Wehrmacht* officers who came from town with their own material to have clothing made by him. He was too busy catering to the officers needs to pay any attention to me, and I became more isolated from him every day.

The Altered I

1942:
The Plaszow camp, established in 1942 under the authority of the SS and police leaders in Krakow (Cracow), was initially a forced-labor camp for Jews. The original site of the camp included two Jewish cemeteries.
http://www.ushmm.org/wlc/en/article.php?ModuleId=10005301

March 1943:
The average barracks contained 150 people in an area of about 80 square metres. By the second half of 1943, its population had risen to 12,000, and by May - June 1944 the number of prisoners had increased to 24,000, including 6,000 - 8,000 Jews from Hungary.

The daily food ration for each detainee was 200 grams of bread, 150 grams of cheese, 300 grams of coffee substitute and hot water soup. The rations were distributed once a week; occasionally one egg was added. Any Jewish labourers caught smuggling food in were executed.
http://www.deathcamps.org/occupation/plaszow.html

"Who's the big guy?" I asked.
"That's Amon Goeth. He's in charge here."

Chapter 18

Plaszow (pwa'shuf) was in the process of being built, established and run by the SS. They started eliminating independent civilian labor camps such as Rakowice, which didn't report to the Gestapo or SS.

On July 3, 1943, two SS men came to Rakowice. We were told to assemble in the courtyard. Twenty people were picked out from the assembled group, including Dolek and Dr. Hilfstein. Management said these were essential workers and were needed in providing services for the Germans. The rest of us, totaling 130, were told to take our belongings, no money and get on trucks that were waiting to take us away. We were threatened with death by shooting if they discovered any money on us. I didn't have any money to hide; I brought only my trunk. I knew we were going to a camp outside the Krakow ghetto, now *Judenfrei*.

Plaszow was situated on a rocky hill. In the summer months grasses and wildflowers grew in profusion. The meadows and marshlands were filled with reeds. To me it was a dismal place. I was miserable, alone and confused.

There were stone and lime quarries nearby and a railway siding. Plaszow, still under construction, was the first big camp I had ever seen. I felt scared and uneasy. None of us knew where to go or what to do. If I had anything of value at that moment, I would have given it all away just to escape from this place.

We got off the trucks and were led by the OD like sheep, directly to a big, empty square. I looked around and could see at one end of the square a wooden structure with two hooks on the top. I never saw a structure of this type before and wondered at its use. There were barracks on one side of the square and a steep, sandy hill on the other. Next to the hill was a bulldozer—its use a mystery to me. Foremost in my thoughts were: *Where am I? Where's my trunk. What's going on?* I was scared, hungry, tired and confused.

We stood there until the early afternoon. Men and women began arriving in groups until the whole square was filled with thousands of people. The ODs were shouting at the groups to line up. The women had been arranged in separate groups from the men. At last, we were arranged in large groups of several hundred people with the ODs surrounding us. I couldn't tell what was happening. Then the SS started to arrive.

"Something unusual is going on," said someone nearby. "Normally there's no *appell* in the middle of the afternoon. Today, everyone was pulled from their *kommandos* and sent to their barracks."

"*Appell?*" I asked.

"Yes, roll call. The *appellplatz* is the place we meet for roll call. We were marched here to see something special, nobody knows what it is. But it's never good." We stood waiting for something to happen. Then a big man in an SS uniform arrived. I didn't know his name, or who he was in the camp, but he walked with great authority.

"Who's the big guy?" I asked.

"That's Amon Goeth. He's in charge here."

Soon the guards led two people in: an adolescent boy and a man both dressed in civilian clothing. They brought the man forward. According to his accusers, he had been found writing a letter.

"Where's the crime in that?" I asked.

The man near me said letters were not allowed to be written in Plaszow, it was a crime punishable by death.

"He's being punished because the SS need some victims," another man nearby said.

I learned that the wooden structure was a gallows and that they were going to hang the two offenders. There was a stool on the gallows with three steps. The man stepped up on the stool, and then the Jewish policeman, named Katz, previously a butcher in Krakow, put the noose around his neck. He then kicked the stool out from under the man. He wriggled around for a while. I wanted to turn away from it—I had never seen a public hanging before, but the OD in charge of my group shouted out, "Keep your head straight and your eyes open." Finally the hanging man was still.

Once he was dead, the guards pulled him down. Two skinny undertakers, called *totengraber*, came to take him away. They were dressed in yellow uniforms.

"They handle death so much they look like the dead." Someone said behind me. I thought they looked like skeletons. They walked in a numb, robotic way, as if what they were doing was of little significance—as if they were handling sacks of grain not human bodies. They placed the body on one of the two stretchers nearby.

Next, the boy was brought forward, about fifteen years old, close to my own age. His crime was whistling Russian songs. This, too, I learned, was punishable by death. Apparently, this Jewish boy picked up the song while working and was caught whistling the tune. The SS needed a scapegoat, and he was punished on trumped up charges of whistling a Russian song. I was told, however, that it wasn't a Russian song, but a Ukrainian one. The Ukrainian guards were in the general supervision and were differentiated by their black uniforms. They marched around singing Ukrainian songs, which were catchy and pleasant. Ukrainian songs were considered OK because Ukrainians were pro-German.

It was difficult to see the boy as he was some distance away, but I imagined he was very scared. He was put on the stool, Katz the butcher put the noose around his neck, the stool was kicked away, and he was hanged. It was the same rope used on the first hanging, and it was beginning to wear. The boy was very slight and lightweight, he hung there not choking right away, but jerking and twisting, wriggling wildly until the rope broke. He fell to the ground before Goeth. He scrambled to his knees, bowed his head in submission and grabbed onto Goeth's leg and begged him to spare his life. Goeth took out a pistol from his holster, aimed it at the boy's head and shot him.

The two undertakers in yellow uniform came forward again and put the dead boy on another stretcher. They had some people help carry the two bodies away. They took the bodies over to the right side, by the bottom of the sandy hill, and somebody started up the bulldozer. They put the bodies on the ground and with the bulldozer pulled down some sand from the hill. They buried them there while everyone was standing at full attention, mutely observing.

This was my welcome to Plaszow. I thought perhaps the public hanging was to intimidate the new group from Rakowice, but the real reason why Goeth picked this date I will never know.

After the spectacle, we were taken to a special barrack for people from Rakowice. All our belongings were piled up outside along the side of the barrack. I was very tired from the day of travel and in shock from the public execution. I was hungry, confused, and all I wanted to do was lie down.

An OD shouted, "Find your belongings from the pile!"

Looking for my trunk was difficult in the jumble of other people's belongings, but finally I found it. Now that I had it, I didn't know what to do with it. One Jewish guy, who I didn't recognize as being from Rakowice, was our *blockalteste*, block leader; he yelled at us and told us what to do next.

First, we were assigned to bunks. Bunks were stacked in three levels, each level one above the other, made out of wood and a thin straw mattress on top. One long stretch of bunks extended the length of the barrack. I was sent to my assigned bunk with my trunk, where I waited for the next set of instructions.

Toward evening, we were called to go outside where we were arranged in groups of five. Everyone was given a metal dish and spoon. We were counted by the *blockalteste* several times, and then we were marched to another barrack. There were so many barracks it was confusing. We were joined by other groups marching to the same barrack. When we arrived, we were told this is where we are going to get dinner. We stood in a long line. At the front of the line, there were prisoners dishing out food; then the people in line took their bowls and sat at long tables to eat. People had to eat in a hurry to make room for others. When our turn came for the soup, I could see it was a very thin, hot liquid with turnips floating in it. Another guy gave us a very thin piece of bread. We were told to line up to be assigned a table.

I hadn't eaten anything since that morning in Rakowice; I gulped the hot liquid down. The bread seemingly evaporated from my hands. After eating, we had to go outside and form yet another group to be marched back to our barrack. Other people, after they were done eating, simply dispersed, but this was our first time here, and we had to be kept in our group.

The *blockalteste* told us where the latrine barrack was, and followed with, "Go wash your dish, wash up, and take care of your private business." The latrine was in another long barrack. In the center was a long trough. Above it, stretching across the barrack was a long pipe where water dripped out. The water was cold; there was no soap, and no cloths to dry our hands and faces. The latrine barrack was very crowded, as several

135

barracks used this same latrine. There was no courtesy: people pushed and shoved each other to get to the trough. Along one wall was a long horizontal board with holes cut in it for toilet seats. We had to stand in line and wait for a vacant hole. I didn't know what to do with my dish and spoon, but a bit of advice I was given was never let go of those two items. Others had their dish tied to a string on their pants and the spoon looped through a buttonhole. I followed their example. Finally, I had my turn and afterward made my way back to the barrack. I wanted more than anything to go to the bunk and sleep, but I had to wait for instructions for every step I took.

When I arrived at the barrack, I was told by another prisoner, "Wait here until they tell you that you can go inside."

"Why?"

"They said we had to wait outside until given the orders." I didn't like it, but I had no choice. I milled about with some others and found out about this camp.

"There's a women's section a bit further," someone said.

"When can we go there?" I asked. "I might have friends there."

"They open the gates in the evening for an hour or two. We're free to go there, but we have to leave by curfew."

Immediately I thought of Anita and Renata. I was excited at the prospect of seeing their friendly faces. It was impossible to go there now. I wasn't familiar with the way, and Plaszow had already overwhelmed my senses. I stayed by the barrack until evening, when the barrack door was opened, and we were given permission to go to bed. Several people squeezed into the bunk together; there was no space between us. We were sleeping head next to head against the wall with our feet toward the center of the barrack. We had very thin blankets and no pillows. The only thing we had was a raised bit of wood at the head end of the bunk. We were left alone. I felt a little comforted that all the people in the barrack were from Rakowice. I was with people I knew. I fell asleep with the knowledge that the women's section was nearby, and I would soon be paying a visit to my old friends.

In the early morning hours, I was awakened by sharp yelling from the OD, "Up, up!" Seemingly, it was the middle of the night, and I had hardly gone to bed. After a rushed visit to the latrine barrack, we ran back to our barrack. I was learning that everything had to be done in a hurry. Some of the prisoners assigned to the task brought out steaming kettles. We lined up with our dish and everybody got a little bit of steaming, dark liquid. The guards called it "coffee," but it was tasteless and bore no resemblance to real coffee. We were given a small piece of bread and a tiny square of margarine. I gobbled it down before being rushed back to the bunks. We were told to straighten and square off our thin blankets. We lined up outside the barrack and were counted again, then marched off to the *appellplatz* for roll call. There I found the whole camp assembled, men and women, in formation by barrack groups. We had to stand quietly in rows of five, one behind the other with our heads facing forward. The OD and SS men went from one group to the next and counted us.

This lasted for some time until a loud order was given to form a unit or command, called, *kommando*. There was a great rush of people as the groups broke up. Each *kommando* was made up of fifty people including the Jewish *kapo* in charge of the work group. *Kapos*, or prisoner functionaries, often had a violent, criminal past. They pitted prisoner against prisoner and used cruelty to ensure their position in the camp. Because of them, fewer SS personnel were needed. All the *kapos* were identified by a white armband with the word *kapo* displayed.

The Rakowice barrack wasn't assigned to a *kommando* yet, we stood in place until all the other groups were marched off to work. Later, I learned some groups stayed in the camp while others went off to a work assignment in Krakow. After the *appellplatz* had emptied, some ODs came in with folding chairs and small tables and all kinds of paperwork. We were made to line up and wait for them to call us to the tables individually.

When it was my turn, an OD officer asked, "What is your name? Where do you come from? What is your age? What is your profession?"

I told him my name, but lied about my age, "I'm sixteen." It was still dangerous to be young. I had no profession of any kind, but I hit upon the idea of calling myself a painter because I had painted the yellow stuff on the lumber in Rakowice. "I'm a painter," I said. He took me at my word and wrote all the information down.

I was the only painter in my group, so they sent me off to the barrack where the painters work. The *kapo* painter was a big, unfriendly guy who looked me over in suspicion. He looked upon me as an intruder in his clique.

"Get a pail, some paint and a brush," he growled. "Climb up that ladder and paint those eaves under the roof." I did what he said, but the ladder was rickety, and I was nervous. He looked at me doubtfully. I knew I wasn't a painter and I never had done work like this before. I held onto the pail, dipped the brush in the paint and started splashing paint where he told me. I was clumsy and paint splattered all over the place. I got more paint on myself than on the barrack. The other guys in the work group yelled at me, but it only jangled my nerves.

The *kapo* came over to me yelling, "You're not doing it right!" Then again a few moments later, "You're not going fast enough! What kind of painting did you do?"

"Barracks, like this."

"How long did you do that?" he said

"A while," was my short response. He was suspicious. I was afraid he would report me. Finally, we broke for lunch in the same procedure as before. The prisoners served the same soup as the day before, but I didn't dare complain.

We ate at the inner camp, and after lunch, we had to form groups, be counted by the Jewish police, then go through the gate and be counted again. Then, we broke up to go to our work assignments. I went back to painting the barracks a sickly, light green color, and before long, I had green paint on my clothing and hands. I worked hard, but felt like an interloper. The group knew what they were doing, and I was just trying to make it through the day.

1943

Triumphant on the ground for the Soviet Army, the year 1943 was gruesome for Jewish survivors in urban ghettos that still lay behind enemy lines. As the Wehrmacht retreated, the Nazi leadership hastened to hide the evidence of its extermination policies. Jews who had been confined to their ghettos, where squalor and starvation slowly diminished their numbers, were violently routed from their quarters to be shipped west, or were killed on the spot.

http://www.soviethistory.org/index.php?
page=subject&SubjectID=1943holocaust&Year=1943

October, 1943
On October 4, 1943, Reischsführer-SS Heinrich Himmler gave a speech to a secret meeting of SS officers, in Poznan, Poland. In this speech, he spoke frankly about the ongoing extermination of the Jewish people.
This is one of the most chilling documents of the Holocaust.

http://www.holocaust-history.org/himmler-poznan/

1943
15 years old

For prisoners in Plaszow, often their
lives depended on whom they knew. I
didn't know anybody. I didn't have
skills.

Chapter 19

In Plaszow, as I later learned, there were many workshops specializing in creating whatever the German military needed. There was a tailor barrack where military uniforms were made. Also, here in the camp were workshops for the cobblers, blacksmiths, electricians, laundry workers, and bakers, to name a few. Just about everything imaginable was made for the military, right down to hairbrushes and bristles. A majority of prisoners were used as laborers in these special workshops. Some of the prisoners were employed in their professional fields as locksmiths, jewelers, carpenters and painters.

The camp had its own sewer, electricity, and water systems. Roads and paths were under construction as well as special camp buildings used for the purpose of storing property looted from the Jews of Krakow.

I was learning the ways of Plaszow. There was a certain hierarchy. The head of the Jewish Police in Plaszow was Chilowicz. His wife, *Pani* Chilowicz, was head of the women's barracks. She was frequently heard throughout camp shouting out her favorite expression to the women: "*kurwy wienieckie*" meaning Venetian Whores. Most of the prisoners were from the Krakow ghetto and knew each other. If somebody knew an influential person in this hierarchy, then they had the possibility of better, softer jobs. This led to the possibility of being chosen to work with the OD and gaining more privileges and maybe having access to more food.

Some prisoners maneuvered for special work assignments for the military outside the camp. These had no SS supervision and were out of the camp all day. They had access to food and managed to develop contacts, which could help them in some way. Occasionally, a prisoner smuggled in extra food, but this was highly illegal and punishable by death. However, I considered these prisoners to be safer than the rest of us, who worked inside the camp under direct SS supervision.

There was a word in the camp called *protekcja*, protection. The people within a protection group took care of their own. To be in a *protekcja* one needed to use friendship, family connections or bribery. Before leaving the Krakow ghetto, some people swallowed their jewels, wrapped inside a mouthful of bread, or they sewed Polish money into their clothing. They used these valuables to barter for better jobs or to buy items on the black market. Taking a risk against barrack inspections, they hid their valuables. Often, through some connection to an OD, or because of the *protekcja*, these people were given an advance warning. Still, there were discoveries, and people were executed every once in a while. I had nothing, so I didn't worry.

For prisoners in Plaszow, often their lives depended on whom they knew. I didn't know anybody. I didn't have skills. I didn't know how to maneuver people to gain advantage for myself. The people who didn't have *protekcja* were assigned to groups used for hard labor building barracks, roadwork or stone quarry work. This was called *barrackenbau*. And it was ugly work—the most dangerous and brutal. I knew that *barrackenbau* was the worst assignment. I knew enough to say I was a painter. Based on my skills, I only hoped I could remain in my current position.

Outside the camp was the German housing. Inside the camp, Jewish men and women were kept separately. Poles, who had broken laws of the German occupation government, were imprisoned separately from Jews. I learned that Anita and her family had survived the Krakow ghetto liquidation and were brought to Plaszow. She, her mother and Aunt Carolla were housed in the women's barracks, located at the north end of the camp. A fence separated the men from the women, but in the evening the gates were unlocked, and we were permitted to visit them for a period of time until curfew ended at 9 p.m.

The one thing I looked forward to after a hard day of labor, was visiting with Anita. I still maintained a certain pride in the way I looked when calling on her; I wouldn't see her without my fancy coat, my *jopka*. After painting all day, I went to my barrack, cleaned up as best I could, and, filled with excited anticipation, I went to see Anita.

She was in a barrack similar to mine. Her allocated space was in one corner of the barrack on an upper bunk. The first time I visited, she was sitting on the bunk with her mother and aunt. They were stunned to see me. After exchanging news, I described my first day of painting, which made Anita laugh.

"We have privileged jobs in the camp. We can get extra food. Uncle Trauring still takes care of us."

"Is he here? I haven't seen him yet," I said.

"No," was all she said, careful not to say too much.

I guessed that he was still working for the Germans, wielding his special privileges and taking care of them.

We talked until curfew. It was just as if we had never said goodbye that last day in Krakow. Although I had plenty to tell her, it was never of any significance. We were two young people who wanted a normal life.

As I was leaving, Anita's mother handed me a piece of bread. I was very appreciative. I was hungry and took it, but I experienced a deep flush of embarrassment. I came to see Anita, not scrounge for extra bread. I felt ashamed that Anita's mother might have thought that.

The next day, the whole cycle began again: marching to *appell*, forming barrack groups, being counted, forming work groups, being counted, then marching to the work assignment. I thought of Anita each time I saw the women being marched to the *appellplatz*. I could hear Chilo-wicz' wife shouting to the group of women, "Move faster, my Venetian Whores!"

At the painting assignment, the *kapo* had enough of me. He was gruff and unfriendly.

"Follow me," he said. We then marched to the *appellplatz* where he found one of the OD's. Pointing back at me, the *kapo* said, "He's not a painter. I don't want him in my unit anymore."

"Why?" asked the OD.

"If I'm going to get my work done, I need someone who can accomplish what we have to do. He's just slowing us down."

I couldn't say anything. I was only employed one and a half days as a painter, and then kicked out. To my dissatisfaction, I was immediately assigned to *barrackenbau* with the rest of the riffraff. There was no way out of it. We were the most expendable, the rejects of one type or another, assigned to fill in wherever work was needed. Almost every day, we worked in a different place. The ODs assigned to us were harsh. They not only hated guarding us, but they were responsible for the quantity and quality of work.

"Move faster, faster! You're too slow!" was the constant command. In addition, we were exposed to the SS. If we didn't please them, we risked getting shot, as was the case with a famous lady architect named Diana Reiter. A wall had collapsed under her supervision, and when she tried to convince Goeth that the quality of work on the foundation of the barrack was poor, she was shot and killed by Hujar, on Goeth's command. This happened just one barrack over from where I worked. My group was shaken to the core and determined to work faster.

Later that evening when the gates opened between the sections, I went to see Anita and poured my heart out to her. I was so disappointed to have been removed from my painting *kommando* and put in *barrackenbau*. Anita felt sorry for me, but neither she nor her mother said anything, nor offered to help me get out of it. I was learning that no one commiserated with the troubles of others. I learned not to complain. Still, at the end of each day I always looked forward to wearing my *jopka* and visiting Anita.

As happened the first time, each time I visited, her mother gave me something to eat. Each time I accepted it gratefully, but my embarrassment increased because I knew Anita's mother viewed my coming as a way of seeking a handout. During our visits, Anita and I walked around to the different parts of the women's camp. One evening I happened to find Renata.

When I found her, she smiled her familiar bright smile and greeted me with a warm hug, "How are you Joziu? Is Dolek here, too?"

"No," I said, "He's still in Rakowice."

"I hope he is OK?" Slight lines crinkled her brow.

"He was the last time I saw him, but we didn't have much chance for good-byes. We were taken away so quickly."

We talked for a little while longer and parted with a hug. I couldn't help but compare her welcome with that of Anita's mother. Renata greeted me with more joy and happiness than Anita's family. They were becoming rather cool and not overly friendly.

For the next several days, whenever I could, I would see Anita. I got some bread, but felt it was becoming an obligation on their part. Obviously, Anita's mother didn't understand that I came to see Anita and she failed to see how important these visits were to me, but I still took the bread.

Less than two weeks later, on returning to my barrack after the end of a workday, those from Rakowice were told by the OD we could not enter. "All detainees from Rakowice are to stay here for a new barrack assignment. All your things will be moved to your new barrack. Do not to return here."

We silently fell in line and were directed to barrack, No. 20. When I arrived at the new barrack, I went looking for my little trunk with my *jopka* and few possessions inside, but I couldn't find it anywhere.

"Where's my trunk?" I asked the OD. I began to feel panicky and suspected it had been stolen along with my other things. The OD ignored me.

Another prisoner said, "Forget about it. It's gone."

"Gone?" I was stunned. This was quite a blow. These were my only possessions. Losing them was a significant loss. How could I see Anita without my *jopka*? My pride wouldn't let her see me without it. Foolishly, I never visited her again. That was a horrible mistake, one that would forever change the direction of my life.

More and more prisoners began taking risks smuggling food into the camp. Because the inspections didn't take place often, the prisoners were lulled into a false sense of security. As they were counted off by the OD and food was discovered, yet not taken away, they developed the notion that they could get away with it. Once in a while, however, Goeth was present for the count. He inspected the prisoners himself, and if he caught someone with food, he immediately shot the offender. At first, he only shot the one who had the food, but because it was happening so frequently, he began to shoot the entire *placowka* of fifty workers as they came in.

Within a few months of my arrival, a number of prisoners were able to escape. In order to discourage the prisoners from further escapes and punish the remaining people in the work group, Goeth shot every tenth person from the escapee's group.

On the outskirts of the camp was a hill called Chujowa Gorka (who-hu'ya gorka). A remnant of World War One surrounding the hill was a large, deep pit, full of stones and rubble. When people were killed at random by Goeth and his cohorts throughout the day, they were brought to the hill by the skinny, yellow-clad gravediggers and dumped into the pit. New bodies were thrown on top of old bodies, gravel layered in between.

Later on, when the count didn't come to the full fifty, instead of shooting people at the *appellplatz*, the remaining forty-nine men would be isolated until about six o'clock in the evening, and a report made to Goeth that there was a missing prisoner. Then the men were marched to the top of Chujowa Gorka. Hujar or Strojewski, two dangerous SS killers, were there waiting. The people were ordered to take off all of their clothing, place it neatly in a pile and, while naked, wait their turn. When their turn came they knelt down with their back to the SS and were shot in the back of the neck. The yellow *totengraber* stood by waiting to carry each body away. Strojewski carried out his orders in a relaxed manner sitting at the edge of the ravine, swinging his legs, smoking a cigarette, enjoying the day, shooting until all forty-nine men were killed.

Because Chujowa Gorka was located nearby, the shots could be heard ringing out throughout the camp. We stood stock still wherever we were and counted the shots out loud. After reaching 49, we turned and said to each other, "Another group has someone missing."

The Altered I

September 12:
Benito Mussolini, under arrest at Abruzzi's Hotel Campo
Imperatore, is freed in a dramatic raid by German troops, on
Adolf Hitler's order.

http://history.howstuffworks.com/world-war-ii/allies-bomb-
northern-nazi-germany8.htm

1943:
Following American involvement in the war manufacturers
around the US became as efficient at producing war machines
as they had been producing other goods with companies like
Ford and GM managing to change from cars to bombs and
aircraft engines and at the same time due to the number of men
overseas fighting the war using more women for
manufacturing a total of 18 million women were employed.

http://www.thepeoplehistory.com/1943.html

September 1943
15 years old

I felt as good as dead already. I became envious of the living. Even if they had only a short time to live, it was still longer than I had at the moment.

Chapter 20

Through various channels the Szajniak (shy-nek) group, an excellent group of workers, named after the *kapo* in charge, came to the attention of Goeth. He received a report that the Szajniak group could not only get the job done efficiently, but the quality of work would be good. To other SS men in town Goeth bragged, "Whatever Szajniak promises me, I will get it." They didn't believe him.

One day, I was taken out of *barrackenbau* and put in the Szajniak group. This was a fortunate event. They happened to be short one person and picked me because I looked strong and healthy. They were a real crackerjack team of workers. We had a certain amount of pride in what we could accomplish together. Szajniak was an unusual leader, a go-getter with an enormous amount of enthusiasm for his group. Under his direction we could do anything.

Some important SS had offices in a building in Krakow. At that time, there was the danger of British air raids. One day they asked Goeth whether he could send a group of workers to build air raid shelters and he replied that he had a real good team of workers.

Air raid shelters had to be built in a certain way, not against the wall or in a straight line, but in a zigzag pattern with a covered roof and camouflage grass placed on top. Goeth wanted an especially fancy shelter for the SS. Being a betting man, Goeth announced, "I'll wager that I'm going to have that shelter built in one day." The SS officers thought this was an incredible bet. How could they lose with such an impossible job to accomplish? The bet was on.

Goeth knew that if he wanted anything special built, then the Szajniak group was assigned to the task. Goeth sent the Szajniak group to Krakow. We had strict orders that this shelter had to be built in one day, or else. Szajniak drove us relentlessly to completion. I worked strenuously, but I was young and fit. I felt satisfied in doing a good job and being useful. After inspecting our work with a critical eye, Szajniak deemed it a job well done. We had accomplished building the shelter in one day. Under Szajniak's leadership we became enthusiastic about our work and supported Szajniak in whatever he wanted us to build. I was very pleased to be a part of this special group.

September 3, 1943, there was another *Aktion* in the Bochnia ghetto. This was a final *Aktion* resulting in everyone taken to Auschwitz or killed on the spot. I never knew what happened to Babcia and Mamusia. But, I didn't say *Kaddish* for them. As a rule, if we weren't certain someone was dead, we didn't say the prayer.

That same month, nineteen prisoners from Rakowice, including Dolek, were brought to Plaszow. Dr. Hilfstein was not present. When I asked someone from that group what had happened to him, I was told this story: The SS had assembled the twenty prisoners and announced they had to give up any money. If money was found they would be shot. Dr. Hilfstein, who had so callously shaved my head because he saw a louse on my jacket, was in this group. When the SS came around to him and searched his clothing, they found twenty *złoty* in his shirt pocket. Before the war twenty *złoty* was perhaps worth $4 in American currency. When the SS discovered the money they shot him. He died for something so worthless. Often I wondered whether he forgot the money was there or if he just didn't care.

After the shooting, the twenty remaining prisoners were taken by truck to Plaszow and assigned to work groups. Dolek was immediately assigned to the master tailor shop. He worked for Madritsch, a very kind man and a friend of Oskar Schindler. Again, Dolek had a pretty good position in the camp. He was assigned to a different barrack from mine. I heard he had visited the women's camp. I hoped he had a happy reunion with Renata, but I never saw him when I went there. I only saw him that brief time when he first arrived in the camp and he didn't see me. In

Plaszow, there were strict rules of interaction. There was no freedom during the day to go see someone just because I knew him, or as in my case, even if he was my brother. More than ever, I felt lost and alienated.

One morning after *appellplatz* and barrack roll call, I reported to my Szajniak work group and was counted again. The count was forty-nine. Someone had escaped during the night. This was unusual. When someone escaped, they usually did it from town and would be discovered at the evening roll call. ODs immediately surrounded us. While guarding us, they made a search of the barrack for the missing man. When they couldn't find him, they realized they would have to give a report to Goeth at 6 p.m. on the *appellplatz*. We were put under strict orders to be guarded by the ODs at all times; however, we were permitted to go to our normal work assignment. That day, we were in a barrack breaking open the walls. Inside one of the walls I found a brand new pair of shoes. They were perfect, without holes. They had laces and thick soles. This was quite a find. My own had no laces, and were torn apart and had many holes. I looked at the brand new boots and ignored them. What do I need them for? Death was guaranteed for us that evening; I wouldn't need new shoes, so I left the boots behind.

None of us said a serious word all day. Either we were completely silent or we spoke in hangman humor. We didn't really know what to say, but joking about our fate made us feel better somehow. At lunchtime we were taken away by the OD and we were closely supervised. We couldn't be left alone even to go to the latrine or any other place. Since there was nothing we could do, we sat down to eat. The two *totengraber* in yellow uniforms came by to look over the goods. There was no pity in their eyes. There was no pity from anybody.

I felt as good as dead already. I became envious of the living. Even if they had only a short time to live, it was still longer than I had at the moment. During this hour I allowed myself to think in final terms. *This is my last meal, no matter how terrible it is. This is the last time I will see this soup or this kitchen barrack. This is the last time I will see these people.*

I said good-bye to everything because there would be no tomorrow.

This is it. This won't happen again. This is the last thing.

After lunch, the ODs marched us back to work. While climbing the hill to our worksite, I teased the guys saying, "Well I'm going to go after you."

"No, I'm going to go after you," someone else said. Nobody

wanted to be the one to "go" first.

There was a siren blast. The rule of the camp was to drop whatever we were doing and immediately return to camp. This blast struck fear and confusion in us.

The OD ordered the Szajniak group to disperse to our various barracks and wait there for instructions. I turned to my friend and asked, "Why do we have to go back to our barracks?"

"I don't know," he replied.

When I arrived at my barrack, I climbed to my bunk on the top level and waited. At 2 p.m., there was another siren, this one indicating that we had to go down to the *appellplatz*. The sounding of the siren to meet was another unusual occurrence. There was never any kind of signal to meet at the *appellplatz* when someone escaped. The whole situation was perplexing to me.

Word had gotten around that Goeth had enough of taking people to Chujowa Gorka. Instead, there was to be a public hanging of the forty-nine prisoners from the Szajniak group. In one horrifying moment, I realized they were going to hang my group but no one in the barrack knew it was my group. I kept that knowledge a secret.

Earlier, I had resigned myself to being shot, but hanging! This was too much for me to bear. I didn't want to be hanged. I racked my brain searching for a way out of it.

When the whistle blew for our barrack to go out to the *appellplatz*, chaos erupted within the barrack. Everybody was running pellmell. A siren call in the middle of the afternoon was a sign that something was horribly wrong and it set off total confusion among the prisoners. Our *blockalteste* was panicky, agitated and yelling. His agitation brought fear and anxiety to everyone else. I was able to linger behind on my bunk without being seen. When everyone was gone I climbed down to the bottom bunk. Carefully, I pulled on a board. To my relief the board was loose. I looked around, checking to make sure I was alone and nobody saw me. I had to act quickly because there was the possibility that if the *blockalteste* counted before the march to *appell*, as they almost always did, they would find one person missing and come back inside to find him. I took a chance, but didn't know if anyone was going to come back to look for stragglers. I was simply doing the first thing that came to mind—an act of complete desperation. I only wanted to escape from hanging.

As I lifted the board, I quickly worked myself under the bunk, wriggling and stretching with all my might to squeeze into the small space.

There was about six or seven inches of room, and I had to lie as flat as I could. For the first time I was grateful for being so thin, otherwise I would never have fit. I brought the board back over, covering myself and waited, terrified, in darkness and silence.

I knew with every fiber of my being that once they arrived at the *appellplatz* and discovered that I was missing, they would come back to the barrack and drag me outside. Eventually I'll get caught and they'll kill me anyway. I can't get away with it; they'll find me and shoot me. But at least I can escape hanging. They won't have a big execution just for me. They'll beat me and shoot me, which is what I prefer to hanging. I had witnessed one hanging and didn't want to see another, let alone be in one. If I was going to die, *I* would choose the manner that was best.

I waited under the bunk for what seemed forever thinking crazy thoughts. *To wait here is death and to go to appell is death. Every way for me is death.* I waited about six hours and nobody came back. I was beginning to hate this small, confined space. I was as desperate to escape it as I was to escape the hanging.

Finally, I heard the men coming back to the barrack, but I was determined not to come out from my hiding spot until I heard whether or not they were looking for me.

This was a terrifying time. *What happened to the Szajniak group? Were they killed? Am I the only one to survive? Are the ODs still looking for me? Am I endangering this barrack because I hid myself?* I was on high alert, keeping a sharp ear out. There was a lot of talking, but I couldn't hear what I was specifically waiting to hear. To my gratification, they began to discuss what had happened at the *appellplatz*. Many men were talking excitedly at the same time. It was loud and difficult to make out the words, but I knew I couldn't come out yet. Also, I had the added problem that someone was sitting on top of the bunk. Then I heard them say the Szajniak group had not been hanged. Others were taken to Chujowa Gorka instead.

I pushed up on the board. I heard a surprised voice say, "Hey! What's going on? Who's under there?" Then the man jumped off the bunk. I worked myself out of the tiny space. When I popped out of my hiding place, I could see a group of surprised looking men.

"Who is that?" someone said.

"It's me, Jozef!"

"You were hiding?" another man asked.

"Yes, the siren scared me. I didn't know what to do," I said.

"You're lucky no one thought to count, little idiot," I heard someone mutter.

Nobody in the barrack had a clue that I was in the group slated for hanging, and I didn't bother to explain. I just sat there along with the others and listened to the stories.

As I heard it, Goeth initially wanted to isolate the people from our group for the hanging. Chilowicz knew we were Goeth's pet group. "Why hang this group of people?" Chilowicz said. "They're your special Szajniak work group. Why not have a selection of the sick and those who can't work? Spare these people." and Goeth agreed.

Everyone had to assemble holding a piece of lumber or something heavy. Individually they paraded before Goeth and his henchmen. He picked out 161 people who he found to be defective or simply not good enough. They took them away to Chujowa Gorka and shot them.

In the meantime the OD arrested Szajniak, but they released him eventually, returning him to his barrack. Essentially, our group was saved because of our reputation and the intercession of Chilowicz. The influence Chilowicz had over Goeth amazed me. He had the ability to choose who would live and who would die.

September 19, 1943, was a significant day for me. When I thought about it I realized I should have been dead. I was alive due to a stream of unusual circumstances. I was saved because of the panic in the ensuing rush to get to the *appellplatz*. There was no count, and I was over-looked in the crowd, enabling me to hide. Then a higher-up in the system interceded on behalf of my special work group.

That same evening I paid a visit to Renata. She was the only person I liked and trusted in the camp. Before the war, when Dolek introduced her to the family, I thought she was a wonderful girl: pleasant, pretty and happy. I remember her always smiling. She was the only one I could turn to now in my time of need. I knew she could give me comfort and friendship. I rushed to the women's barracks and found Renata in her barrack. "I escaped a death sentence today!" I blurted out breathlessly.

Renata's eyes went wide. "What happened?" she asked.

"It's a long story," I said. "I was in a hopeless situation, but my life was spared." I felt the most incredible lightness. I was so happy to be alive, as well as relieved that my group was safe. But I felt a deep underlying sadness, too. I needed to unburden my heart to Renata.

"I'm so glad you're safe. How terrible that must have been for you," she said. Letting out a deep sigh, she patted the bunk next to her. "Joziu, sit here and tell me everything."

I proceeded to tell her the whole story from the beginning.

The next day I rejoined Szajniak group and we went back to work as normal.

1943

Last major deportation of German Jews
www.ushmm.org/w/c/en

September 20-October
Approximately 7,200 Danish Jews escape to Sweden with the help of the Danish resistance movement and many individual Danish citizens.

http://www.ushmm.org/wlc/en/article.php?
ModuleId=10007767

In November
The Riga Ghetto is liquidated.

The U.S. Congress holds hearings regarding the U.S. State Department's inaction regarding European Jews, despite mounting reports of mass extermination.

November 3 - Nazis carry out Operation Harvest Festival in occupied Poland, killing 42,000 Jews.

http://www.historyplace.com/worldwar2/holocaust/#1943

Fall to Winter 1943
15 years old

While I was gone, the OD took the count and it came up as 49. One missing: me.

Chapter 21

I was learning that every decision I made came with a consequence. Some decisions cost dearly. One day after the lunch hour, we were lined up waiting at the gate to be counted before heading back to our work assignment when I had a sudden attack of diarrhea. I knew I was not allowed to break ranks and run to the latrine barrack at this time. The ODs were taking the count and if I was missing I knew I would get into trouble. I tried to hold it as long as I could, but soon I couldn't take the pain and pressure building up in my bowels any longer. I fled from the line and ran to the latrine. While I was gone, the OD took the count and it came up as 49. One missing: me. The entire group had to be set aside to wait while they looked for me. Making the group wait was a bad thing to do. When I rejoined them, someone told me that I had missed the count and they were looking for me. When the OD came over to me, he took down my name and number, then left. I hoped that would be all there was to it, but I was filled with a deep foreboding.

In the middle of the night the OD came into our barrack and called out my name. I responded and they took me to the OD headquarters where I had to wait for the OD commander, named Finkelstein. A cruel man, he was second in command from Chilowicz. Finkelstein came to the room where I was waiting. I saw that he was holding a whip in his hands. He checked my number and then he silently looked me over from head to toe. I didn't look up at him but instead kept my eyes focused on the floor in front of me.

"You endangered the group by being late," he said. "Pull down your pants and bend over the chair."

Now was the time to take my punishment. I did what he said and he started whipping me with his full might. The pain was excruciating, but I bit my tongue and kept quiet. My backside felt on fire from the stinging strokes. As it was happening, the whipping seemed incredibly slow, as if without end, but finally the lashes stopped. He sent me back to the barrack. My behind was sore for days afterward and was covered with large, red, swollen welts.

Later, on another occasion, I felt sick with fever. Customarily, when someone is sick, he reports it while at the *appell*. Instead of going to work he is sent to *revier* (an abbreviated German word for *krankenrevier*, or field hospital). A Jewish doctor named Gross was in charge of this barrack. Once at the *revier*, I had to stand in a very long line and wait my turn for inspection. Even if I said I was sick and had a fever someone else had to verify this as a fact. Someone took my temperature; it read 102. I was told I could have a day off from work and stay in the barrack. At the time, it seemed like a relief not to go to work, but to my disappointment, I learned that lying down was not allowed. I was given a work assignment cleaning the barrack all day.

The next day, whether I felt better or not, I had no excuse to stay away from work, so I marched to the *appellplatz* as usual. After the count I went to join my Szajniak work group. "We have our fifty already," the group leader plainly said. "When you didn't report yesterday, we filled your spot. You have to go somewhere else." Discouraged, I watched them disappear from view. I liked this group and I didn't want to find another group, but I didn't have a choice. With heaviness in my heart, I marched over to my new group.

My new work assignment was with a *barrackenbau* group, considered the lowest position, the bottom layer of the camp. I knew I would be exposed to deadly situations in this group. I was depressed and vowed never to report sick again. Reporting had cost me my placement in a group I liked and had pointed out to those in charge that I had a weakness.

My new group assignment was to dig ditches and push heavy, rock-laden, dilapidated wheelbarrows up from the ditch onto a narrow plank and onto the road. The wheelbarrows had wooden wheels and mine had the added feature of a crooked wheel, rendering it constantly off-center. I struggled just to keep it in a straight line. Like all things in Plaszow, I learned there was a trick to it. By steering it crookedly, it seemed to stay straight. To make matters more difficult, there was the narrow wooden plank to contend with. I feared slipping off it and tumbling down into the ditch with my wheelbarrow landing on top of me. Once I had gotten the wobbly wheelbarrow onto the main road, I had to push it to a dumping ground some distance away.

While we were working in the ditch, loading up our wheelbarrows with the rocks, there was an incident. We were near Goeth's house when I heard a loud gunshot. This in itself was nothing unusual; in Plaszow shootings throughout the day were common. As I was muscling my heavy load up the gravelly road, struggling to keep my wheelbarrow straight, I saw an OD ahead of me standing on the road directing all the wheelbarrow traffic.

He was calling out in a loud voice, "Careful! Corpse on the road!" He stood next to a body bleeding from a head wound. Instantly, I recognized the dead man. He was the camp fool. Someone who was out of his mind, always laughing, whether it was at other prisoners, *kapos* or the OD, he didn't recognize anyone in authority. On this day he must have displeased Goeth in some way, and he shot him.

As I passed the body, I went by a work group building a barrack across the road. At that moment, they were using caulk to prep the barrack. Just then a breeze wafted the scent of caulk scent toward me. Thereafter, whenever I smelled that chemical substance, I associated it with the scent of blood.

Another day, my group was assigned to dig fence posts up near Chujowa Gorka. Up there, the ground was hard and filled with big rocks and small stones. We were just off to the side of the road when two buses full of people drove by on their way to the top of Chujowa Gorka.

I could tell by their manner of dress that they were civilians, not prisoners. There were men and women dressed in clean, nice clothing. As their bus passed by, they regarded us working alongside the road with curiosity, and I, just as curious, looked back at them. They appeared Aryan with their blond hair and fair complexions. I couldn't figure out who they were or why civilians would be here. I turned to my workmate Gross (not the doctor) and asked, "Where are they going, do you think?"

"The only thing up there is Chujowa Gorka," he said.

We proceeded with our digging, but soon after, we heard gunshots from the direction of the hill.

After about an hour or so, some OD men came to us. One pointed at me and Gross and said, "We want you two with wheelbarrows to come up to the hill."

When we went up, we could see they had executed all those civilians. There were 75 or 80 of them. I speculated that they must have been people who knew too much. Maybe they were Polish collaborators who the German officers had to get rid of, in order to cover their tracks. I knew they were different because instead of finding them naked and their clothing in a neat orderly pile—the manner of execution used on Jews— these people had been executed while still fully clothed. The two *totengrabers* in yellow were undressing the bodies and stacking them in a pile, like stacks of firewood. They swung the bodies up and over by their arms and legs, one on top of the other. I saw that they were piling up the clothing on the side. Naked men and women were lying to the side of the stacks of bodies and I caught myself staring at the nude body of a blond woman. I only saw a side view of her, but I realized at that moment that this was the first time I had ever seen a naked woman.

Then the OD man said, "Take all this clothing down to the clothing chamber."

We scrambled to load the bloody garments into our wheelbarrows. I knew in the camp there was a barrack especially for the purpose of storing clothing. There were heaps and heaps of clothes in there from people who had been killed.

After loading up our wheelbarrows Gross and I went back down the hill, unguarded in our task.

Gross turned to me. "Wait a minute, nobody's looking, let's go through this stuff and see what we can find," he said.

We searched through the things and found some personal belongings, but we had no use for them. We searched for food and found a wonderful large loaf of white French-style bread coated with a thick spread of butter. Unfortunately for us, it was covered in blood, but that didn't deter us. It was a real find and I was eager to eat it. We divided it between us, picked out the bloody parts, and had ourselves a terrific butter sandwich. To us, this was a feast.

At this time, I was still living in the segregated barracks for the underprivileged of the *barrackenbau*. Around three or four in the morning two OD's awakened us. They were making a lot of noise and seemed agitated. In loud voices, they ordered everyone to get up, get dressed and go outside.

One OD walked up and down the length of the barrack hurrying people, shouting at them as he paced, "Get dressed! Get outside!" He was hitting us with his *reit peitscher* (horsewhip). Prisoners began scrounging around for their clothes and shoes, whatever they could find, but they were startled out of sleep and were confused.

Meanwhile, waiting outside, was the other OD. As each person got dressed and ran outside, I could hear him counting each one off. He yelled back to the OD man inside, "I've got seven. I need forty-two more!" Right away I recognized the magic number. Someone had escaped and now 49 would die because of it.

The OD inside the barrack was still shouting and hitting people with his *reit peitscher*. He appeared nervous and anxious to move the people up and out for the count. I could hear the count and knew they needed 49 prisoners so I kept stalling. Every time he strode by I pretended to put my shoes on, put my clothing on, but just as soon as he wasn't watching, I took them off again. I was never ready whenever he passed by my bunk. He was so nervous, dashing up and down the barrack, rushing around in a panic, he didn't even notice. He was young, inexperienced and didn't know what he was doing.

"We have forty-nine!" I heard. There was a marching of feet and then an abrupt silence.

I had no evidence at the time, but I assumed they were taken to Chujowa Gorka and shot. Later, I found out the true story. There was a work group comprised of some prominent people in the camp. One of these men escaped. As usual, when Goeth found out someone had escaped, he would have the person executed on the hill. Goeth was away at the time, so the execution was scheduled for the following day. In the meantime, he wanted the prisoners kept in an isolation barrack overnight. When Chilowicz found out who was in the group slated for execution, he wanted to save them. In order to save his friends, he had to substitute another 49 prisoners. What better group to choose from than my barrack full of undesirable characters. So, in the early morning hours he sent his OD men to pick us out.

I felt an extreme fear at the time, but I had a strong will to survive. After it was over, I felt a flood of relief. *It's over. I'm OK.* I didn't dwell on past experiences; each day had its own problems. I only thought about surviving the current day.

January 29, 1944:
Cracow; Five Poles are put to death for helping Jews.

March 4, 1944:
Warsaw; Four women were shot in the ghetto along with 80 non Jews. All their bodies, dead and wounded alike, were thrown into a building that was then lit on fire.

April 15, 1944:
Ponar Execution Site: Diggers in the pit, having unburied tens of thousands of bodies, then burning them as part of the Blobal Commando Action, attempt to escape to freedom. They had been secretly digging a tunnel within the burial pits. 40 managed to get through the tunnel. 25 are found and shot, 15 were able to escape. The remaining 25 diggers were shot in punishment of the actions of the others.

June 6, 1944:
THE ALLIES LAND IN NORMANDY------- D-DAY

July 24, 1944:
Sarvar, Hungary; Deportations continue despite the retreat of the German Army. 1,500 are sent to Birkenau. This day, Soviet forces entered Majdanek. For the first time, allied observes gaze upon the gas chambers, crematoria and the remains of thousands of charred human remains.
http://www.neveragain.org/1944.htm

We weren't going to Krakow for the special work assignment at all. We began to suspect that we had been set up to be sent to the gas chambers.

Chapter 22

The prisoners in Plaszow caught something of a break in January 1944, when the camp was changed from a forced labor camp, to a *zwangsarbeitlager*, a concentration camp, controlled by SS. This action saved many lives because now that Plaszow was a concentration camp, it came under the jurisdiction of Berlin. Each death now had to be accounted for. Paperwork had to be filled out properly and reports were sent to Berlin for review. Life was still hard for a prisoner of the camp, but the random shootings at the sudden whim of Goeth lessened.

The construction of Plaszow was nearing its completion. Encircling the camp was a double barrier of barbed wire fencing with twelve watchtowers spread out at intervals around the camp perimeter. These watchtowers were equipped with machine guns, telephones and revolving searchlights. It was now like a small city with factories, workshops and several different kinds of hospitals, including epidemic and quarantine areas. There was a building, workshop or laboratory for everything needed by the Germans, all of which of course was provided by the slave labor of the Jews.

The winter of 1943-1944 was bitterly cold. There was very little food for prisoners. We were served a watery soup without any nutritional benefit. As a result prisoners were becoming weak and sick.

In March 1944, an OD approached my friend Gross and me with

a clipboard in hand. He said, "There's going to be a special job in town. They're looking for volunteers. I can sign you up right now." He took out a pen and prepared to write our names on a sheet of paper. This seemed like a good idea at the time. Anything we could do to get away from this place and work in town where there was more access to food was considered a privilege.

"Sign us up!" we said in unison.

On April 13, 1944, the SS gathered the 150 prisoners who had signed up. They had us stand in formation and assigned us to a special barrack for work in Krakow. Instead of going to our usual barrack they marched us to the *auffangslager* or isolation barrack. This was a holding barrack made up of two barracks separate from the camp behind barbed wire fencing. Word had gotten around that whenever they were going to send a shipment of Jews to Auschwitz or some other camp, they isolated them here.

We weren't going to Krakow for the special work assignment at all. We began to suspect that we had been set up to be sent to the gas chambers. The prisoners knew about gas chambers by this time and I had been told that Auschwitz was a bad place. We knew people died there. Beyond that, we knew nothing. To us, Auschwitz meant certain death. The cold realization that I had made a terrible mistake, perhaps the worst mistake of my short life, lodged itself firmly inside my brain. All the old warnings came back to haunt me. I knew them by heart, yet foolishly threw them aside with the prospect of a better job and access to food. The saying "Whatever you do, don't volunteer for anything!" came back to haunt me. But I tricked myself into thinking it would be OK since I was in *barrackenbau*, the worst position I could be in, as it were. I was already doing dangerous work, putting myself in the way of a loaded gun and whip. What situation could be worse than that? I had made a fatal decision.

Inside the barrack, fully covering the bunks were hundreds of messages from previous occupants, engraved with sharp objects or scrawled in blood. One word that jumped out at me was *nekhama*, a Hebrew word meaning "vengeance." Those doomed souls knew they were going to die and wanted to leave a grim reminder to those following them down this path. We resigned ourselves to the idea that we were going to Auschwitz. The German SS kept us waiting in suspense for two days. After two days, they came and got us out of the *auffangslager* and marched us to the train station.

They loaded 150 of us into several cattle cars. Surprisingly, the cars were roomy. There was straw placed on the floor and we settled down for our final ride. However, there was something very different about this situation that none of us could figure out. This wasn't what a transport looked like. We were still under Nazi guard, yet it was quiet. It was their custom to shout and beat us into place, squashing us all together. But we weren't beaten or even crowded. This was not the usual way things were done. Typically, the cars were packed with people; the doors were locked and sealed closed. The doors to these cars were wide open and the guards were sitting with us, their legs hanging over the edge of the car, dangling and swinging their feet gaily. Their guns, instead of pointed at us, were lying beside them. They were relaxed and gradually we became relaxed too.

Then the train started to move. We couldn't tell exactly what direction we were going, but the signs we passed seemed to indicate we weren't headed west toward Auschwitz. We didn't know what was going on, and nobody would tell us, but we could tell we were traveling east.

After a while, the train stopped and the guards gave us bread and water. Now we were really confused. They are feeding us before gassing us? We traveled in this state of confusion the whole day until we ended up in the mountains in a town called Zakopane, a famous resort area. This was a total surprise and a great relief. None of us expected to be alive by the end of the day, yet we had arrived at one of Poland's top mountain resort areas. Once the train stopped and we were let out, we were ordered to march with the typical screaming, yelling and bullying. We walked a little bit out of town to a beautiful chalet surrounded by barbed wire. We were led inside, organized and eventually assigned bunks. The chalet was fairly large with two floors. We still didn't know what was going on or the work they expected us to do, but we were not totally unhappy with our new situation. At night the SS guards, who lived outside our prison chalet, in a chalet of their own, locked up the camp.

In the morning, we were led out to *appell* and then marched out on the snow-covered ground to work. April, in these mountains, is bitterly cold. We were sent down a very steep incline to a fast-moving mountain stream and ordered to drag rocks out of the frigid water. The steep canyon walls blocked the sun from reaching us with its warmth.

We learned that the Germans wanted to build a hydroelectric plant at this spot. They wanted all the stones removed from the river so the water could move freely. It was a terrible, miserable job. We splashed down into the freezing water and began hauling out large rocks. They were too big for us to pull out and carry to the waiting lorries at the edge of the river. We had to use sledge hammers and chisels to split them up into smaller, more manageable pieces, while at the same time maintaining our balance in deep, rushing, cold water. Fighting against the strong current, I feared losing my footing and being swept downstream.

Once we had our rocks piled onto the lorries, about twenty prisoners then had to pull it up a steep, 300-foot hill along rails. I was afraid that if we lost our grip, the lorry would fall back down the hill causing a disaster. We pushed and pulled the lorry at all times until we got it to the top. Once we reached the top we tipped it over and spilled the stones into a ravine far below. Then the process started all over again. I was just as afraid of the downhill trip. We had to hold on tight to the lorry for fear it would slip from our grasp and jump the tracks, hurtling itself down the steep incline. There was no rest at the bottom. Once at the river's edge, we slopped back into the freezing cold water. Our shoes were soaking wet. My bare feet were slipping around in my shoes. My hands were red and raw from the freezing water and soon they felt like frozen lumps of flesh. This was deadly work, much worse than anything I had encountered in Plaszow.

We returned to our prison chalet, cold and tired; then we were fed bread and soup. The food wasn't bad here—they gave us much more than in Plaszow. We went to bed, but we were scared and discouraged about the next day. People were already getting sick from the cold and exposure.

The SS here were as diabolical as they were in Plaszow. The head of the work group in Zakopane was Strojewski. We were terrified of him and did whatever he asked of us. There was a noncommissioned officer in charge of us named Wurzel. He also was a terrifying bully, constantly ordering, screaming and beating us the whole day. We never had peace from him. He had access to the locked-up camp and came in during the evening. He woke us up, pulled us out of our bunks and sent us outside where we were made to do all kinds of special exercises and numerous drills: push-ups, jumping up and down and crawling on the ground. Despite the extra food, we were underfed, as well as sleep deprived and overworked. The physical effort to perform Wurzel's tortuous calisthenics was staggering.

As we were marching from work, somebody called out, "Hey, Wurzel!" He heard it and thought someone was calling to him in a disrespectful way. Actually, the call was directed at another prisoner, who also was named Wurzel. When the "Terrible Wurzel" found the "Prisoner Wurzel," he picked on him specifically. Anytime during the day, he might put him through needless exercises. "Terrible Wurzel" was a bad man. We learned to dread every waking moment.

Each morning at *appell,* we stared at the mountain range and tried to decipher what the day would be like by looking at the clouds. We could tell if it would snow or rain depending on where the clouds were situated over the mountain range. Each morning and each evening, there was frost on the ground and on the trees and bushes. Overall, these mountains, though beautiful, were cold and deadly. During this time, 18 people out of the 150 became sick or hurt and were sent back to Plaszow.

On May 1, 1944, two weeks after our arrival, we went to the *appellplatz* and saw bundles of striped uniforms that had been sent up from Plaszow. Before this time, we wore our own civilian clothing. Now, we had the striped uniforms, which were evidence that Plaszow was now officially a concentration camp. I felt the new uniform. It was made of a thin material, and when I held it up to the light I could practically see right through it. The SS wanted us to strip naked, throw our old clothing into a pile and put on the new uniform, consisting of a pair of pants, a jacket and a thin shirt. We still didn't have socks, and we were still wearing our old, worn-out, run-down shoes.

I was wearing my ironclad, canvas pants Dolek had made for me when we were in Rakowice. I loved them and didn't want to wear the new uniform. I felt awful having to throw them away in a pile with everyone's clothing. I put the new, clean uniform on. Straightaway I felt an icy blast of air through the thin material.

In early May, without any reason, the attitude of the SS changed toward us. We weren't ordered to dig in the river for the rocks anymore. Now, they had us digging ditches. We were no longer tortured with beatings and night exercises. Strojewski became very nice. Wurzel was quiet and the elderly staff sergeant, who ran everyday affairs, became quite friendly with us. Even the weather became mild and warmer. We didn't know why they were now friendly or what was really going on. We were surprised, but pleased with this turnabout in attitude. I surmised that the Germans realized the job they were trying to accomplish would never be finished if they continued to abuse us. They were going to end up working everyone to death; then they would have to go back to Plaszow for more slave laborers. Away from the supervision of Plaszow, they decided to make it a vacation in Zakopane and included us in their scheme.

As far as work was concerned, we felt the project didn't need to be done at all. Often the SS would disappear from guard duty. As soon as that happened, we stopped working; we just didn't bother with it. We assigned someone as lookout and we sat there relaxing, basking in the sun. We had a signal: it was a made-up word, *seks.* This was a word we had used in Plaszow to signify danger: something is happening, someone is coming. Once we heard *seks,* we knew the SS were coming back and we immediately started to look busy at our work. Otherwise, we got away with doing nothing all day long. We made no progress with our work, but the SS didn't complain about the ditches not getting dug.

Remarkably, Strojewski became the friendliest person around. With enough bread and very little enforced labor, it was like a wonderful vacation. The next day was a holiday. Our now friendly staff sergeant got us out of our prison chalet in the morning and led us down to the river. He then instructed us in a very kind, amicable manner to bathe ourselves in the cold water.

Looking around at our huddled, shivering group he said, "Let's have a little contest. Run up the hill back to the chalet. Whoever gets there first is going to get a loaf of bread!"

This took a few seconds to sink in. *There was extra bread?* I sized up the competition and felt I could easily beat this crowd. They were pretty slow.

"Go, now!" he shouted.

We ran like mad. I was doing quite well, but I had underestimated the desire for extra bread and somebody else beat me to the top.

Later, we sat together at the top of the hill, a companionable group. The staff sergeant, in the mood for music, said, "Sing some of the songs of the mountain people." After conferring together, we picked a song all of us knew about some mountain people who had to leave their home because they couldn't make enough of a living to buy bread. This was a sad but beautiful song. We sat there singing happily on this wonderful, lovely day.

Terrible Wurzel began to look at us in a different way. He no longer derived pleasure from harassing us day-in and day-out. Instead, he now wanted to turn us into proper German soldiers. He was tough—a typical drill sergeant—but we learned the correct way to goose step.

"When you get back to Plaszow, you will be different people," he said. When you march back into camp, you won't be the stragglers you were when you left! We'll make fine soldiers out of you!"

I believe the SS wanted to stick it out in Zakopane as long as possible and have a nice vacation. In the process, they took us under their wings and trained us. They wanted to show the others back at Plaszow what they had made of us. We were not just a bunch of stragglers and depressed people; we were going to march like proud soldiers. Plus, it would show the other officers that if Wurzel got a handful of prisoners, he could make something of them which would demonstrate his abilities, proving what he could do with nothing.

We remained in Zakopane a total of three months until July 15, 1944. Going back to Plaszow after such a nice time was depressing; it felt like a huge loss of freedom and happiness. We were loaded into trains again, but instead of a cattle car, we rode in a passenger car. We were given leftover moldy bread from the camp. I picked off the mold and dealt with what I had.

When we disembarked, we were placed in formation and marched, heads up straight. We had been trained for this moment, and it seemed our guards were actually proud of us. We still felt that Zakopane spirit, marching with dignity, feeling good. Because the German officers were pleased with us, we felt honored by their approval.

After our marching demonstration, we were once again allocated to our different barracks. Our eyes had been opened for a brief period of time to camaraderie, life in the outdoors, some food and friendly masters. But once back in Plaszow our nightmare began again. The place was truly horrifying, now even more than before. The mood in the camp had changed entirely. The SS were nervous and angry. They were pacing about anxiously and a panicky feeling transmitted down to us.

Back in my barrack, I was told about a health *appell* that had taken place in May, organized by Goeth. The prisoners, both men and women, were again forced to strip naked and carry lumber, trying to demonstrate their good health, marching straight and strong in front of the assembled SS people. As they marched past, doctors examined them closely for signs of weakness or defect. This so-called health *appell* was just another word for "selection," as more than a thousand people were deemed unfit for work and were transported to Auschwitz for immediate extermination.

Even the children of the prisoners were not spared in this *Aktion*. In March, Goeth set up a kindergarten area, making it appear as if he were doing the prisoners a favor. The kindergarten area was inviting to a small child, complete with a playground, lawn and flowers. Coming from the Krakow ghetto this would have been an incredible sight for a child. During the health *appell*, happy children's music played over loudspeakers, while parents watched helplessly as the SS escorted hundreds of children to trucks waiting to transport them to Auschwitz.

In July 1944, we didn't know the world scene, but we knew that the camp was going to be evacuated. The Russians were moving in, was one account I heard. I guessed the German military realized they were losing the war and couldn't leave any witnesses behind in Plaszow. ODs and some of the functionaries (*kapos* and *blockaltestes*) were shot, including Chilowicz along with his entire family. The Chilowiczs' were shot trying to escape. The SS were eliminating prisoners—either shipping them out or killing them off. People were sent out daily and most of them went to Auschwitz.

Goeth was in an uproar trying to cover his tracks. The thousands of bodies they had buried with a bulldozer in the mass grave at Chujowa Gorka were dug up and burned to hide the evidence. I saw the smoke-filled sky and smelled the stench of burning corpses. The scent reminded me of burnt chicken feathers.

Somehow I was reunited with Dolek. He was reassigned to my sleeping barrack. The factories were closed and he was no longer working or sleeping in the tailor barrack. He hadn't changed a bit; he was as negative as ever. I wasn't a pessimist; I was numb. I didn't look to the future. Dolek was different. In a rare moment of communication, he said, "Joziu, I know I am going to die."

I tried to reassure him. "Don't say that. Don't talk about the future. Just live day-to-day. Don't even think about the future."

"I'm afraid of what's coming," he said.

The Altered I

August 8, 1944:
Berlin: After a kangaroo trial, overseen by Goebbels, Hitler hangs the German officer corp of conspirators who tried to kill him. They are hung on meat hooks with chicken wired around their necks. The butchery is filmed and sent to Hitler for review. Over the next months many more conspirators would be sent to trial.

http://www.neveragain.org/1944.htm

The World Jewish Congress in New York asks the War Department to bomb the crematoria at Auschwitz, **August 9, 1944**. The War Department turns down the request (**August 14, 1944**)

http://www.pbs.org/wgbh/amex/holocaust/filmmore/reference/primary/bombworld.html

"We are going to die before we get to Auschwitz!" somebody cried out.
"They're trying to cook us alive," someone else moaned.

Chapter 23

In August, our barrack was ordered to form lines outside. We were marched to the railway station and herded into cattle cars. Normally, seventy people were crammed into one cattle car. Under these circumstances, sitting or moving was difficult. This particular, hot day the SS loaded 140 people into each car. At some point during the loading process, without my being aware of it, I became separated from Dolek.

Once inside the car, movement of any kind was restrictive. If I managed to lift my arm to scratch my head, I wouldn't be able to bring it down again. I was loaded face to face with another prisoner. We were so close together we were practically nose-to-nose. The heat in the car was intense: sweat poured out of me, running into my eyes, but I couldn't even lift a hand to wipe the sweat away. I could do nothing but stand there in misery. The SS closed the door with a loud bang. The only bit of light we had filtered down from a tiny slot, covered with barbed wire, at the upper edge of the car. We were left in the intensely hot box car all day long. The heat became intolerable.

"We are going to die before we get to Auschwitz!" somebody cried out.

"They're trying to cook us alive," someone else moaned.

The smell of unwashed, sweaty bodies permeated the car. Soon, because of a lack of water and air, people began to scream and some fainted.

"Whether we die in here from overheating or of thirst, it doesn't matter," I heard someone say. "We're all going to Auschwitz." As far as any of us knew, Auschwitz had only one purpose.

Out of nowhere, we heard the gushing sound of a heavy stream of water on the metal roof. Beads of water rolled down through the barbed wire window and sprayed down on our heads. None of us could understand what was happening. The cool water pouring onto us was an incredibly good feeling—it seemed like an offering of goodwill from the German officers. We felt euphoria and a tremendous sense of relief.

"They won't kill us!" prisoners cried.

"Of course they mean to kill us!" someone countered.

"Why are they trying save us with the water, if they mean to send us to Auschwitz?"

"Maybe they don't intend to kill us. Maybe they're trying to keep us alive!" somebody suggested.

"Who can know the mind of insane men!" someone said in disgust.

Whatever it was, we believed it was the Germans giving us the water. Everybody became hopeful that perhaps we weren't going to die after all.

Before the miracle of the water I could have so easily given up hope. Enveloping me was the terrible heat like a woolen blanket. I was crazy from thirst and the panicked screaming of the others was frightening. We believed we would die, either there on the rails or at Auschwitz. Then out of the blue a sudden uplift with the provision of water, as if someone was saying to us, "You aren't going to die. They are keeping you alive. You will live." This alone gave a sufficient bit of hope, which gave us the extra determination to try to live. We didn't know at the time that Oskar Schindler had arranged for the water.

We continued waiting on the rails for the afternoon, but I had lost track of time because the August days were very long. Remaining on the rails far longer than we expected, our newfound hopes faded.

"They are probably going to kill us anyway," someone muttered.

"It's just like the sick games they like to play, making us think they were going to keep us alive."

Soon, we became resigned to the idea of dying and some people did die. The immense heat had begun to take its toll on those who were weak or sick.

Sometime in the afternoon, the train finally began to move. I couldn't tell the hour; I could only watch the changing light from the tiny, slotted window. However, the further we traveled away from Plaszow, the cooler it became. The cool air was some relief, but it was still hot and sticky. I was parched, my body tired and in pain from standing still for so many hours.

Sometime during the night we arrived at an unknown destination. Someone heard voices outside and they yelled out the window, "Hey! In here! Where are we?"

"Auschwitz!" an unknown voice pierced the night.

The reply chilled our blood. Our train was standing just outside the camp. None of us actually saw the camp, but some saw the bright lights shining into the sky from our position on the rails. Our train stood waiting there for quite a while. I felt terrified, completely frozen in fear. But more than that, I suffered from leg cramps, my mouth was dry as a bone, and I was exhausted. After a while I didn't care anymore where I was. I felt a total resignation within me and gave into the idea of the gas chamber. *My leg is numb, I don't know if I'm standing or not. I'm thirsty. I'm tired.* These were my concerns. The gas chamber didn't seem as frightening as my immediate problems.

The spirit inside our car was also one of resignation. Everyone was waiting for the doors to clang open and the unloading process to begin. But, our train lurched into movement, startling us into a surge of panic. Someone shouted, "This is it. We're going in!"

"We're going to die!" someone yelled. We didn't know which direction we were moving, but we were convinced we were going to be gassed. As the train began to slowly move, the lights from the camp began to fade.

"Where are we going?" someone asked, but no one in our car could answer that. It was a mystery.

Gradually, the train increased in speed, and we could tell that we were moving away from Auschwitz.

"We didn't go in!" I shouted out in amazement. We were close to going in, but never went inside.

Now the middle of the night, we still didn't know where we were headed. The biggest problems for us at the moment were thirst and tiredness. Drumming continuously through my mind was: *I have got to get some water! Water! WATER!*

The man standing in front of me had a canteen attached to his pants. I could hear liquid sloshing back and forth in it. The idea that he had a canteen full of water lodged itself into my brain. He had died at some point after leaving Auschwitz, but due to the press of people all around him, he didn't fall to the ground. He certainly wouldn't need it anymore. What if someone else takes it first? I reached out and grabbed it and held it in my hands like some great jewel. I twisted off the cap, and took a long, deep swig. To my horror, instead of sweet refreshing water, the canteen was filled with the man's hot, stinky urine. Given the circumstances, this wasn't entirely surprising. There wasn't any kind of sanitation in our cramped car, people just urinated—or worse—right where they were standing. The stench permeated deep into my clothing, my skin, my nostrils, until I forgot what fresh air smelled like.

As people died off they were piled up to the side of the car. The dead were stacked one on top of the other in order to make more room, but it was still tight, and I couldn't sit down. People began to get restless, and moved as much as they could from space to space.

Somebody cried out, "What a beautiful country!" I had no idea what he was talking about. I later found out we were traveling through Czechoslovakia. He was so enthusiastic about the view, that it made me want to see it too.

"I can't see!" I said.

"Here, I'll lift you up." I caught only a brief glimpse, but it was one of the most spectacular scenes I had ever seen. Beyond the beauty of the countryside, there was something else that filled me with the strangest sensation. I saw blue sky and a forest in the distance. There were pastures and a farmer was plowing his fields. Cows were grazing. I didn't think a world like this existed anymore. I hadn't seen a normal life for years. With the exception of a few relatively easy, but nonetheless wholly subjugated, days at Zakopane, all I knew of life was camps, work, beatings and killing. Compared to what was happening in the train, outside that tiny barbed wire slot seemed another world, almost fake, the contrast was so great.

I was confused for a moment. *What is the real world?* The real world as far as I knew it, was in this cramped boxcar. I had forgotten about the people going about their normal lives, harvesting grain, tending their farms, their cows grazing in the fields. These were parallel worlds. Side-by-side, we were traveling with the other world at the same time, in the same space. My world in the boxcar was death, stink and fear. Outside the barbed wire slot was something entirely different. My existence was real. *What was it outside the window? Was it a dream, a fantasy?* I was shocked to the core and I couldn't accept it as real. For me, the real world was inside this cattle car.

Our train kept to its course, destination unknown, and I began to wonder what was to become of us. For perhaps several days, I lost track of time. The train would slow and come to a stop now and again during the journey so we never could tell if we were at our final destination or not.

I wasn't especially hungry, but was incredibly parched. I thought dying of thirst was the worst possible death. My mouth felt so dry, my tongue felt swollen and was sticking to the roof of my mouth. I tried to remember what I had read about dehydration. I knew I was supposed to keep my mouth shut so that any kind of moisture would not escape, but the choice between breathing through my mouth or breathing through my nose was impossible to make. If I kept my mouth shut that would lessen the dehydration, but then I would be forced to smell the odors in the boxcar. I felt weak and dizzy, breathing hard. I could feel my heartbeat pounding as spots flashed before my eyes. My vision became blurry and darkness enveloped me. At some point, I fainted and crumpled to the floor. In the car, the mood was getting worse. People were moaning and crying. Slowly, people were going out of their minds.

At last, the train came to a complete stop. The SS screamed and shouted, "*Raus! Raus! Schnell!*" Get out! Get out, quick! I was tired and totally confused, but quickly scrambled out of the boxcar with the others. The bright light of day blinded me. I was bewildered and scared, "Where are we?" I said to no one in particular. The train was standing on one side of the track and in front of us was a big river.

We were ordered to pull out the dead bodies from the boxcar. Then we were counted. Some prisoners were ordered to carry the dead. By some miracle I found Dolek in the crowd of straggling people. He had been in another car near mine. Then we started marching in tight groups, up a steep, rocky trail, full of overgrowth. The climb was made more difficult because we were weak, hungry and thirsty. We climbed higher and higher without any idea of where we were going. The trip seemed very long and always the strain of climbing uphill was incredibly difficult. Finally, we saw an opening. We had arrived at a big square, a courtyard. In front of us was a big wall with a big gate similar to Auschwitz', except there were no railroad tracks. The structure was situated fairly high on a hill and the railroad station was far down below.

We stood outside the gate and were counted again. Then we

waited for a time until eventually the gates slowly opened up, allowing us entrance to the large interior courtyard. It was full of people sitting or lying on the ground. At the far end of this courtyard was another set of large doors. The prisoners carrying the dead bodies from the train brought them to the closed doors at the far end and dropped them there. The first thing I wanted was water, but I was told there was no water. Discouraged, I fell to the gravel-strewn ground where I was left undisturbed.

We had arrived in Mauthausen.

The Altered I

On **10 August 1944** a transport of 4589 Jewish prisoners came from the Plaszow Labour camp near Krakow. The last large transport in 1944 arrived in late September bringing 6449 prisoners of whom half were Jews. According to the camp records a total of 13,322 Jewish males and 504 Jewish females entered Mauthausen in 1944. The number of Jews who died that year was 3437.

http://www.holocaustresearchproject.org/othercamps/mauthausen.html

Aug 25, 1944:
Liberation of Paris
On this day in 1944, French General Jacques Leclerc enters the free French capital triumphantly. Pockets of German intransigence remained, but Paris was free from
German control.
http://www.history.com/this-day-in-history/liberation-of-paris

August 26: On the Fuhrer's orders, German forces begin their withdrawal from Greece.

http://history.howstuffworks.com/world-war-ii/the-battle-of-the-bulge-timeline6.htm

August 1944-Mauthausen
16 years old

The whole barrack was filled with people crawling blindly, searching for their places. After a while I gave up.

Chapter 24

I had never heard of Mauthausen. As I found out, Mauthausen was the only Category 3 camp operated by the Nazis. It was a true Nazi death camp. Not an extermination camp, which systematically killed Jews by gassing, but a *"Vernichtun durch arbeit,"* death by harsh labor camp. Our papers were stamped *"Ruckkehr unerwunscht,"* "Return not desired".

Located twelve miles from Linz, Austria, Mauthausen appeared like a medieval fortress: cold, gray, squat and formidable. Mauthausen also had satellite camps: Melk, Ebensee, Gusen, to name a few, but Mauthausen was the main camp. There were at least two thousand prisoners remaining in the shipment from Plaszow, and each of us had to be processed. During the long ordeal, the SS kept us outside, waiting in the courtyard. The prisoners working there didn't bother us, and we could sleep undisturbed, though we were without food, water or toilets. There was an open manhole nearby that the prisoners used as a toilet. We never had toilet paper in any of the camps, but near this hole I could see a big pile of German occupation money that somebody must have brought with them from Plaszow. In a place like Mauthausen money was valueless. It had only one practical use: toilet paper. The paper was stiff and uncomfortable, but better than nothing.

As we were vegetating there, periodically, prisoners wearing striped uniforms counted people off and then the main gate opened up and allowed them admittance inside. None of us knew what happened to the prisoners after that. We waited about two or three days in this gloomy, sad place before we too, were processed. Eventually, my group of about two hundred people were counted, led inside by *kapos* and processed into Mauthausen.

The *kapos* lashed their whips until all two hundred of us were inside the doors. We stood in front of the building, but didn't know what it was. Then we were marched inside a large room and ordered to strip off all of our clothing and throw it in a big pile. A large door opened up. Peering inside, I could see it was a shower room. By this time I had been told about shower rooms: They were really gas chambers. They handed us a bar of soap and instructed us to wash all over to disinfect ourselves. There were letters engraved on the soap: RIF. I recognized the meaning at once. There was a rumor circulating that the letters stood for "*Reines Judisches Fett*": Pure Jewish Fat. I am not sure if the soap rumor was true or not, but some of the Jews were trying to make us believe this soap came from rendered down Jewish bodies.

I wondered if this shower room was a gas chamber. There were signs affixed to the outside of each chamber indicating "Shower Room," but once we entered the room, we couldn't tell if it would be water or gas.

We crowded in on the cold cement floors, naked and terrified, waiting to see what would happen. I looked up at the pipes running along the ceiling and gazed with some expectancy at the interspersed shower heads. Would it be gas or water? The minutes dragged by. With a sudden hiss, hot water came pouring out. It ran for just a short time, just enough to get us wet, and then it was abruptly shut off. This was our opportunity to soap ourselves, but I was so thirsty I didn't care about soaping up. I wanted to take the water in my mouth and drink my fill, but it only lasted a few moments and the few drops that came out only wet my lips. My thirst was not allayed. After a few moments the water blasted us again signaling that we rinse off. When the shower shut off for the final time, a door at the other end of the room opened up. We were herded out to a courtyard where we waited naked, wet and shivering for new orders. We were shown a big pile of haphazardly thrown, striped clothing and ordered to pick out trousers, a shirt and a jacket. Everything was mixed up together and I had difficulty seeing what was what in the frenzied, mad dash. I had to grab whatever I could get my hands on and hope it was pants and a shirt. I didn't worry about sizing; all the clothing was the same size. None of it ever fit properly. The *kapos* were beating us to hurry. We could never move fast enough to please them.

I had just managed to grab a pair of pants and a jacket before we were taken, barefoot, to another building and made to stand in a single-file line. At the end of the line were prisoners sitting at tables, who, as we approached, one by one, wrote our names down. After I gave my name, the prisoner handed me a red metal bowl and a spoon. These were valuable items in the camp—without either of them we couldn't eat. I held onto both for dear life. Then I was given a number: 87719. This was my I.D. Next to the number was a red triangle. Jews normally were identified by the colors red and yellow and the political prisoners were identified by a red triangle. But for some reason, we all had the red triangle, the political identification. A number of threaded needles were passed around and right away we sewed by hand the strips of cloth to our clothing. One strip was attached on the left chest area and the other went on the right pant leg.

Afterward, *kapos* lead my group to the barracks. There were four barracks, each surrounded by a barbed wire fence. There was also a barbed wire fence surrounding the entire group of four barracks. When we arrived at our barrack, we were not allowed to go inside. Hundreds of people milled around the area. I found out from someone that these four barracks housed all the newcomers to the camp. We weren't allowed to sit down. I could walk, but there was nowhere I wanted to go; the courtyard was hot and studded with sharp stones that cut into my feet.

Later, in the evening, some prisoners brought out kettles of soup. We lined up again and, after some time had passed, I finally had soup ladled into my bowl. The soup was typical, watery and awful with little nutritional value, but at least it was wet. I quickly slurped it down. Then we were given orders to line up in rows of five and were counted by the *kapos* and the SS. They took their time inspecting our uniforms for numbers and locations. Many people were beaten when the SS or *kapo* found something they didn't like. It took hours for them to complete counting and inspecting to their satisfaction. Finally, they began to let people into the barracks.

We entered up the center of the barrack. There was what looked like a small washroom in the center and two large, empty rooms off the center wash room, one to the left and one to the right. A barrack of this size could accommodate four hundred people, but we were two thousand. I wondered how they were going to make us fit. Typically there were bunks stacked four high, however, there were no bunks in this barrack. We were told to go directly to the assigned place on the floor where we were supposed to sleep.

With the *kapos* supervising, their whips at the ready, we were made to sit on the floor. The first person in the row sat with his back against the wall and their knees open. The second person sat in front of the first, with their back tight up against the stomach of the first prisoner. Each person in the row had to sit the same way and no matter how tight we were against each other the *kapos* beat us even closer together. After the first row was snug, they started forming the second row. There were perhaps six inches separating the rows from each other. The *kapos* walked up and down beating us and screaming at us. Sometimes they walked between the rows disregarding our feet and hands. When they were finally satisfied with the arrangement, they left us alone in the dark.

Order was maintained only up to the point of being left alone. The air was hot and humid. I had cramps in my legs and arms. After a while my legs fell asleep. Nobody could move to find a more comfortable position. I was exhausted but found it impossible to sleep because the other prisoners were noisy, screaming and shouting. After the *kapos* left, it seemed that everybody, all at once, wanted to get up from their place and get water. The only water source came from the washroom. Stepping over people to make one's way to the bathroom in the dark became an ordeal. When I got up to get water, I couldn't see my hand in front of my face. I kept tripping over people. Once I was able to get to the bathroom, I couldn't get to the water because of the crowd jostling each other in the small space. There was a line, but no one gave anyone any consideration. People were shoved out of the way so they could get to the water first. Soon, it was my turn for a sip of water. Just as I took one sip I was pushed from behind and lost my place at the faucet. Then, a second later, I was just as thirsty as before, maybe even thirstier. But, by this time the crowd had grown so big, I couldn't get back in line for more water. I had little choice but to try and find my place back on the floor.

The whole barrack was filled with people crawling blindly, searching for their places. After a while I gave up. I dropped down, in what I thought was an empty space on the floor, but turned out to be a person. He screamed and kicked me away. In my haste to get away from him, I fell on someone else. Every time I took a step I fell on someone. People came at me, too. I had to act defensively or else suffer the consequences of them stepping on my bare feet. To protect myself, I eventually had to stand.

All night long, there was complete bedlam. People were screaming and moaning in pain and discomfort. Anyone who needed to use the toilets couldn't use them because of the crowds trying to get water. We had no choice but to relieve ourselves where we stood or sat. In addition to being stepped on, kicked and yelled at, now there was the strong odor of urine and feces in the barrack.

Early the next morning the *kapos* came in and screamed at us and beat us again. We were ordered to line up at the *appell* for the count. As usual, some people were sick and not fast enough. They had to be dragged out. Some had died during the night. Their bodies were carried out and piled up in groups of five. Nobody checked them to make sure if they were dead or merely sick. If they didn't stand up and walk out on their own, they were carried out and piled up. The *kapos* counted us over and over again.

I didn't know where Dolek was in all of the confusion of the night before, but after the *appell* we found each other and tried to stick together. After *appell*, they brought out kettles of the typical brown water they called "coffee," but at least it was liquid and my thirst was somewhat satisfied. We spent the day in the courtyard again. We were not allowed in the barrack to get water or go to the bathroom except by special arrangement and in small groups formed by the *kapos*.

The August sun was beating down on us and we were tired, sweating and stinking. The general talk amongst us was about what would happen next. Nobody knew, but we didn't expect it to be good.

That night after evening *appell*, we were allowed back inside the barrack. This time they decided to place us in a different formation. We were still crowded together, but instead of making us sit back to front, they beat us into position flat on the ground. We were head to foot, very much like sardines in a tin can. There was no room between us. They continued to beat us until we were pressed tight against each other.

In a way, I thought this was a better arrangement than the night before, because at least we were lying down. Again, as soon as we were left alone, the migration to the bathroom for water began anew. As soon as we left our place on the floor, we couldn't get back to it. I tried to lie still for as long as possible; if I got up I wouldn't be able to sleep. But soon my thirst and need to go to the bathroom forced me up. The third night was spent in this same format, squashed up like sardines. Some people died and were taken away, their deaths creating more room in the barrack.

At *appell*, the morning of the fourth day, some *blockaltestes*, block elders, came in before us. They were not from our area, I didn't recognize them. After *appell* we were told to stand in formation and remain at attention while the *blockalteste* walked up and down in front of the assembled group, scrutinizing the ranks carefully. He pointed out some people and they stepped forward. On one of his passes, he pointed at me. I stepped out and joined the other five, all around the same age as me. Then we were ordered to leave with the *blockalteste.* I looked back at Dolek, but didn't say anything.

We were brought to a new barrack crowded with prisoners. The barrack had the normal formation of bunks stacked four high and accommodated a standard number of people. Then the *blockaltestes* took us to the showers. We were given the same uniform, but still no shoes. When we came back to the barrack it was completely empty, everyone was out at work. We were told to clean this barrack. We spent the whole day washing the windows, sweeping the floors and doing general house duties. I thought it was nice, as jobs went. The block leaders were observing us, but staying out of our way.

That night, the prisoners assigned to this sleeping barrack came back from work. They looked totally beaten down. "Where do you work?" I asked.

"At the Wiener Graben stone quarry, carrying rocks all day," one man said.

They looked with envy at us because we appeared clean and not work weary. They were newcomers and barefoot like us. I felt sorry for them, but I was glad I didn't have their job.

That night, however, I was told by the *kapo* of the stone quarry, "You're not going to work in the barrack tomorrow. Instead you're going to the stone quarry with the others." I was disappointed to leave this easy work assignment and barrack with bunks. The next day I was called out with the rest of the prisoners.

Only two of the young boys, twins, were allowed to stay and clean the barracks. The *blockaltestes* were pederasts and handpicked their victims. I was not chosen; I was rejected and sent out. Using sex or favoritism was another form of survival.

I learned that the *kapos* of Mauthausen were recruited by the German SS to take charge of the rest of us. Some had prior records as criminals, some were even murderers. Their brutality against us was tremendous. They were usually given more food and other special privileges, such as a separate room in the barrack. The *kapos* formed the main part of the *"Prominenz,"* prisoners who were given prominence over other inmates.

The *kapos* were beasts who beat us worse than any German. The *kapos* and *blockaltestes* had the ultimate power in the camp. They could choose life or death for us. The concentration camp was the best thing that ever happened to them, it seemed. A Nazi had to follow orders, whereas a *kapo*, or *blockalteste*, used any means to get us to do what he wanted. The *kapos* maintained their positions by being as cruel to us as possible. They used strict discipline to create fear. If they were humane, they would lose their coveted position and find themselves among the other prisoners, who would make them suffer because of the ill treatment they had inflicted. They couldn't risk it. Because of the *kapos* handling the prisoners, the German officers didn't have to remain in the camp. They could depend on the *kapos* to do their dirty work for them.

1941-1945

Two-thirds of Hungarian Jewry was destroyed between **1941** and **1945**. More than half a million people fell victim to the labour service, the deportations organised by German Nazis and their Hungarian henchmen, the brutality of the Hungarian authorities, the death marches, the gassings in Auschwitz, the mass executions, and the terrible circumstances of the concentration camps.

http://degob.org/index.php?showarticle=2031

August 23, 1944

Zigeunernacht ("Night of the Gypsies"): All Gypsies who remained in Auschwitz were gassed.

http://history1900s.about.com/od/holocaust/a/Gypsies-Timeline.htm

August 1944-Todesstieg
16 years old

> **Two SS men stood, one on each side of
> the plank, yelling at the prisoners,
> rushing them, calling them names.**

Chapter 25

Our work started before dawn and ended when it was dark again. We had our so-called coffee, were counted and formed into groups, then marched off toward the stone quarry. We followed the line of a wire fence. I saw a hole in the fence and wondered about it. I asked an old-timer when I had the chance and he told me the hole was a device used to kill prisoners of war. He said that, at one time, they caught and imprisoned forty American paratroopers. They forced them to crawl through the hole in the wire. As they crawled through to the other side, they were gunned down by Nazis with machine guns. The German officer couldn't shoot a POW unless he was trying to escape. The use of chicanery had been mastered by the Nazi's.

On our march to the stone quarry, the *kapos* closely guarded every move we made. If we did anything wrong, they hit us on the head, our back or our rears with their whips. We were careful to remain quiet. Because of the sharp rocks underfoot, marching was difficult. Finally, we arrived at the stone quarry. There was a long, gently curved stairway winding down before us. The prisoners called these the 186 steps, or "*todessteig,*" the stairway of death.

There were two groups of workers: workers who chiseled away at the rock, cutting the stones, and others who carried the stones to a certain destination. There were also two locations to pick up a stone. One was across the flat rocky surface of the quarry and the other was across a ravine that was perhaps ten feet deep.

Getting stones from across the ravine was dangerous. There was a narrow wooden plank, about six inches wide. Two SS men stood, one on each side of the plank, yelling at the prisoners, rushing them, calling them names. Their German shepherd dogs stood nearby, growling and ready to attack. They were specially trained to tear a man apart. As each prisoner passed them, the dogs barked and nipped at their legs and feet. They frightened the prisoners, compelling them to rush across the plank. This caused some to lose their balance and fall into the ravine below, causing serious injury or sometimes death.

At the start, my group was assigned to cross the flat land of the granite quarry to get the stones. The quarry floor, with its sharp-as-glass gravel, was treacherous to our bare feet. My feet became cut right away. We walked single-file to the area the workers were cutting the stone. When it was my turn, I turned my back toward the cutters and two men put a heavy stone on my shoulders. The stone could weigh 70, 80 or even 100 pounds. The stone was sharp, rough and cut into my skin. Then I made my way back as best as I could to my waiting group. We were all wobbling around trying to balance our stones. The stone had generally been carelessly placed on our backs; some weren't exactly centered. We had to wait there until all two hundred prisoners in my group were assembled.

Our group now complete, we began the long climb up the stairway. This is when the true, terrible test of the fittest began. The steps, although wide, were cut unevenly out from the rock. Some steps were irregular in size and shape, some were deep or shallow and some were loose. We were made to climb the stairs at a steady, quick pace, stopping for rest was not allowed. All the while the *kapos* yelled, screamed and prodded us with their whips, making navigation up the steps difficult, as well as deadly. There was the added danger of tripping and falling directly on the person behind. Or, the stone could fall off our shoulders or backs at any given moment. In many cases, the stone did fall and it would crash onto the person behind. The falling stone started a domino effect, first rolling off the bearers' back and then hitting the person behind, hurting or killing them, causing that person to drop their stone and injuring the person behind him.

If someone's stone fell off, they scrambled around trying to pick it up again. They didn't want to continue up the stairway without their stone because waiting at the top were the SS guards who liked to severely punish any who arrived at the top without a stone. In desperation, people tried to pick up their stone and carry it in their arms, but it was impossible to carry them this way. The only way was to carry them on our backs. No one was in a position to be of help to anyone. Usually, the other prisoners ignored the person with the problem and continued marching up the stairs.

Once we arrived at the top of the stairway, the prisoners without a stone were separated from those who still had one and put under special guard. Then they were taken around a corner to the infamous "*fallschirmspringerwand*": Parachute Wall, a sheer cliff wall down to the bottom of the quarry. The SS lined the people up and pushed them over the cliff edge where they fell about eight stories to their death. The rest of us with our stone intact, continued to lug them in the hot sun down the path about a mile and a half. No one was allowed to fall behind; we had to march together. I was drenched in sweat and incredibly thirsty. The thirst itself was again driving me crazy. With each step, the stone became heavier. I could feel it slipping from its position. The only thing I could do was bend over so my back was more horizontal to the ground. I couldn't adjust the position of the stone, and I was terrified of dropping it.

We came to a big pile of stones and were told to throw our stones onto the heap. What a relief to get rid of the burden. But it was short-lived. Immediately, we lined up again. In this brief moment of stillness, I realized how deadly tired I was. My feet were bloody and hurting. The other prisoners without shoes were in the same condition. Before long, the ground were we stood became smudged with our blood.

"Quickly, run back and get another stone!" the SS guard ordered in German. I was about to drop from the first go-round, now I had to do it all again? What choice did I have but to run, get another stone and resume the whole cycle again? We made many repeated trips all day long, and as a result I was learning through experience how to survive this vicious cycle.

Whenever possible, I ran on the outer edges of my feet. In this way I avoided putting any pressure on my soles. After many repeated trips up and down the 186 steps, I learned the trick of how to navigate my way up. I left my formation and started going up on the left side of the steps. Some steps were so high that it was very difficult to step on them and pull myself up with the stone on my shoulders. I realized that this is where many people failed and dropped their stone. If I walked next to the wall, I could manage the steps better with the heavy load. I put one leg on the edge of the rock wall with my shoulder against the wall for balance. In this way, I made two smaller steps for myself rather than one large step and was able to maintain my balance.

Throughout this miserable first day, we ran up the stairs, ran to the drop off place, threw our stone on the pile and ran back for another one, on and on ten to fifteen times. We worked without lunch or breaks.

By my account, the stone quarry was one of the worst experiences of the camps. People were crying and moaning in misery; some were sobbing. In order to survive, I didn't allow myself to notice them or hear them. I had to make myself go completely numb. I couldn't look at anyone and feel their grief. I could only focus on how I took the next step and keep on taking that next step until the SS ordered me to stop.

Some of the prisoners were in their thirties or forties. Most of them, however, were young like me, although I couldn't tell anyone's age. Covered in gray dust, we all looked the same. Sweat ran in rivulets down our faces, leaving dusty tracks, but by the end of the day we stopped sweating. Our lips were parched, split, cracked and bleeding. Our eyes were filled with quarry grit, making it painful and difficult to see. I looked at the other prisoners and saw their eyes were sunken deep into their faces with fatigue.

During the day, at any given time, many people collapsed from the heaviness of their loads and extreme exhaustion. They gave up, collapsed and died on the ground. Their bodies were picked up and carried to a designated spot. The unfortunate ones who lay broken and dead at the bottom of the ravine remained there until workers came back to pick them up later in the day. Those who survived the day marched back to the camp carrying the dead on stretchers or when the stretchers ran out, carrying them slung over their backs.

The SS wanted high casualties in Mauthausen. The work conditions in the quarry made it easy for them to accomplish that goal. At the end of the day, all the dead had to be counted at the *appellplatz*. They were placed beside us in piles of five. After the endless counting, the bodies were taken to the crematorium and the living sent back to their barracks.

Soon they served us bread and soup. I kept my bowl attached to my pants with a thin wire, and my spoon was weaved between two buttonholes of my shirt. During the workday, I was constantly aware of where these two items were.

Since I had been rejected by the pederasts, I was sent back to my barrack without bunks. By this time, our barracks were not as crowded because prisoners were dying off in huge numbers every day. We still slept on the floor. As happened every night I spent here, the migration to the water began as soon as the guards left. This was still a challenge because we had only one faucet and everyone was thirsty. Even so, it wasn't as bad as before. From two thousand prisoners to begin, we were now reduced to several hundred. The barrack was hot and noisy with moans of pain and misery. I was filthy, and there was no way I could wash myself. My feet were now caked in dirt and dried blood. I was too hurt and worn out to care about anything except sleep. I slept despite the noise in the barrack. When I fell into a deep and exhausted sleep, I dreamed I was being chased by dogs or I was carrying stones.

The *kapo* woke us up while it was still dark outside. He was screaming, "*Auf, auf!*" Up, up! This was only our second day at the stone quarry and it started the same as day number one, except now I was terrifically sore. Every part of my body ached. As soon as my feet hit the floor, the wounds opened up and started to bleed. By day two, all of us knew what to expect. I had learned a few tricks, but this didn't solve anything because I didn't know how I would survive another day.

New groups of two hundred people were formed and off to the 186 steps we trudged. Day-in and day-out nothing ever changed, with the exception that each night our barrack was getting emptier and emptier. Every day I dragged myself from the quarry was a miracle. I had resigned myself to the fact that I wouldn't survive this ordeal. Every day I grew more morose. Others must have felt the same way because there were no conversations, only the sounds of pain and sorrow.

I was alone, Dolek was gone and I didn't know where he was. Although we weren't close, I missed him. There was no one around me who knew me or cared about me. Although my group was from Plaszow, Mauthausen had changed everyone in so many ways, I didn't recognize anyone anymore.

At this point, I was concerned only with my own survival. Every day I faced death and those who wanted me to die. In the barrack at night we became irritated with one another for no reason at all. We shouted at each other, or pushed and shoved. I didn't want anyone in my way, especially when I was trying to get water. People, it seemed, were hindering me from the water, and this only annoyed me. I am sure I was in their way, too, but this is what the struggle for survival had come to.

I.2 The Mauthausen main camp was constructed in 1938 at a site near the Upper Austrian town of Mauthausen, roughly 20 kilometers east of Linz. A second, nearby camp, known as Gusen I opened in 1940.These two "main camps" were designated "Category III" or extermination camps, designed to eliminate enemies of the German Reich through a combination of overwork, starvation, and violence.

http://www.archives.gov/publications/ref-info-papers/rip115.pdf

World War II—1944

France
Paris is liberated from Nazi occupation **August 25th**
United Kingdom
Germany Launches the V1 rockets / Doodlebugs against London

United States
The **Battle of the Bulge** beginning on December 16th is one of the deadliest battles in World War II with 19,000 US soldiers killed

Germany
The Allies assemble the largest force of **Air Power** used who bombed railways and other targets in Germany
http://www.thepeoplehistory.com/1944.html

**My belief in God was gone. To me,
having faith in God was useless.**

Chapter 26

Beginning from the time I left my family in the forest, the
last two years had been horrible. My life was threatened several times a
day and my mind couldn't deal with it: it was too much to cope with. I
was becoming detached from my living conditions.

If someone was beaten next to me—beaten to death in many
cases—the first question I asked myself was am I in any way affected
by this? If I am not affected, if it only affects the other guy, then it just
leaves my mind. I am OK. I wasn't the one beaten, and I am still alive.
The incident never crossed my mind again, and I walked away
uncaring.

There were different stages of survival and gradually, all of us
went through them. One stage was detachment: to go numb, to
become mentally unfeeling and uncaring. I was brought up in a good
home, to love God, to love my neighbor, to have a good conscience,
and to have feelings of compassion for my fellow man. All these things
vanished in the camps.

My belief in God was gone. To me, having faith in God was
useless. I could have prayed all day long and nothing would change my
immediate situation. What was the purpose of asking him for anything?
I didn't stop believing there was a God; but he wasn't there for me.
What kind of God allows this? I wanted improvement in my life, I

wanted help, hope, but I couldn't get even the least of these. I couldn't depend on him to help me in any way at all. I had to depend on myself. I reasoned that if he doesn't do anything for me, then I don't need him. If I am going to survive, it will be based on what I and I alone, do.

All things connected with humanity vanished as well. How can I love anyone if I don't care? I didn't have feelings. So what if the person next to me died, as long as I was alive. That day in the forest when I left my parents, the love had to be cut off suddenly, so I wouldn't feel the anguish that came with it. For me, love was a forbidden emotion, ultimately bringing only pain.

People living in the camps became completely morally degraded. We were no longer human. For the sake of survival, we had lost our humanity. All of us became like animals. But, we were worse than animals. Animals kill for food when they are hungry, not out of hatred. Animals are not evil in what they do.

There was no human behavior in the camp on any level. Everyone took on a different depraved form of behavior. The SS hated and didn't stop the killing; the *kapos* punished mercilessly; and the prisoners detached themselves. We were beaten down, trying to survive at any cost. We became automatons: we moved and felt like robots, numb and dead. Yet, at the same time, I felt a keen awareness of my surroundings, but it was a very narrow scope for the purpose of survival only. I was constantly on guard watching for any danger, any threat.

The dehumanization reached an extreme state for me. I felt there were no humans left in the world. I had no hope. Why should I survive? For what purpose? The whole world must be the same way. Since the age of thirteen, I experienced nothing except a totally inhumane environment. At sixteen, I should have been having a real life. I should have been concentrating on my education, my relationships with others. I should have been connected to the world. But for me, my brain was only connected with one subject: survival. The idea of surviving at any cost became utterly paramount; nothing else was important. Surviving the war was too remote an idea. Survival meant only now, sometimes minute-by-minute and never longer than a day.

We had our own language in the camps. For instance, if somebody wanted to say "never" they would say "tomorrow." There was no such thing as tomorrow—life didn't extend past this one day. I couldn't plan anything in the future. Each day was so bad that I could only think of the immediate present. We all lived in the present, although it wasn't really living, it was literally how to survive the next minute. After the minute passed, then we thought about the next minute.

The whole idea of a future was a very difficult thing to face, and for me there was also no past. Thinking of the past was a dangerous practice. Unfortunately, waiting around in the roll-call area, I found that I had plenty of time to think about the past. Often the roll-call count lasted for hours and hours. If someone escaped, then it was even longer, sometimes twenty-four hours and not one of us could leave the square.

It was during these times that I allowed myself to dwell on the past. I thought about the Friday night suppers with Tatus, Mamusia, and the rest of the family. I thought about all the food we had prepared and went over the entire process of the meal. I focused solely on the food, bite by bite, every little thing. I tasted all of it in my mouth: The Challah bread, *gifilte* fish, boiled chicken, pieces of boiled beef, carrots, boiled potatoes, *mizeria* (pickles in vinegar) and then dessert. We always had a variety of sweets. No matter how long we were detained at the *appell*, I never finished the supper. It was a total escape into fantasy. I took my time and entered the realm of the past. When I relived the Friday night supper, I didn't feel as tired, as hot or cold. I escaped mentally and physically, as if I had taken a drug creating a sense of euphoria.

For some people, however, thinking about the past was a very dangerous pastime. Eventually the person would have to come back to reality. Coming back to the present situation was as dangerous and painful as if the person was waking up from a pleasant dream and presented with a real nightmare world. As a young person in the camps, I had some advantages. I could think about the past for a little bit, but some older people couldn't handle the reality of the present once they lost themselves in the fantasy of the past.

One night while in the barrack, there was an air raid. Allies, American or British, were bombing the camp. We were not allowed to go anywhere for shelter, and this frightened me. We were lying in the barrack completely helpless. The Germans went to their air raid shelters, but we had to stay in the barracks, shut off, unable to protect ourselves. I didn't want to die like this, but I didn't have a choice. I heard the loud sounds of an intense air raid with shooting and bombing. I didn't want to get killed, and although it seemed a contradiction, in my desperation I turned to God in prayer. If God helped me live through this, I would make some kind of an agreement, but I had nothing to deal with, what could I offer him? After I thought about it I prayed, "God, if I survive this night, I'll be willing to go to the stone quarry without complaining."

The Altered I

September 2, 1944:
Holocaust diarist Anne Frank was sent to diarist.

September 5, 1944:
"Mad Tuesday" 65,000 Dutch Nazi collaborators flee to Germany

http://www.historyorb.com/date/1944/september

On September 19, 1944, a few days before the Soviet army liberated the Klooga slave labor camp in Estonia, the Germans and their Estonian collaborators murdered more than 2,000 Jews, mostly from the Vilna Ghetto.

September 1944-Melk
16 years old

**Melk had its own crematorium, complete
with a tall chimney that could be seen
from far away.**

Chapter 27

We spent a month toiling in the stone quarry, and I don't know how I survived it. I can't imagine where I got the strength to face it every day. I called this particular treatment a form of natural selection. We had thirty days of this treatment, and those who survived were taken to other satellite camps of Mauthausen, but many didn't make it.

In one instance, after the count at the *appellplatz*, instead of being ordered to the stone quarry, we were instructed to march to our barracks and wait there for further orders. When the *kapos* came, we were commanded to get shoes from a big heap piled up outside our barrack. The shoes were flat, with a wooden base and scratchy canvas top that came up to the ankle. The canvas was attached to the wooden base with nails hammered around the edge. There was no difference in size, nor was there a left or right shoe. Once commanded to get the shoes, we made a hurried grab for them.

All the shoes were recycled. When someone died, all his clothing went back into the system and they were issued to the living prisoners. We never received new shoes, but they were new to us. When I grabbed for shoes, my primary purpose was to find ones that weren't in too bad shape with plenty of wear left in them. I especially didn't go for ones with any tears in them. We didn't even have a pair of socks. The shoes were ill fitting on everybody but our feet were cut up from the stone quarry and there was a certain relief they provided.

Walking in them for the first time was awkward. They were stiff and made flexing difficult. The only way to walk in them was to pick up the foot without bending it and put it down flat. The canvas was rough on our bare ankles. Now I had the dual challenge of not bending my foot and at the same time keeping the canvas from rubbing my skin raw.

Next, they assembled all the survivors of the quarry in the courtyard. We were marched from camp down to the railway station. I remembered the path from the time we first arrived and had the arduous climb up the rocky, uneven path. This time, however, we were marching down an evenly paved road. We were put on board a regular passenger train, not a cattle car. I could sit down in an actual seat like a person, not an animal.

Getting away from Mauthausen and the stone quarry was a complete relief, but I took little enjoyment from the train ride. The earlier days of fascination and excitement with train rides were long gone. What I cared about most was sitting down, getting some rest and getting away from the horrors of Mauthausen.

The train moved slowly, then stopped someplace off the main track. Again, the train picked up speed until we finally arrived at the camp of Melk. I didn't know this camp. Later, I learned that it was one of the larger sub-camps of Mauthausen, located just outside the small town of Melk.

The town of Melk is situated on the south bank of the Danube River and the Wachau Valley of Lower Austria. It seemed quiet and peaceful. Our train passed by quaint stores and houses, but these were lost on me. I was a broken-down human being. I had just spent thirty days in the most brutal and horrendous place of my short life and I was numb to everything.

Melk had its own crematorium, complete with a tall chimney that could be seen from far away. Many said the chimney resembled an index finger pointing upwards, stabbing the sky. For many of the prisoners here, the chimney pointed the way to freedom. Up the chimney was the only way out.

We disembarked from the train and marched in groups toward the camp. As we approached the camp, we saw no barracks, but instead a multi-storied building. We found out this was a *Wehrmacht* garrison occupied by soldiers. Farther on we saw the electrified barbed wire and the gate. As we approached the gates, the ramp opened up and the *kapos* leading us shouted, *"Mutzen ab! Augen recht!"* Caps off! Eyes right! We promptly obeyed. We marched to the *appellplatz* just beyond the gate. Although it was late afternoon, the camp was empty. We were told to stand at the *appell*. We remained standing still for several hours. Even though this was hard, it was much better than laboring in the stone quarry. Toward evening, many prisoners started arriving at the *appellplatz* and formed into groups. Soon, the area was crowded with people. We were all dressed in a similar way, wearing striped pants, wooden shoes, red dish hanging in the back, and the spoon woven through the buttonhole of the shirt. The only difference was the identifying triangles. There were different colored triangles next to their numbers. Most triangles I saw were red like mine; some of the *kapos* had black or green. Green meant they had a criminal record.

Overall, Melk was totally different from any other camp I had been in. Until now, I had only been with Jewish prisoners, but in Melk there were people from thirty-five countries; almost every country in Europe was represented. There were people such as Spanish republicans who were kept here from the Spanish Civil War. There were French and Russian prisoners of war. A large number of soldiers from Russia were not kept in a prisoner of war camp, but instead in concentration camps.

Again, people carried bodies on stretchers which were stacked next to the living. There was the usual count by the *kapos*, then by the Germans. There was one prisoner who marched with the Germans writing everything down on a notepad. I noticed that he had a purple triangle next to his number; I didn't know what that indicated.

After the whole camp was counted, they brought some funny looking benches to the front. Then they began calling out numbers, one by one. Those called had to step forward, drop their pants and bend over the bench until they were almost horizontal. Two *kapos* one on either side with a *reit peitsche* (leather horse whip) began to strike the man on the butt with mighty, full-strength blows. The prisoner had to call out the number of strokes delivered to them. We could hear them, in between their cries of pain, count out in German, "One, two, three …!" up to twenty-five. Because of their pain, they either fainted or lost the count and then they had to start all over again from number one. For many of them, German wasn't their first language and they had a hard time of it. One, two, three, is easy enough: in German it is *"eins, zwei, drei,"* but twenty-three is *"drei zwanzig"*, and twenty-four *"vier und zwanzig,"* literally four-and-twenty and *"funf und zwanzig,"* five-and-twenty, were much harder to say. The prisoners had to pronounce the numbers correctly too. If they said twenty -and -four or twenty-and-five, this wasn't recognized by the *kapos* and they beat them with more strokes, always starting from number one until they said it correctly. Not all the blows landed on the butt, some were on the waist and the kidney area. Some of the prisoners fainted and couldn't stand up again so they were taken to *revier*, the camp hospital from which many never came back. The punishment was meted out based on the report of the *kapos* for committing some minor infractions, such as not working hard enough, or dropping a tool or whatever lame excuse they chose to create.

After *appell*, we were dismissed. We were given some turnip soup plus a portion of bread from a round loaf weighing more than four pounds, cut in sections. This was distributed by the *blockalteste* who cut it into eight sections. All totaled, we each got just over a half pound each. Then we were marched off to a barrack. It was a stone structure, not really a barrack with garages and storehouses underneath. We walked up a ramp to our quarters in the upper part of the structure. This particular building had been damaged in a recent air raid, a bomb had landed on it and killed some prisoners, but it had been rebuilt since. We were each assigned to a section of the barrack. In this stone barrack, there was one long stretch of bunks three rows high, four to a bunk. I was assigned a place in one of these rows. We were squeezed together. Each of us had our own space and blanket, but this changed later.

I went to work the next day and was assigned to a group. Our *kapo* was a one-eyed guy named Adolph. He was an old timer in the camps. I could see he was limping and weak. Because of his crippled condition, his own life was in danger. His infirmity made him exceptionally cruel with insults and beatings. He appeared to crawl rather than walk and his strange gait resembled that of a monkey.

After the groups were formed, we had to walk about two and a half miles and then we had a fifteen-minute train ride in cattle cars to Loisdorf. There, the prisoners were building tunnels for factories. I had no idea what they were making at the time. The idea was to build the rockets deep in the mountains away from the American bombers in Austria. These tunnels had to be very tall for the equipment to fit properly.

Many years later, I found out that the tunnels were designed to house and manufacture the V1 rockets. V meaning *"vergeltungswaffen,"* weapons of reprisal. The scientist who invented the V-1 was Wernher Von Braun. His rockets were the first unmanned rockets that flew to England

and bombed London and other places, killing thousands of civilians including many innocent children.

There were three shifts. At first, my group was assigned the day shift, but our group had to alternate every few weeks. When we got back to our barracks after a hard day, sometimes the *kapos* and *blockaltestes* invented devious exercises for us to perform such as picking up stones from the ground and piling them up neatly. They stopped at nothing to make us as miserable as possible and keep us busy around-the-clock.

Each day after *appell*, we were assigned to blocks. Before we could eat, we had to be shaved. Prisoners couldn't possess a razor or scissors, but we always had to be clean-shaven. The assignment fell to a prisoner barber. The men lined up outside the barrack where they stood in place for hours. There were only two barbers for a barrack; the place was always full; and it took a long time to get through the crowd. Because I was too young to grow a beard, I was saved from the mandatory shaving. But, I still had to have a haircut. The hair was cut close to the scalp, 1/8 inch, or even less. Then they shaved a part in the middle, shaved right to the skin. This was done so that if somebody escaped they would be recognized as a prisoner. We referred to it as the *"Lousestrasse,"* Louse Street.

Next we had our food ration. If we had the day shift, we received the soup. But if we worked the night shift, we didn't get soup. At this time, I was on the day shift, so kettles of soup were brought out and issued by the *blockalteste*. The soup was practically nothing, a few turnips and some potato peels. We also got a meager ration of bread.

I wanted to go to sleep, but none of us were ever allowed into the barrack to sleep at will or when we were tired. We had to wait for the time the SS dictated. Once we heard the order, "Go to bed," then we could stumble into our barrack, find our bunk and sleep. Once I was in my spot on the bunk I quickly fell asleep. All too soon I would be forced awake and made to complete the work cycle again.

September 19, 1944:
Armistice between Finland and Soviet Union is signed. (End of the Continuation War)

September 28, 1944:
Nazi murders in Marzabotto, Italy (SS-major Reder)

> "What kind of people live there? Even in
> the camp they're not allowed to move
> around. Why are they kept separate from
> the other prisoners?"

Chapter 28

Ordinarily, everything in the camp was based on rank. The prisoners couldn't decide anything for themselves. We responded to our hunger, thirst or exhaustion when the *kapos* gave us the order to eat, drink, or sleep. However, occasionally after the shave, bread and soup, we were allowed to walk around the camp. We had a half hour to an hour, depending on their schedule. During these "free times," I could walk around. I was allowed to go anywhere in the camp within the barbed wire.

One day during my so-called free-time, I spied a barrack surrounded by electrified barbed wire. I had never seen this type of barrack before and it mystified me. Normally, all the camps were surrounded by electrified barbed wire—literally two rows of it. This particular barrack was special because it was surrounded by its own high voltage wire. This prevented its prisoners from moving about as freely as we did. The other barracks in the camp had unrestricted exits and there was relatively free circulation when permitted.

I was already surrounded by some rather dangerous characters and they weren't put behind special barbed wire. I concluded that the prisoners in this barrack must be especially dangerous to others.

I asked a fellow prisoner, "What kind of people live there? Even in the camp they're not allowed to move around. Why are they kept separate from the other prisoners?"

The fellow prisoner answered, "They aren't criminals. All those people in there are *Bibelforscher*, sometimes called Jehovah's Witnesses. They worship their God Jehovah."

This was puzzling information. I had never heard of a *Bibelforscher*, or Bible student, before. What was especially confounding was their name. I knew the name Jehovah. This was the name of the Jewish God, except our religious traditions forbid us from pronouncing it. When the *Tetragrammaton*, the four Hebrew letters "YHWH" that translates to the name Jehovah, appeared in the scriptures we said *Adonai* which means Lord.

"If they worship Jehovah, they must be Jews because Jehovah is the Jewish God," I said.

"No, they're not Jewish. They're Aryan Germans and Austrians."

I stared at him in astonishment. These people were all Aryan Germans? There were no Jews in there?

I wanted to know more about this group of people who were not Jews but called on the name of Jehovah. I asked what they did to deserve imprisonment and learned that the *Bibelforscher* would not join Hitler's army or give the mandatory salute, "*Heil Hitler*." Even in the camp they refused to participate in any war-related work. All we did in Melk was war-related work. *Was this a resistance group in the camp?*

"What do they believe?" I asked.

"We don't know but they don't believe in the Pope or the Saints."

This was the sum total of what we knew of the *Bibelforscher*, or BIFO for short, which wasn't much. They believed in the Bible and they worshiped Jehovah. Nobody knew exactly what kind of group this was.

Later, alone with my thoughts, I tried to figure these people out. *What are they doing? They are suffering for the Jewish God, the God I just abandoned and have no use for. They are suffering for him?* In addition to the loss of my religious faith, I had deadened my emotions. In spite of my numbness, what I learned about Jehovah's Witnesses really struck me. I knew the name Jehovah, but I had lost my faith in God. From my viewpoint Jehovah was useless to me. I could have prayed all I wanted, but I knew I would not receive answers to my prayers. We Jews felt that Jehovah failed us, and yet we had done nothing wrong. I began to ignore Jehovah and eventually grew to hate him. If I was going to survive, it would be by my own effort, not by praying about it.

Because of my own feelings toward God, I was impressed by the Witnesses faith. Many years later after the war, I concluded that these people were not criminals. They just wanted to remain politically neutral, a stand that Hitler would not tolerate. They were in the camp because they wanted to show love to others and not fight in the war. The concept of love was out of place in the environment of a concentration camp. My experience was that no love of any type was shown toward each other there.

Then, on another day, an old-timer in the camp noticed me watching the Jehovah's Witnesses' barracks and told me something even more astounding.

"You know, they can go free the very same day or the next, if they'll only sign a statement renouncing their religion. But they don't sign it!" he said.

"I don't believe it. You're pulling my leg. If this were true, the barracks would be empty. Who wouldn't sign it? If they gave me a chance like that, there wouldn't be a question that I would do it!"

I reasoned that they could believe what they wanted without anyone knowing. They could just sign the paper, and then go free, continuing to believe what they wanted.

"They view signing this paper as a denial of their religion and as a transfer of their allegiance from God to Hitler."

"It must be a temptation," I said.

Nodding he said, "There's a stack right at the entrance to the barrack on a shelf. They don't have to ask; it's always there. All they have to do is sign it, and they can go free."

The Jehovah's Witnesses faced the decision to sign every day. Resisting the temptation of freedom must have been hard, especially when conditions in the camp were most difficult for them.

"There's a special torture the Nazis invented just to break their loyalty," the old-timer said.

"What's that?"

"They hang them on a pole with their arms tied backwards and upward."

"They do this just to Jehovah's Witnesses?" I asked.

"No. They hang others like that too, but for the BIFO they nail bolts into the pole, spread their fingers between the bolts, and then tie their fingertips together."

"They don't give in even then?"

208

"As far as I know, they don't give in," he said.

I wondered what gave these people the extraordinary strength and integrity to withstand these trials. This was worse than our situation. We didn't have a choice; we didn't have to make a decision. We were here until we died. Nobody in the camp understood the Witnesses for refusing to sign their way to freedom, an opportunity extended to no other group.

My fascination with the Witnesses stemmed from my Jewish training. I remembered the Jews who were forced to renounce their religion during the Spanish Inquisition. Many died as martyrs burned at the stake. I remembered the Hebrew expression *Al Kiddush Hashem,* meaning "for the sanctification of God's name." I was astonished to discover that these people were dying for the sanctification of the Jewish God's name.

Their fortitude was in extreme contrast to the life going on around me. In Melk, the conditions became so extreme, so desperate that we remained automatons, existing without feeling toward our fellowman, dead to everything. We couldn't distinguish one person from another by their actions or personality. Now I faced a group of people, who, under this type of pressure, acted differently from the rest of us.

The idea of surviving into a world of inhumanity was horrifying. In my daydreams, I hoped that, if I survived, I would one day live in a labor camp but work someplace inside, sheltered from the weather. I would have a gray coat that I was proud to wear. I would have a little compartment of my own in a locker room. I would lock it carefully because inside I would keep a loaf of bread. This was as far as my dreams went. I could not imagine a better world. But to see people who acted human in the midst of such inhumanity gave me an emotional lift, similar to the time when water was sprayed on the train outside of Plaszow, giving us some blessed relief from the oppressive heat. The water gave us hope because we thought we weren't being sent to Auschwitz to die.

If there were some people like the Witnesses who were still human in this world, then it began to seem worth surviving.

Still, I queried, "Why the barbed wire? Why would they put electric fences around them if they are just Bible students?"

The old-timer said, "Before they had wire, the BIFO would go and talk to other people, whoever they would meet. They talked to them about their God, Jehovah, and told them to put faith in God because bad times would be over soon."

The one thing the Nazis wanted to do was remove all hope from the hearts and minds of the prisoners. They wanted to break down our spirits, making us easier to control. To give us hope and a source of strength was more dangerous than a revolt. The only way to prevent the spread of such ideas was to seclude the Witnesses from others.

By this time the Jehovah's Witnesses had been in the various camps up to eleven years longer than I had, enduring these trials day-in and day-out. For their courage, they were greatly admired by everyone, eventually even by the Germans. Of course nobody knew exactly what the Witnesses believed. What they believed didn't matter to me, but under these particular conditions, it was their conduct that mattered.

On another occasion, I saw an unusual incident. After the *appell*, we were marched out in work groups and brought to the closed gate to be counted again by the *kapo*. I saw a prisoner wearing stripes walk to the ramp, the gate opened and he walked out unguarded. He didn't have to wait at the gate as was required by us or take off his hat with head turned left toward the Nazis, eyes lowered in submission. As far as I knew, no prisoner ever left the camp without a guard. In disbelief, I turned to the prisoner next to me and asked, "Hey, where's he going? What's he doing?"

"He's going to work," my companion said. "That guy is a BIFO. The Nazis know he's not gonna run away."

Gradually, I learned about the Witnesses. They were known for not escaping. They would never take advantage of the possibility of escape. They were in Melk proving the point to themselves, their God and any others who observed them, that they could remain loyal to God under any conditions. They were put in Melk and other camps because they would not follow Hitler as their leader. Escaping would not accomplish their purpose.

Daily, the prisoners in the camp had difficulties with each other. There was much fighting and struggling for survival. People didn't care about one another; however, there was a set of unspoken rules amongst the prisoners. Stealing bread, for instance, was considered a crime. But prisoners stole from each other if their own survival was involved. If the thief was caught, there was the potential threat that another prisoner would kill him. To me, everyone in Melk was for himself and only himself, even if it cost someone else's life. The Witnesses were completely different. I felt that the Witnesses were special, almost beyond human. They were honest; they didn't steal, from each other or the camp. Because of this, as I was told by prisoners who were in Melk longer than me, they were put in trusted positions in the warehouses and kitchens.

SS officers were now assigned to Melk permanently and many of them brought their families. They lived in nice homes outside of the camp. They had a community there and needed servants. They needed help with gardens, children, cooking and cleaning. They could pick from anybody in the camp for these jobs. But there was a problem; how could they trust prisoners, who they had persecuted and who hated them? It could be dangerous to bring them into their homes and expose their families to them. However, the Witnesses were making a good reputation for themselves as trustworthy workers. Who better than the Witnesses to choose to be the SS officers' private servants? So, rather than killing the Jehovah's Witnesses they used them in caring for the officers' homes.

The Witnesses were obedient servants, faithfully doing everything commanded of them, as long as it didn't violate their conscience (performing a military function, such as cleaning a uniform). They even cared for the Nazis children as if they were their own.

At night they were locked in their separate barracks, but I felt that this worked to their advantage. They were protected when they had their meetings in secret, or prayers or whatever they had going on. Due to the extra barbed wire and gates surrounding their barrack, they could hear a guard coming with ample time left to hide what they were doing.

During regular work hours, the Witnesses were not locked up and they moved about amongst the other prisoners on their way to their work assignments. However, we were not allowed to talk to them about religious matters under threat of severe punishment. If caught, the Witness and the prisoner would be given the famous twenty-five strokes, administered on the naked buttocks with the *reit peitsche*. As a result, people were afraid to talk to them. We even avoided them in casual conversation about work. There was always the chance that someone would falsely accuse us of having a religious conversation.

Because of the difficulty and the danger of being whipped, I personally never spoke to a Witness in Melk. They wore the purple triangle as their identification badge. If I saw a prisoner wearing the purple triangle, I knew I could trust him. I knew he would never hurt me like the *kapos*. I didn't have to avoid the Witnesses. I could tell it was a purple triangle coming down the camp street even before I saw the color of their triangle. They walked differently. The Jews and other prisoners shambled along, scuffling their feet, eyes downcast. The Witnesses always walked erect and looked us in the eye. I believed they thought it was their mission somehow, to encourage us and lift our spirits. They were the talk of the camp and everybody felt in some way a sense of pride in them. We felt beaten, and lost. But, they showed love; while I had forgotten that word even existed.

The Gypsies

The Gypsies are one of the "forgotten victims" of the Holocaust. The Nazis, in their strive to rid the world of undesirables, targeted both Jews and Gypsies for "extermination."

http://history1900s.about.com/od/holocaust/a/Gypsies-Timeline.htm

Desperate Acts

A Jewish policeman shakes the hand of one of more than 1000 Jews who are about to leave the Westerbork, Holland, concentration camp in early September, 1944.

http://www.holocaustchronicle.org/staticpages/561.html

September 1944-Decisions
16 years old

In the evening, while in our barracks, we often took the time to sit down on the hard plank floor and pick the lice off our bodies.

Chapter 29

The work of digging and building tunnels was immense. There were three different shifts working around the clock to get it done. Each shift was eight hours of work, but our day lasted anywhere from 12 to 14 hours. First, we were assembled for roll call at the *appellplatz*, which always took a long time, then we were marched to the train station, over two miles away and waited for the train to arrive that would take us to Loisdorf.

I was now on the night shift. This was a rough time to work the tunnels or *stollen*, as they were called in German. First, the work group had to drill into the mountain and remove all the rocks and debris, making the tunnels ready for the cement to be poured, forming the ceiling, walls and floors. Trucks brought in steel girders. My group carried the girders from the trucks to the tunnel.

It was September and still warm outside, but I knew colder days were coming. We left our barracks in the late afternoon and were counted and recounted at the *appellplatz*. When dismissed, we had to march five in row with our arms linked together at the elbows to prevent us from escaping. Then we marched to the train about a mile away, climbed into the cattle car and took a short ride to Loisdorf.

As one shift arrived, another was leaving. We passed at the train station in Loisdorf. While waiting on the platform for the new arrivals to disembark, the returning prisoners sometimes yelled across the tracks to the newly arrived, hoping to gain some new information about camp. Most of the people I worked with were Hungarian Jews and called over to the other group in their language.

They yelled in Hungarian, "What is the supper?"

The others answered, "Soup!"

It was either *krumpli levesh*, potato soup, or *kapushta levesh*, cabbage soup. And, we had *kacsi kenyret*, meaning a little bread. If it was the afternoon shift that was leaving, the question asked was, "What's for lunch?" It seems food was always first on all of our minds.

After the night shift I returned to camp and headed to the *appell* for the count. Then we were dismissed to the barracks. Once in the barracks I wanted to sleep, but this was not allowed. Sleep wasn't a right in Melk. Instead we lined up for the shave or haircut. I skipped the shave since I hadn't grown a beard yet, but I had my "*Lousestrasse*" cleaned up. Afterward, we each received our "coffee." Next, the *block* leaders came with their devious plans to get us to work harder and keep us miserable. Usually, this meant cleaning the barrack or performing tortuous calisthenics. Finally, we were allowed to line up to enter the barrack. Each day the beds were stripped, exposing a bare straw mattress, so each time we came into the barrack we were issued a blanket.

I received a blanket that was usually in bad condition. Either it was so badly torn it didn't cover me up at all or it was sopping wet from someone's urine. Then, blanket in hand, we were randomly assigned to bunks and I could finally get some sleep. It was the same cycle every day.

I had barely closed my eyes before I was awakened to a shrill whistle signaling the time to get up. I went to the latrine barrack to try to wash my face or do something to be clean, but it was impossible to keep clean there. Although the latrine was better here than at other camps, there was always a long wait for the toilet. Many prisoners had diarrhea. There was a long strip of wood planks with holes cut out for toilets stretched across the barrack. The latrine barrack wasn't designed for washing. There was no soap, towels or toilet paper, just cold water with low water pressure. Plus, everything had to be done in a hurry; otherwise we could miss out on the "coffee" ration and slim portion of bread.

As far as shifts went, I preferred the day shift. It was better in the sense that I could sleep undisturbed from the troublesome *kapos*. We never could get enough sleep. One time while walking to the train for Loisdorf, I was so tired I just closed my eyes and let the other prisoners pull me along. It was so comfortable resting in their linked arms.

In the evening, while in our barracks, we often took the time to sit down on the hard plank floor and pick the lice off our bodies. There were so many of them it was terrible. Our mission each night was to kill as many lice as possible, but they were still there, and no matter how many we killed it didn't help much. The conditions were such that the louse population continued to thrive and multiply.

There were different kinds of lice, each one living on different parts of the body and our clothing. Each one had its own, unique appearance. They crawled over us continually. We hated them more than the Nazis. At least the Nazis weren't on us 100 percent of the time. When I tried to sleep, they crawled into my mouth and ears. I couldn't run or hide from them. There was no way to find a peaceful moment. I loved to kill them. Some of them were big fat ones, full of blood. These we called a *rasowa*, Polish for "pure bred." I squashed them between my fingertips and nails. They made a loud, satisfying, snapping sound: "Oh that was a *rasowa!*" I held it up to my prison mates.

Often this was how we entertained ourselves, picking at lice, laughing to each other and saying, "That was a high pure-bred louse!" We made jokes out of things that terrified us. Survivors often did that.

By the time I arrived in Melk, my survival skills were finely tuned. I had learned many of the techniques for improving my chances of survival. One was to know when it was good to be up front, in the middle, or in the back of the group. Every one of these decisions could be crucial to survival. Survival meant being aware without the distraction of anything or anybody else.

Every camp was different and one wrong move could mean bad trouble, even death. When entering a new camp, part of the survival technique for me was to get informed from the old timers. I did this right away. Finding out the ins and outs of the camp was very important. I was sharp in the survival techniques, acutely aware of what was going on around me. I had to be this way; I had no friends amongst the hierarchy or the *kapos*. Nobody had friends in Melk. Someone who was formerly called a friend could quickly change into an enemy. Though, it was possible to have "friendly connections." Perhaps it was someone in control of soup or bread portion. Whether it was a *kapo* during the day or a *block* leader in the evening, they would hold out the best for their close friends dipping from the bottom of the kettle where the chunks of food settled, or slicing a bigger piece of bread for their "friend." My portion of soup was usually served from the thin, watery surface. The bread and soup were issued by my *block* leader. When he sees me he knows I am nobody to him. I put my bowl down for the soup and he, just for spite, skims the ladle right off the top. I have to endure it and make no complaints. He pulls out the ladle in such a way that most of the liquid drops back into the kettle. The *block* leader is challenging me and wants to see my reaction. But I am powerless against him and do nothing.

Not that the soup was good and worth a second bowl, it was horrible. It was made of potato peels but sometimes we didn't even get those. With our bowls of soup in hand my fellow prison mates and I stood leaning against the fence and compared what we got.

Nudging me, another prisoner asked, "How many peels did you get?"

"One," I said.

"Oh, I got four." He bragged.

When the bread was cut, I received the thin slice of the triangle while friends of the *blockalteste* always got the thick slices. We always compared the slices of bread too. Did someone else get a bigger piece? If they did we were jealous of them.

We were each given one-eighth of the loaf. Because we were starved, there were countless decisions and discussions on what to do with the bread. The decision on how to handle the bread ration was pure torture. There was no specific tactic on how to eat it.

"Do I save it, or do I eat it now while I have it?" One asks.

"What do I do? Maybe I'll eat half now and save half for tomorrow." Another wonders.

The decision was a painful one. We were all so hungry—the soup and bread were never enough. Personally, to eat just a little bit and still feel hungry knowing full well that I had some bread saved was tormenting. The questions I faced were: *Should I save the whole thing for the morning? But, then I have to hide it because somebody will steal it. Where do I hide it?* There just wasn't any good way of handling the decision, and in the end I couldn't make one.

Prisoners tried all sorts of things. One said, "I'm going to hold on to the bread, keep it in my uniform, safe from thieves." If the weather was wet, then our uniforms were soggy and not an ideal place for bread. If it hadn't rained and we were dry, the uniform was a good place.

When my uniform was dry, I kept the bread on top of my chest. But, once I had the bread there, it was a terrible temptation to take a small piece. If I took just one tiny piece, my fear was I would want another and another. In the end I couldn't escape the temptation. I couldn't tolerate having the bread on me and not being able to eat it. So, after I took a chunk, I ate more of it than I intended, and then I felt bad that I took the chunks and had no more saved.

There was a prisoner who secretly made a sharp blade. He offered, "I can slice your bread in many, many slices, very thin slices."

"What is the payment?" There was always a price for such services.

"A slice of your bread," he replied.

This seemed like a good idea. I reasoned that if I take a piece of bread and just take a chunk, I would know I was going to swallow these chunks without even knowing I ate them. But, if I took just the thin slices and pretended—just look how many slices I would have left! In the end, I couldn't fool my empty stomach. Nothing really worked no matter what method was suggested.

One evening, we had just been given our portion of bread when I was called away for a work detail. I couldn't take the bread with me. Now what am I going to do with the bread? There was a boy who usually slept next to me on the bunk and who was also in my work group. We were about the same age and sort of friendly. I trusted him and asked if he would hold my bread until I got back. He readily accepted. When I came back and asked for my bread, he said it was gone. He was very upset and kept saying he was sorry.

Now I was upset and heartbroken. Somehow the bread had been stolen when he wasn't looking. This was an unimaginable tragedy to me. Losing a half a day's portion of bread was a major disaster. I was shocked this had happened to me as stealing bread was an unforgivable, heinous crime. My friend extended his hand toward me and said, "Here, Jozef; have a piece of my bread." This was really quite a sacrifice, and I was grateful to him.

Survival in the camps sometimes meant choosing the right tools to work with. On some shifts, I worked inside the tunnel doing work that required tools. There were big cement mixers outside the tunnel mixing the cement which was then poured into waiting lorries that ran along a rail into the tunnel. These lorries were V-shaped and could be tipped over to unload the wet cement onto the track. After the lorries were emptied, two people shoveled cement and built the wall. After ten minutes, the next lorry arrived with a fresh load of cement to be scooped up and thrown on the walls. I had to hustle to shovel the wet cement off the planks and throw it behind on the framework. If we didn't get all the cement removed before the next load arrived, a beating was guaranteed. Although this was hard work, it was bearable. Throwing the cement against the walls was easier than throwing it at the ceiling. For the ceiling I had to throw the cement way up above my head all the while balancing on tall scaffolding. We couldn't drop any cement on the ground or else the civilian contractors supervising the work threatened us with a severe beating. This kind of work took strength and dexterity and, of course, having use of the right shovel.

All the shovels were kept in a deep metal tool shed outside the entrance to the tunnel. The first thing we did when we arrived was to run into the shed and grab a tool. There were different kinds of shovels but it was so dark it was difficult to make them out. The *kapos* were beating us with their whips and yelling at us to rush. Usually we just grabbed the first shovel we could find. I wanted to take my time and search for the one I wanted, but there was no time.

One night I happened to grab a shovel ideal for scooping wet cement off the scaffolding. Not overly heavy, with a flat bottom, cement could be thrown over my head. This shovel was practical compared with the other ones. I felt pleased with my discovery and wanted to make sure I worked with this particular shovel every time. But I couldn't mark it. There had to be a way I could save it for myself. I devised a plan: In order to have it available every day, I had to put it in a specific place. When we put the shovels away I went deep into the shed and placed it in the right rear corner.

Prisoners were allowed into the shed in groups. Other waiting groups couldn't enter until everyone from the previous group had come out. Searching for my shovel took up valuable time, which prevented the next group from getting in. Each time I arrived at the work site, I went to that far part of the shed to retrieve the shovel, invariably I was beaten by the *kapo*. He cursed at me and beat with the *reit peitsche* over my head and back. But I took the risk; keeping the same shovel contributed to my survival.

I developed a smooth pattern of work. While on the upper scaffolding, scooping the cement up, I would, in the same swift motion, hurl it upwards over my shoulder, aiming it where I wanted it to go. One other guy, a Hungarian, was working with me. He was a weak, older, tired man. He was working with one of those big, heavy coal shovels with a round bottom. He couldn't throw the cement up and over. As much as he tried he couldn't keep up with my pace. I was in a rush to get through the pile of cement so as not to get beaten by the civilian contractors. I found them to be bad men who didn't care how cruel they were. They were under the gun to get the work done and they didn't want to be delayed by incompetent workers.

Because my Hungarian partner was so slow, I wound up doing his part. He was trying, but I had no pity for him, my patience was wearing thin. The burden of the cement throwing fell on me to finish. As hard as I worked, I just couldn't shovel through the old pile of cement before a new pile was dumped at our feet. The Austrian overseer stomped over, screaming at me, "What's taking so long? Why are you so slow?" Then he began to beat me.

"I'm doing my part!" Pointing at my partner, I said, "But he isn't!"

The Austrian went out and brought an SS man back with him. Together, they took the Hungarian away. I never saw him again; I don't know what they did with him. Usually, if someone couldn't work they got rid of him one way or another. Whatever they did with him, I didn't feel guilty about it. I automatically did the thing I needed to do to protect myself and ensure my own survival. I had the right shovel, I did my work, and he didn't do his. This was heartless, but at the time I had no heart.

October 23, 1944:
On this date, young Alice Ehrmann wrote about the brutal deportation of young children.

Alice Ehrmann was sixteen years old when she was sent from Prague to the ghetto at Terezin (Theresienstadt). She was the child of a Jewish father and a Catholic mother. According to Nazi racial laws, she was considered to be mischlinge of the first degree (half-Jewish).

http://www.holocaustedu.org/education/student_center/this_week_in_history/alice_ehrmann_october_23_1944/

October 7, 1944:
On this day, a mini-revolt took place. As several hundred Jewish prisoners were being forced to carry corpses from the gas chambers to the furnace to dispose of the bodies, they blew up one of the gas chambers and set fire to another, using explosives smuggled to them from Jewish women who worked in a nearby armaments factory.

October 10, 1944:
On this day in 1944, 800 Gypsy children, including more than a hundred boys between 9 and 14 years old are systematically murdered.

http://www.history.com/this-day-in-history/eight-hundred-children-are-gassed-to-death-at-auschwitz

October 1944
16 years old

> As I said, being barefoot was an
> advantage for me. I had no problem
> going to the latrine and had no fear of
> anyone stealing something I didn't have.

Chapter 30

October and November were gray, dark and wet. The rain drenched our uniforms and soaked us to the skin. While trying to sleep in our bunks, our blankets, dampened now from our uniforms, gave us little comfort. We were freezing cold, shivering all day and all night. In the barrack we huddled close together trying to keep warm, but nothing helped.

The mud on the road was so heavy that walking was difficult. Our wooden shoes were laborious to walk in on any given day, but on a rainy day, our feet were sucked down into the wet, thick mud, making it especially impossible to navigate our way. We walked clumsily along, slipping, sliding and pulling our mud-plastered feet out of the sticky ground. Somehow we all got used to it. I became so used to walking in these ill-fitting shoes that it seemed quite natural to me. (When I finally had a real pair of shoes after the war, I still walked in this clumsy Frankenstein way, clomp, clomp, clomp.) Because of the thick, sticky ooze, the wooden part of the shoe frequently became stuck. I had to pull my foot up with force, which put pressure on the nails holding the canvas tops to the wooden bottom. Eventually, the nails tore through the fabric and, to my dismay each time I pulled my foot up, the tears became bigger.

On my way to work, while trekking through the sludge, to my consternation the bottom of one shoe came off. I picked it up and stared at it. This was a crisis situation. What can I do? I can't nail it back on. I shoved it in the waistband of my pants and proceeded to walk with only the canvas part of the shoe hanging around my ankle.

During the mid-day break (no food, just some time off) I found some used and discarded paper cement sacks on the side of the road. I scouted around and found pieces of thin wire. With the wire, I wrapped the cement sack around the remaining part of the canvas, hoping this would hold throughout the day. I walked as gingerly as possible, but feared it wouldn't hold. We were made to walk quickly and in a short time the cement sack fell apart.

At the end of the shift, we marched to the train hooked together at the elbows, but I couldn't keep up with the group. I stumbled along as best I could. I ripped off the remaining shoe, shoved it in my pants and walked barefoot. This was much easier, and I could keep up.

At the work site the next day, I searched for a cement sack and started over again.

Soon, while marching to work, my one intact shoe began to rip away from the bottom. We were marching quickly, and before I could grab for the wooden sole, it got stuck in the mud. I couldn't break loose from the row of interlocked prisoners. I was pulled right along with the marching group, leaving the wooden sole behind. Eventually, I threw away the remaining wooden sole and decided to forgo shoes altogether. I pulled out the nails that were hanging from the canvas and walked with just the canvas tops around my ankles.

Winter was coming. As the temperature dropped, the road became frozen. On the night shift, I was assigned work outside sorting pebbles that were mixed in with the cement. The work itself was largely stationary, making it difficult to keep warm. I had no shoes or any hope for being given new ones. If I reported that I had lost my shoes, I would get a beating for losing government property. I had no choice but to remain in this shoe-less state, and I envied the others who had shoes.

Although I had work-hardened, rough feet from my time in Mauthausen, they were always cold. I don't know how I could stand it, but somehow I did. Here in Melk, they grew calloused from the sharp, pebbly frozen surface of the ground.

I went barefoot about six weeks. There was an advantage to being barefoot. We had received an order: if we went to the latrine at night, we were forbidden to take our shoes or trousers. These had to be left behind in the barrack. Running wasn't allowed. We had to walk to the latrine barrack slowly, even though it was cold outside. There were watchtowers all around the camp and lights on all the streets. If we were caught wearing shoes or trousers while going to the latrine we would be charged with an attempt to escape and would be killed.

This was problematic. If someone left their shoes behind to go to the latrine, there was a probability that they would be stolen by the time they returned. There was no trust among us. As a result, the prisoners were too afraid to go to the latrine. Instead they did their business right on the mattress where they lay. They used all kinds of tricks. For instance, they would spray the entire mattress with their urine, distributing it evenly so there wasn't just one wet place. This was terrible. There were three tiers of bunks and the mattresses were thin straw. The urine leaked down onto the person below. Also, many prisoners had diarrhea, and that, too, dripped down onto the person below.

The consequences of these actions were dreadful. Every once in a while the *block* leaders came around in the morning to inspect the bunks. If they found the bunk was soiled, they grabbed the prisoner, tied him to the bunk, strapped him down tight and beat him. To my shock, sometimes they made him eat the excrement. There was no discretion involved in who the *blockalteste* grabbed. Sometimes the prisoner they grabbed was not the actual one who did it. Maybe this prisoner was innocent and the urine or excrement dripped down from somebody in a bunk above him. Nevertheless, the *blockalteste* had to grab someone and punish him for being in the unclean bunk. If the prisoner didn't die from the beating, he was taken to the hospital. As we were all very well aware, if anyone went to the hospital they might not come back alive.

As I said, being barefoot was an advantage for me. I had no problem going to the latrine and had no fear of anyone stealing something I didn't have. I thought of the Jehovah's Witnesses (*Bibelforscher*) barracks. They had a reputation in the camps for being completely honest. They would never steal anything from anyone, even under the direst circumstances. I was sure they weren't afraid to leave their things behind. They could go to the latrines with absolute confidence, without fear that their possessions would be stolen.

During the winter months of 1944, the population of Melk grew with new arrivals. There were Poles from the Polish uprising in Warsaw; there were Yugoslav partisans, Italian partisans and Hungarian Jews. These men were big, robust, healthy fellows, straight from the outside world. But many of them were dead within six weeks. By comparison, I had been in the camp a long time and had learned the ropes. I had acclimatized to the harsh and brutal lifestyle, but for those coming in from the outside; they couldn't take the extreme conditions under which we survived. The shock of it was just too much, and as a result many died off quickly.

One night while on the night shift and waiting on the *appellplatz* for the final count, I noticed a newcomer to our group. He was a Hungarian Jew, tall, intellectual looking, but quite weak. He was shaky on his feet. His brand-new government regulation shoes caught my attention. I stayed close by him in the group lineup. Usually, if somebody looked weak or sick, we avoided being near that person because this might bring trouble. Since we were linked by the elbows, if someone fell, the entire row was dragged down or the others in the row would have to pull the sick, weak one along. This delayed the group and if anyone fell behind, they were punished. But I saw the newcomer's shoes. I thought he wasn't going to last very long and I would soon get an opportunity to grab his shoes.

As soon as we got the order to march, the newcomer took one step and fell flat on his face. Instantly, I crouched down beside him and began removing his shoes. I worked as fast as I could, but he was yelling and crying, drawing the attention of a *kapo,* who came running over. This was no time for a disturbance; we had already started to march and we were at the gate. The *kapo* beat both of us in earnest.

In between the blows, I cried out to him, "I don't have shoes. He doesn't need any—he's not going anywhere!"

Then the *kapo* turned to the Hungarian and beat him forcefully. While this was going on, I ripped the shoes off the man. He was screaming now, but I didn't pay attention to him. I had to rush off and rejoin the group otherwise, I would get beaten again. Ultimately, the group was delayed because of our tussle and I got a beating anyway. I was now the owner of a new pair of regulation shoes. I was happy with my acquisition and never gave another thought about what had happened to the other man.

Even though we were hooked by the elbows when we marched outside camp to prevent escapes—if one prisoner escaped, the four remaining prisoners in his row were punished. There were a few occasions when people escaped anyway because we marched under cover of night.

One night as we were marching to the trains, an entire row of five prisoners broke rank and ran into the nearby woods. They took off like flying arrows. I heard shouting and our entire group was held up. The SS went tramping through the woods, their flashlights casting out wild beams of light as they desperately searched. Because it was dark, they couldn't do much. Besides, the escapees would be easily identified by their *Lousestrasse* down the middle of their scalps. All they had to do was wait for a villager to report seeing them.

Every once in a while the SS recaptured a prisoner. During the evening *appell,* the SS had a special "welcoming" ceremony. This happened on several occasions while I was in Melk. First the prisoner, with arms and feet manacled, was brought out standing on a little wagon. Around his neck hung a board with the words *"ich bin wider da"*: 'Hurrah! I'm here again." This was an example of typical SS humor. Next there was a public beating. The SS put the prisoner back in the wagon and took him away never to be seen again.

With all the rain, we had hoped the lice would drown but they didn't. They were worse than before. Always hiding in any warm place on the body they could find. We killed as many lice as possible but it didn't help. When I went to bed, I couldn't lie still; the insects were constantly crawling over my skin and biting me. The biting wasn't so bad, but the creeping and crawling over my body made me toss and turn.

In late February 1945, we had a louse inspection. Everybody had to show up at their barracks stripped naked. We were called out, one barrack at a time, and marched before the *kapos* who looked us over. We were threatened with a beating of twenty-five strokes if they found a louse on us.

As the camp was preparing for lice inspections, in my barrack, we were anxiously picking off lice and killing them, waiting our turn to be called out. As soon as we thought we were louse free they were back on our bodies again. When we felt clean of lice, we asked our neighbor to inspect us. Whoever inspected us always found more lice. We could never rid ourselves of them entirely. When it was our barrack's turn for the inspection, we filed out. Fortunately, by the time the inspecting *kapos* got to us, they were tired of the job and gave us a cursory once-over without looking too closely.

March 27, 1945:
General Eisenhower declares German defenses on Western Front broken.

March 30, 1945:
World War II: a defecting German pilot delivers a Messerschmitt Me 262 A-1 to Americans.

April 10, 1945:
Allies liberate 1st Nazi concentration camp, Buchenwald (Czech)

http://www.historyorb.com/events/date/1945?p=2

April 1945
17 years old

There were rumors being passed around. Some said the Nazis were abandoning the camp and were going to kill all of us.

Chapter 31

The situation in Melk was going from bad to worse. Although we didn't know the status of the war, we saw British and American planes flying overhead nearly every day. I always enjoyed seeing the fleets of planes flying above. There were so many of them, the sky was darkened. We could tell something big was happening, but we didn't know what it was or where the planes were headed.

In the meantime, we were feverishly building tunnels under the intense pressure of our German masters. In front of the tunnels, covering the work area, was equipment draped with camouflage netting. When we heard the sound of the air raid siren, everybody outside the tunnel had to sit absolutely still. We saw the planes coming by the hundreds, and we relished the idea that the Germans were being bombed. We realized the planes were a sign of something positive, and it gave us hope, but it didn't effect change in our life. The allies flew over, and then they were gone, and we were sent back to work.

About mid-April there was unrest in the camp and we weren't sent out to work. Something was going on. There were rumors being passed around. Some said the Nazis were abandoning the camp and were going to kill all of us. Still, nobody knew for sure what was going on and it worried us. There were a lot of activities going on amongst the guards. Trucks were loaded. The *kapos* were unusually quiet, but they were nervous too.

When the soup kettles were brought in, we were all surprised.

The SS were feeding us the best meal we had ever had in the camps. The soup was delicious; it was creamy and thick with beans and noodles. We never had anything like it all the days we were in the camp. This didn't make sense. There was no work; we were allowed to sit in the barracks and then they served us this wonderful soup.

April 12, 1945, was my seventeenth birthday. This cold and rainy day we lined up for the morning *appell* and the routine seemed back to normal. We stood there for hours while the *kapos* ran around looking for someone. The count was off. Somebody had escaped.

Oftentimes, when someone went missing for the morning count, it was because they were dead or lying sick in the barrack. The *kapos* searched for them and brought them out, but this time they couldn't find the missing prisoner. In the meantime, we weren't dismissed until the *kapos* had found the prisoner. We stood in the rain getting sopping wet. We weren't given any food or water. The guards wouldn't allow us even the small luxury of wrapping our arms tight around ourselves for warmth. We had to stand straight and silent. Some people in the ranks fell over from exhaustion, but not one of us who were still standing made any move to help them up. We left them lying there.

The entire camp spent that day and all that night standing on the *appellplatz*. In the morning of April 13, after what was close to twenty-four hours standing at attention, an order came. We were told to line up in groups by the hundreds, facing toward the gate. At the signal we were marched out of the camp.

There were so many of us. I never saw the beginning or the end of the stream of people. Our camp was being evacuated. We marched out of Melk down toward the Danube River to waiting passenger boats. We were loaded on like cattle, squashed into every available space, top to bottom. Somehow I found a spot on the stairway but it was very uncomfortable. My legs were sticking out in front of me, and everyone who came along tripped over them. We were so crowded together that after a while movement was restricted entirely. Someone was sitting on my legs and soon I couldn't feel them anymore.

I was superstitious and felt this day, Friday the Thirteenth, was a bad day. After a while, the boat began to move away from the pier. We remained on the boat about a day and a half. We weren't given food or water. The one positive thing to be said was that it was a calm river and no one got motion sickness, but it was a miserable trip. When we came to Linz, Austria, the boat docked. I was relieved to know I would be on dry land, stretching my cramped legs.

We were herded off the boat and immediately started marching to who knew where. We marched for an hour and then were told to rest for ten minutes. The weather was warm, and I was comforted by the sunshine. I reflected that an hour-long march was nothing. *This is easy and they even let us rest. This marching isn't so bad.* After ten minutes had passed, the SS roused us up and we began marching again. Another hour went by and we had another ten-minute rest. We did this every hour.

After a while, though, our walking became laborious. We walked in the same manner, our foot placed down flat and then picked up straight, in a pattern of flat, flat, clomp, clomp. My feet were getting quite uncomfortable in the ridiculous shoes. We carried nothing extra except our dish, hooked to our pants and spoon, weaved through the buttonhole of our shirts. The only thing I could be thankful for was that the roads were dry.

Our first stop for the night was in an Austrian town. We came to an area of horse stables where the guards locked us inside for the night. I took a few steps into the darkened building, stopped, and collapsed in a tired heap, not moving from that place until morning.

The next morning we marched again. We had an hour-long march, then a ten-minute rest. We still had not had any food or water. Many of the prisoners were getting tired and lagged behind. Some tried to help the stragglers by dragging them along, but before long they all fell behind. I focused hard on keeping up because if I couldn't, the outcome would be grim. Prisoners who couldn't keep up were shot and pushed into a ditch. I didn't always see it happening when it was behind me, but I heard the shots ring out.

Others had marched through on this same road prior to our group and I saw dead bodies wearing the striped prison garb lying exposed in the open ditches. I surmised the SS were getting desperate. They left prisoners abandoned on the road right in the open and did nothing to hide their murders from the local people.

Again, we stopped for the night. Our customary quarters were becoming the stables located outside the villages. However, there was very little room in them for all of us. Whoever couldn't find a spot in the stable had to sleep in the open field which is where I slept. I noticed some leaves on the ground nearby. Others noticed them as well and soon, we began to pick and chew on them, hoping to get a little nourishment. I saw some prisoners take the leaves, roll them up, and make a "cigarette." Prisoners were permitted to smoke in the camps. In order to motivate prisoners to work harder they were given work incentive coupons which could be traded for cigarettes and matches. So, using their matches, they lit the leaves and tried to smoke them. I thought it might actually work, so I decided to do the same thing. We sat there puffing away at these dried up old leaves, living in the moment and finding what little joy we could. That is not to say that our situation was enjoyable; it wasn't. We were outside in the cold without blankets, but not to be working in the tunnels was a comfort. For now, we had rest without harassment from the *kapos*.

The next day we marched again. As we were marching, SS guards came with bags full of small soup crackers. They were carefully counted out so everyone received ten or twelve each, almost a handful.

That night we stayed in open fields with the SS surrounding us. Although we slept on wet grass, I was grateful there was no snow. Someone nearby caught a small rodent. He killed it and ate it raw, skin and all. This caused jealousy among the other prisoners. They crowded around him, clamoring for a bit of it. I couldn't get in close enough. Some threatened to steal it from him, but nobody was able to get it away from him.

My starvation drove me to continually look on the ground for something, *anything* to eat. One time I found an old, frozen potato. I wanted to eat it so desperately, but the taste was terrible. Because it had been frozen, it had turned a rotten kind of sweet. As hungry as I was, I couldn't eat a bit of it. I gave it away and somebody else ate it with relish.

Several days went by and gradually our ranks thinned. Prisoners remained quiet and concentrated on keeping up with the crowd. I was trying my best to keep up, but marching at this pace was incredibly tiring. Prisoners dropped off right in the ranks; they sat down or lay down and could not go any further.

Finally, we arrived in Gmunden, Austria. There were a few trucks passing by us. One truck slowly rolled by with an SS sergeant among the group. At the time, I didn't know his name but he would come back into my life after the war.

He shouted out to us, "If anybody is sick and cannot walk, load up on the truck!" His words filled me with suspicion. I had developed a great distrust of anything offered by the SS. If it seemed like it was going to help me in some way, then I knew it wasn't being offered in good will. As weak and tired as I was, I didn't get on the truck. However, a few people volunteered, some of whom I knew from sharing the same barrack back in Melk. They climbed aboard, the truck took off and they were gone. I never saw any of them again.

This happened to be the last day of the march. We arrived in the evening but because it was dark, I didn't really know where I was. I saw many trucks going up and down a steep hill. We were directed to climb that difficult hill through a dark forest of towering pine trees. At the top, we arrived at a camp ensconced in the forest itself, surrounded by snow-capped, rugged looking mountains. We had arrived at Ebensee.

May 2, 1945:

President Truman issues Executive Order 9547 to appoint Justice Robert H. Jackson of the U.S. Supreme Court as Chief Counsel for the United States to the UNWCC and as Chief Prosecutor to the projected international war crimes trial. He is authorized to represent the United States during negotiations to create such a tribunal.

The German garrison in Berlin surrenders to the Soviet army.

German forces surrender in Italy.

http://www.scholastic.com/teachers/article/chronology-holocaust-late-april-through-july-1945

April to May 1945
17 years old

We just stood there, naked, waiting, not sure what would happen next.

Chapter 32

Thousands of us left Melk, but only a few hundred stragglers from the death march lived to see Ebensee. We arrived in the evening on April 21 or 22, 1945. The SS marched us in front of the showers and divided us into groups of 100. We were made to undress and stand naked in the freezing cold until our turn came for the showers, if they were indeed actually showers. Our big question was always, "water or gas chamber?"

As we stood waiting our turn, to my growing discomfort, I realized I hadn't seen any of the groups before mine come out of the showers. My anxiety was only heightened by their seeming disappearance. Was I awaiting life or was it a death sentence? Finally, it was our turn to go in. The same fear that always gripped me at this point arose in my chest. We were handed soap and were hustled inside. After a bit of uneasy silence and staring up at the shower heads, to my relief warm, wonderful water sprayed over us. The water lasted a few seconds and then abruptly shut off. We were to use this time to lather ourselves with the soap. Then, after a few more seconds, the water shot back on. All too quickly it turned off and we were herded outside, our skin tingling as the bitterly cold air wrapped around our wet bodies.

We just stood there, naked, waiting, not sure what would happen next. I saw the other groups standing around and realized that no one had been sent to a gas chamber. The exit was on the opposite side of the entrance, which is why I couldn't see anyone leaving the shower chamber.

I stood with the rest of my group all night, totally numb from the cold and still hungry and exhausted. In the morning, we had to locate our clothing by our number from a jumbled mess piled up outside the showers. I had the same number since my first day in Mauthausen: 87719.

Rummaging through hundreds of uniforms along with hundreds of other prisoners, everyone grabbing like mad, was pure chaos. We were cold and in a frenzied panic. Prisoners screamed and yelled as the fierce *kapos* whipped and beat us. We couldn't get dressed fast enough. I was used to it by now, and this treatment seemed normal. By some miracle, I found my clothes and I dressed as quickly as I could. Without further delay, we were marched directly to a train and then to the work site.

Ebensee, located about 47 miles southwest of Linz in upper Austria at Lake Traunsee, was the ideal location for the German military to build tunnels similar to those in Melk. The military supposed the missile testing and research being done deep in the tunnels would be safe from air raids.

As newcomers in the camp, we were assigned to Attnang-Puchheim, a railroad junction town. The Americans bombed this railroad junction almost every night, leaving huge craters in the ground. Our job was to rebuild the damaged tracks, remove the twisted ones and bring in new rails. As we approached the worksite, I saw that there was a steam locomotive lying in a big crater. We were ordered to lift it out. We weren't given ropes or anything to help with the job. Men went down into the pit to try to dig it out, but it was an impossible job. *How could they put weak, starving people to work like this?*

I was put to work on the upper part of the crater but soon I was taken away with a bunch of others to carry new rails from storage and bring them to the site. All day long we worked, always accompanied by abusive screaming and beatings from the *kapos*. At the end of the day, we had the bodies of the dead to carry away.

While waiting for the train from Attnang-Puchheim to take us back to camp at Ebensee, we were told to sit in an adjacent field next to the track. Early spring grasses were shooting up. I poked through the grass looking for thick, juicy blades to chew on. I found some and chewed and sucked on those, trying to get some moisture out of them. When the train came, we were loaded onto cattle cars. Because there was no direct line from the train into camp, we were left a little distance away and had to walk the rest of the way into the camp. Once inside, we were finally assigned to barracks.

The camp was crowded with prisoners, who had been brought in from all over. The SS overcrowded the barracks, squeezing as many as they could into a barrack. This was the first time I had seen the inside of a barrack since leaving Melk. (Our march had taken about ten days.) There were three tiers of bunks. Since my arrival at Ebensee, almost two nights before, I had not slept. I was extremely tired, but no one was allowed to lie down. We had a long wait ahead before the order came to go to sleep. I could only look longingly at the bunks.

In the meantime, the *kapos* portioned out bread from a square loaf. This was also the first time any of us had been given food of any kind since our arrival. We were handed the famous heavy bread that was mostly made from sawdust and difficult to cut into evenly apportioned pieces. Some were very thin, while others quite thick. The *kapo* looked me square in the face to see who I was before he handed me a slice. I was of no consequence to him, so I was given a small slice of about four ounces (but most times it was less.) This was considered the day's portion.

Next, we had to line up, and because there were so many of us, the organization took a long time. We were then divided into groups of twelve. After everyone had been assigned a specific tier and a spot on the bunk, we waited for the whistle to blow, signaling it was time for our group to find our place. We were four to a bunk, pressed up tight against each other. We went to bed fully dressed and had to rely on each other's body heat for warmth since we didn't have blankets. If somebody wanted to turn over, we all had to roll over at the same time. Sleeping in the barrack was an appalling experience: Cold and overcrowded, sometimes a prisoner would die while in his bunk. People were dying all the time. Death had become routine. If someone died while in the bunk, we just threw the body onto the ground.

The next morning at 4 a.m., we were brutally roused by the *kapos*. The *kapos* gave us the so-called "coffee," and off we marched to the waiting train at Attnang-Puchheim.

Here, there were two groups, as the day before, some were cleaning up damage from the bombs and some were building the tracks back up again. Today we had to carry the rails. They were extremely heavy, too heavy for me, but I knew that if I couldn't carry my load the SS would shoot me. To ensure my survival and conserve my energy, I made sure that I was behind someone taller than me. In this way the rail didn't rest directly on my shoulders, but instead it rested on the taller prisoner, who took the brunt of the load on his shoulders. I knew just what facial expressions to make. I grimaced and heaved to make a show of working hard.

By this time, finagling had become natural to me. All I knew was how to survive, and if it meant using tricks or outsmarting everyone else, then that is what I did. I wanted to survive at any cost. Sometimes that meant taking advantage of people who didn't know any better.

Ebensee was reportedly the worst camp in existence. Mauthausen was a category three death camp, but being sent to Ebensee was always a death sentence. It was the "final destination" camp for any who managed to survive their former camp. Ebensee was well hidden and the farthest away from the front line. The camp was bad to start, but gradually got worse as other transferees crowded in from other camps.

After the bread rations were handed out, we had some free time and were allowed to walk around the camp. That evening, I happened to run into a man I knew well from the little village Nieznanowice. His name was Itzek. We had followed the same path from Rakowice, through Plaszow and now Ebensee. He was skin and bones, stooped and crippled. He could hardly walk but he admired how well I was walking. I was young and still rather strong, but he was what we called a *mussulman* by this stage. There are various stages of death for a prisoner; the final stage is the *mussulman* stage. One never forgets seeing a *mussulman*. The word comes from a Polish word "*muzulman*" meaning Muslim. A *mussulman* is a prisoner, who is still walking around, but his eyes are dead, they no longer have a spark of life. His eyes are staring, unfocused. Often a *mussulman* has a fixed smile on his face, and he is drooling. He shuffles along, oblivious to everything and everyone. Then he dies with that same fixed grimace on his face. Every prisoner recognized the stages. If someone began to shuffle in a certain aimless way, then he was beginning to go into the *mussulman* stage; it was usually irreversible. My acquaintance Itzek felt sure that he wouldn't make it and that he was going to die soon. After talking a while we said our goodbyes and I never saw him again.

The bodies of the dead were piling up. They were gathered in stacks and then taken by truckload to the crematorium where prisoners burned bodies twenty-four hours a day. The workers couldn't keep up with the number of bodies, so the stacks of dead kept growing.

The bread, made mostly of sawdust, had very little nutritious value. The soup was just water without vegetables or fat. Combined with filthy living conditions that caused disease, prisoners were starved to death, worked to death or beaten to death.

I walked past the dead bodies in front of the crematorium every day but I paid scant attention to them—they were just bodies. My mind absorbed it but had no reaction. Death was commonplace; everywhere around me was death. I believed that death was the only way out of the camp. I knew I was going to end in the same stack of bodies eventually.

Then there was Barrack No. 26. This served as the camp hospital and housed the sick, the crippled and those who could no longer work. However, they weren't cared for or comforted in any way. They didn't have food, water or even a bunk; yet, they weren't killed. This was where the *kapos* waited for them to die. The people in Barrack No. 26 were crowded on the floor, lying all around. We couldn't walk through the barrack without stepping on someone. They were in a deplorable state. As hard as this is to admit, some friends and I considered it a fun pastime to go in Barrack No. 26 in the evening to look for anyone we might know who had disappeared.

I carelessly walked over people in my search. "Get off me!" One poor, sick prisoner screamed.

I laughed at him and replied, "Don't cry. What is the difference? You are dead, anyway."

I was cruel to say that. I had dismissed him as if he didn't count. I looked at people dying the same way I looked at the dead; they didn't mean anything to me. I don't even know why I went there looking for people I might have known. Even if I found someone, what could I do for him? I think the only reason I had for going there was to have a mean joke at these people's expense. I wanted to show them that I was superior. I was still walking. I was strong and alive and they were dying. What an appalling pastime! To this day, I cannot imagine how a person can sink to this level.

Back in our barracks at night, the lice were completely loathsome. They tortured us. Before we were given the order to sleep, we sat on the floor picking them from our clothing and bodies, snapping them between our fingertips. We took our vengeance killing them.

Starting at the beginning of May, we weren't given any more food. I ate anything just to put something in my stomach. I found some old bark from a partially burnt tree. I didn't hesitate to eat it. Prisoners were desperate to eat anything, even the grass but it caused terrible dysentery the likes of which I never saw before. I didn't realize it at the time, but by eating the carbonized bark I had given myself a cure for diarrhea, which ultimately saved my life. I did not suffer with dysentery as the other prisoners did. They died at a rate quicker than the workers could burn their bodies at the crematorium and the stack of dead bodies was becoming bigger and bigger near the crematorium gate.

In order to get us to work harder in the tunnels, the Austrian civilian supervisors gave out incentive coupons. We could use these for trading at the little camp "store." There was no food in the store and nothing of value. They "sold" combs. These were useless items to us since our heads were clean-shaven. The only items of interest to me were cigarettes. I had half of a coupon so I could get half a cigarette.

There were many Russians in Ebensee, young soldiers, enterprising prisoners of war. Some of them began cutting into the bodies accumulating in front of the crematorium. They began trading the pieces of flesh in exchange for cigarettes or the motivation coupons. In the evening, they came into our barracks with the meat that had been roasted. They offered pieces to us. I only had half a coupon. I went to the Russian with my bit of coupon and traded it for a piece of flesh. The meat was very small, one-quarter inch thick, one-half inch wide and one inch long. I bit into it but the meat was dried out and tasteless. I ate it anyway. At this point I would eat anything at all, even human flesh.

Soon, however, the young soldiers, not content with the flesh of the dead and wanting a better "quality meat," sneaked into the barracks at night and tried to cut away flesh from the living. Cannibalism was practiced in Ebensee. Starvation drives people to desperate behavior.

The Germans were acting oddly, as if our work wasn't important anymore. They didn't seem to care if we got it done or not. We could tell something was changing.

On May 5, 1945, after *appell,* we were not dismissed as usual. By that time we had noticed that some of the watchtowers were empty: There were no German SS guarding us from up there anymore. We were still assembled when we witnessed the unusual arrival of the camp commander, Ganz.

He addressed the group in tender terms, *"Meine Herren,"* or "Dear Sirs," he said. "The Americans are coming and we are expecting a fight to take place. We might have to turn you over into the hands of the Americans and I am concerned for your own safety. I would like you to spend the night in the tunnel and wait there."

In a historical moment, he asked the assembled group: "Will you go there?"

The whole camp gave a resounding, "NO!"

We knew that under normal circumstances this would not be tolerated. This was the first time in the history of a concentration camp that anyone said no to an SS commander. We knew this time they couldn't force us. The guards were gone and Ganz was here with only a few others.

We were sent back to our barracks and didn't go to work. As long as I had work, then somehow, I kept going but as soon as I stopped, my whole organism began to deteriorate. I lay alone in my bunk in a stupor. I didn't feel anything or know anything. Starvation was setting in.

My whole body was swelling up with water and now it was starting to show around the eyes and cheeks. My feet swelled first and then the edema worked up my legs, then my abdomen bloated. The last place it formed was under my eyes, which turned puffy. At this point I knew exactly the time I had left, judging by when my symptoms started.

We were matter of fact with each other when we saw where the swelling was. If someone had swelling in his cheeks, we said, "Oh, you only have twenty-four hours to go." We had seen the harbingers of death all too frequently. We didn't try to comfort each other.

On May 5, I felt swelling in my eye-well. I knew I had very little time left. I lay down on my bunk. By this time, because of the number of deaths in the camp, the barracks were emptying of prisoners and I was alone on the bunk. I sunk into a *mussulman* state. I was barely conscious of the things going on around me. I had no hunger; I had no thirst. It felt like being in a semi-conscious coma.

There was a lot of activity going on in the barracks, noises and prisoners running around. I didn't know why, but the German officers had left. Prisoners were talking but I didn't take any of it in. There was an excitement in the air, but I ignored it. I just wanted to lay there quietly, undisturbed.

Then somebody yelled out, "The Russians broke into the bakery! There's bread!"

At hearing the word "bread," I was somehow revived. I forced myself to get up. When I arrived at the bakery, I was told, "It's all gone. There isn't any more bread." But I was up and for some reason, I was still alive. I should have been dead already. I went back to my bunk and lay there as before and ignored everyone. The day wore on and gradually changed from day into evening. Whatever was going on around me made little sense to me. The sound was like a bunch of flies buzzing around my head. I knew I was in the final *mussulman* stages. I wasn't aware of how I was acting, nor did I care. Nobody else cared, either.

Sometime during the night of May 5, I heard loud explosions. But they didn't signify anything to me. I didn't know where the explosions came from or who set them off. Later, I was told that the explosions came from the tunnel; the one Commander Ganz wanted us to run into "for our own safety." By declining Ganz' fake offer, we actually saved our own lives.

The next morning, May 6, 1945, there was more noise and excited activity. Somebody came running into the barrack shouting, "The Americans are here! The Americans are in the camp!" Ebensee had been liberated.

I didn't move from my bunk. Americans in the camp didn't have meaning for me. I sensed the excitement, but I couldn't respond to it, physically, mentally or emotionally. I heard happy yelling and screaming, signaling good news, but how does a dying person respond to good news? I had no emotions; I wanted only to stay in my bunk with my eyes closed. Breathing was all I could do.

I found out later that the Americans who arrived in Ebensee were a very small group, a patrol unit. They didn't have any food or supplies with them but when they saw the state of the camp their hearts went out to the starving people. In town, they found warehouses full of food. They brought cans of pork and beans back to camp and gave instructions for the food to be prepared and fed to the prisoners. Then they left.

About noon, I heard the call to eat. When I heard there was food, I again came to life. To be resurrected by the word "food" was amazing. Somehow I mustered the energy, got up and stood in line holding my dish and spoon, waiting my turn.

I heard about the Americans but I never saw them. I didn't know where this food had come from. Everything in the camp seemed to be the same except there weren't any German SS around. We lined up in the same concentration camp way. I wasn't thinking like a newly freed person. *Kapos* were still yelling at us. I was still in the camp starving but receiving a miracle portion of unexpected food. In my mind, I was still fighting for survival. I didn't know anything about liberation or freedom.

While waiting in line, I had a heightened sense of anxiety. I saw people walking by with dishes full of food. I was angry and jealous. I worried there wouldn't be enough left for me by the time I got to the kettle. Food was of primary importance for me, not freedom. I was so weak my knees were wobbling. I was visibly shaking.

A short time before the wondrous call for food, I was nearly starved to death. Now I was standing in line getting an unbelievable portion of food.

When it was my turn, I had no problems getting a good portion size. This time I was given a full scoop from the bottom of the kettle. I saw immediately that it wasn't the usual thin, watery soup. It wasn't soup at all. It was thick, steaming, full of meat and beans. My eyes popped open wide. I couldn't believe what I saw. I hadn't seen food like this in years. This food was glorious, big, fat, hot wonderful stuff.

I knew that I should eat slowly and carefully. Chew and digest. As a rule in the camps, we didn't eat our food quickly. We tried to take our time chewing, making the meal last for as long as we were allowed. This was all we were given: We had to make each bite count.

We had discussions among us that if we ever got food again, how carefully we would eat it. But all of this talk didn't mean anything. I held my heavy dish of food grateful it was filled to the top. Standing where I was, I swallowed the food ravenously.

Even before I finished this bowl, my thoughts were turned toward getting more. This was a once-in-a-lifetime opportunity. I hoped to get back in line before it was all gone. But that was craziness. We never would have dared getting in line a second time before. Getting caught in line a second time was a big offense. Usually it meant a beating from the *kapo,* maybe resulting in death.

I swallowed quickly without chewing, eating without tasting. My attention was fixed solely on the line. The *kapos* were still running around screaming like they always did. The danger was still present, but the idea of getting more food was irresistible. I took the chance. Carefully, I wiped the bowl clean with my elbow so that it looked dry and unused. I got back in line, trying to make it look like this was my first time. I looked around to see if anybody had seen me or was going to report me, but everybody was so busy eating they didn't notice me. There was plenty more in the kettle, and they readily gave it to me. *This was so easy!*

I was already stuffed from my first bowl. My stomach was bulging and hurting, but my focus was not to satisfy my hunger. I wanted a second portion, just in case I never got food again. This was all a part of the instinctual survival struggle. With a happy heart, I took the full bowl back to my barrack. I sat on the bunk for the rest of the day. I kept the bowl on the floor, watching it carefully. So that no one would see it and want to steal it, I hid it behind my feet. I was going to save it for later. The next meal might not come. I remembered the time in Melk just before our march to Ebensee. The Nazis gave us a wonderful thick soup with noodles but that was the last time we had food for many days. I felt that I had to treasure my second portion.

With my hunger satiated, I was now exhausted, but I didn't dare lie down. Customarily, we were never allowed to lie down in the barrack after a meal. I sat there the whole afternoon but nobody made me get up. Gradually, the dish of food cooled off and developed a thick layer of fat on top.

In the evening, there came a call for more food. Again, I was in a stupor until I heard the word "food." I was confused at first because I didn't know what to do with the food I already had sitting at my feet. I wasn't hungry but I wasn't going to ignore the opportunity to get more food. *What do I do?* I pulled out the dish, saw the layer of fat on top and puzzled. This was a treasure; I couldn't leave it. I skimmed off the fat and threw it on the ground. Quickly I gulped down the cold stew. I wiped the bowl clean and shuffled back outside.

Everyone else was thinking like me, as evidenced by the long line. No one said, "Oh I better not eat more. This is bad for me." We knew we should eat crackers but when starving people are presented with this kind of food, they are powerless to refuse it, nor can they eat slowly in small portions.

The evening food was the same as the afternoon: thick and hot. It was almost sickening to think of eating it at this point. The food from lunch sat like a rock in my stomach. I forced myself to get another steaming bowl. This time I didn't eat it.

By that evening and into the next day, people began to die. They got sick from eating like there was no tomorrow. One moment they were standing and eating; in the next moment they fell to the ground dead. People were running as fast as they could to the latrines. There were people still sitting on the latrines when they died. The others pulled off the dead body and sat down in his place.

The act of kindness from the Americans became a kind of mass killing. Of course, this wasn't their intention, but that is what happened. There were bodies scattered all over the place. What a cruel irony to survive the war, survive starvation and then die from the kindness of others.

Those of us who didn't die immediately developed dysentery. We couldn't hold it even to run to the latrine. There was no digestion process at all, it just poured out of us and ran down our legs. The food acted like poison. There was a horrible stink all around. The bodies lying on the ground were twisted and contorted in death, but everybody ignored them. Nobody bothered to pick them up. I couldn't tell if they died from starvation or the effects of the food that had seemed to be such a miracle, but was wreaking havoc on all of us.

After a while silence fell in the camp. There were no emotions. Nobody cried or talked. We were left entirely alone without instructions or orders. Those of us who were alive were merely living skeletons shuffling around. We didn't understand what was going on, but still, we didn't think about the future. Everything was "just this instant."

All the survivors, without exception, had to throw their pants away. Our pants were already dirty. People had diarrhea and all kinds of problems for years and never washed, but this time they couldn't even keep their pants on. People were naked from the waist down and some walked around totally naked. I, too, had no pants. The only way we got another pair of pants was to pull them off somebody who had died. I found someone still wearing pants. I pulled them off, inspected them, found them satisfactory and put them on. I was still afraid of not wearing the right number, so I ripped the number from the garment. This was my first day of "freedom."

In the meantime, we stayed in our old barracks, which were still filled with stench and louse ridden. Choosing instead to be with a few of my companions outside in the early spring sunshine, I sat down and spent hours picking lice from my uniform.

1945

May 4–5
Ebensee, a subcamp of Mauthausen, is liberated by the U.S. 80th Infantry Division.

July 5
The Central Committee of Liberated Jews in Bavaria is officially established in Munich.

http://www.scholastic.com/teachers/article/chronology-holocaust-late-april-through-july-1945

May-July 1945
17 years old

> Someone from the Red Cross came over
> to me and said, "We're going to take you
> to the hospital."

Chapter 33

The Americans came and went. After they left, the camp descended into total anarchy. The *kapos*, especially the meaner ones, went into hiding. They were afraid the prisoners would take out their vengeance on them for being so cruel. The *kapos* could only be recognized by being fatter than the others. Many were discovered by the prisoners and some were hung or beaten to death with sticks and stones.

I came upon some prisoners who had caught a *kapo* and were in the process of killing him. I didn't even know him but I wanted to participate in the punishment so I picked up a stone to throw at him. The stone felt heavy in my hand. I heaved it forward only to have it plunk down at my feet and I fell down to my knees from the effort. I was too weak to even pick it up again, so I gave up on the idea.

Now, we were liberated. We had food and some of us had survived. The gate to the camp was open, but I didn't dare come close to it. Some people walked right out and I watched them anxiously. *How could they just walk out?* I had no sense of freedom: Liberation didn't mean freedom to me at all. I was afraid of going outside. I stayed right in the camp, living in my barrack and sleeping in my bunk.

In the first three days after liberation, the Americans issued identification cards for former prisoners of concentration camps. They set up tables and we lined up to receive our cards. The identification paper was two pages long with four sides showing our name, fingerprint, where we came from, our number and how long we were in the camp.

Before our liberation, the Jews were kept separate from the other prisoners. After liberation, the Americans put people into barracks by nationality. There was a separate barrack for the French, the Italians and for the Poles. To their way of thinking this was a good idea. However, they put Polish Jews and non-Jewish Poles together. This was a big mistake. We didn't feel comfortable around the Poles and distrusted them because of their prejudice against us and the treatment we received from them in Poland. The Poles kept together and talked of returning to Poland while the Jews were convinced there was nothing in Poland for them and didn't want to go back.

The Red Cross arrived at the camp a few days later, supplying us with bread and farina cereal. I was still sick and near death.

When they searched the barracks, they questioned everyone inside, "Is anybody sick in here?"

There was only one person in my barrack who was sick and that was me. The others pointed toward me and said, "He's sick."

In the dim light from one lamp hanging from the ceiling, I lay quivering in fear on my bunk. I didn't want them finding out I was sick.

Someone from the Red Cross came over to me and said, "We're going to take you to the hospital."

Hearing this I protested, "No! I'm not sick!" I was terrified of going to the hospital. Sick meant death to me. Going to the hospital meant death. The fact that they were from the American Red Cross didn't matter. My reality was a concentration camp reality and it was impossible to change that kind of thinking overnight.

The Red Cross people were nice. They tried to reassure me, but I insisted I wasn't sick. I had heard the statement before, "We are going to take you to the hospital for your own good." But whoever was taken never came back. I didn't care that these were different people. I wasn't reassured one bit. Since they couldn't persuade me, they finally left me alone.

Although the Red Cross supplied us with food, it was never enough to satisfy us. Some enterprising ex-prisoners began to organize themselves into search parties scouting for food in the countryside. They begged for food from the farmers. At first, out of fear, the farmers gave them anything they asked for. Other former prisoners at camp saw the success this group was having, so they went "scouting," too. Soon quite a few were going on these expeditions, but there weren't very many farms around Ebensee, and the farmers soon became overwhelmed.

Each time they saw a group coming they begged off, "We have nothing. We are poor ourselves." This made some ex-prisoners angry, and in a few cases they broke into the farmhouses and stole food or whatever else they felt like taking. There was no law or police around, so they could get away with it.

One such group, when they saw the pickings were scarce, decided to take me along. I looked like a skeleton walking around. I weighed less than sixty pounds and we said that if someone had wanted to, they could shine a light through my stomach and it would be visible on the other side. The local farmers had never seen anybody like me. They were shocked and took pity. "Oh my, my!" they said, and then they gave me some food. The leaders of the group promptly took it away, leaving me just barely enough.*

I was always looking for ways to get more food. There were American troops in the vicinity living in the fields in pup tents and they set up the typical American field kitchens for themselves. An ex-prisoner discovered that they served the food near the camp. He learned that the soldiers lined up three times a day with their mess kits to get their food. After they got their meal, they sat in the fields eating, relaxing and smoking their cigarettes; then they tossed whatever remained into the garbage. He saw them dip their mess kits in hot water and go off.

He told me about it and we got a group together to scope it out. We sat on a little hill overlooking the campground. The soldiers had gone and only the kitchen personnel were left cleaning up. We gathered our strength, ran down the hill and dipped our red dishes into the garbage can. Just then the Americans saw us and chased us. We ran as fast as we could back up the hill. They didn't come after us too far and soon gave up. Out of breath from our expedition, we lay in the field and began picking out what we could find to eat.

Even though we were liberated and we were fed, we wanted more food. We raided the American field kitchens in this particular dash and grab fashion for a number of days. Then we heard in the camp that some charitable American group called Caritas was distributing food packages to ex-prisoners in Linz. This was some distance from Ebensee, but it was worth our while to receive a Red Cross package.

There were some trains running on and off carrying milk, wood and iron in open flat cars. When the train reached Ebensee, it slowed down and sometimes stopped. We found one particular area we could jump on the train. Starting very early in the morning, four or five of us ventured to Linz, not arriving until late in the afternoon. The city had been bombed and we had no idea where to go. Finally, we saw a long line of ex-prisoners indicating that we had found the Caritas people and their truck.

We waited our turn but when we got to the truck, we were told they were running short on food and could only give us one package for two people. This was very disappointing news but we took the package. It was a big, heavy flat carton. We didn't dare open it until we got back to camp later in the afternoon. Sitting on our bunks in the barrack, we were excited to open it up and see what was inside. We opened it very carefully, so as not to attract the attention of others. Inside were all kinds of treasures, a can of corned beef, a can of spam, a package of powdered eggs, some crackers, a small bar of chocolate and four cigarettes in a small package. But now we had a dilemma, how do we divide it? We drew lots and somehow all of us were satisfied with the results. We immediately devoured it. We didn't know what to do with the powdered eggs, but we had a feast anyway.

One day the Polish Jews and non-Jewish Poles received orders to leave the barrack and take our belongings. We lined up outside the barracks in groups of five, in concentration-camp style. We marched out of the camp to the outskirts of town, close to the mountains. We found ourselves in front of two large, two-story brick houses. Jews and Poles split up between the houses and then we were assigned to rooms. There were many large rooms in this house. Inside it was primitive, two-tiered bunks with straw mattresses, hard military pillows and scratchy military blankets. The room I was assigned to had four double bunks. We were assigned two to each bunk. I didn't especially care for my bunkmate. He took up a lot of the room on the mattress. Our new home was called Ebensee Feuer Kogel, or, Peak of Fire.

Although we didn't mix company with the Poles, we saw them bring in women from some other places. I didn't know what was going on but it was obvious there was heavy carousing between the men and the women. The Polish group printed a one-page leaflet and included in the news and announcements was a warning to watch out for venereal disease.

I was free to move around but I was scared. I had no place to go, no one to go to, nor any money for travel. The only food we received was provided in our building but there was nobody of any real authority in charge. Some ex-prisoners took charge of the distribution. Other Jewish survivors went "organizing" in the countryside. I don't know where they went, but they soon came back wearing civilian clothing. One came back proudly sporting tall, black riding boots. To me, it seemed to me they were adjusting to life and took advantage of opportunities. I was frightened and didn't go anywhere. I never used to be afraid of anything, but now I was too scared to leave the building.

Despite having regular meals, I remained skinny. After three or four weeks, I still couldn't gain any weight. Earlier, I had approached the camp doctor with my health issue. He was also a fellow ex-prisoner in Ebensee. I only learned he was a trained medical doctor after liberation. I had changed my mind about going to a hospital and sought him out.

I met him in a courtyard and said, "I'm weak. I can't gain any weight. Everyone is gaining weight, but I'm not. I want to go to the hospital for ex-prisoners."

"You aren't sick enough for me to send you to the hospital," he said. And then he dismissed me. I was disappointed and frustrated with him. He could easily have given me a pass, but he wouldn't do it.

Finally, one guy who knew the ropes said, "There's something wrong with you. You're skin over bones. You need a doctor or a hospital."

"I tried to get a pass for the hospital, but the doctor wouldn't give it to me," I told him. "Besides, I have no idea how to get to a hospital. I don't have any transportation and I don't know anyone who does."

"Don't worry," he said. "Leave it to me. I'll handle it."

One morning he came for me and we went out together on a freight train from Ebensee to Bad Ischl. He took the lead and I followed him unquestionably. We walked down the streets near the railroad station until he found a building with a shingle on the door stating, "Doctor of Internal Medicine is in the House." We climbed the stairs to the second story and entered a large waiting room crowded with people.

"This will take a whole day before I get to see a doctor. Then it will be night, then what will we do? We have no place to stay," I said.

He patted my shoulder. "I'll take care of it," he said. I was still dressed in my concentration camp stripes, but my companion was wearing civilian clothing. He marched to the front of the doctor's office, opened the door, and burst into the room.

The doctor jumped up in shock and anger. "You dare to rush into my office? You weren't called!" he shouted.

"Shut your mouth!" my friend yelled.

I was cowering at the door. My friend pointed back at me and said to the doctor, "You write a permission to send him to a hospital or I'll kill you—I'll kill you on the spot!"

The doctor turned pale. He was well aware of the anarchy running rampant in the town. He looked me over and said, "I don't know who he is; I haven't examined him. How can I send him to the hospital?"

My friend said, "Never mind, he's skinny. Just tell them he's a camp survivor."

The doctor nodded and quickly filled out the papers.

The Altered I

Third from Right Dziunka w/friends–
Jozef'sSister
(Early days in Krakow before the war)

July-October 1945
17 years old

> "I can't remove the dirt, its
> *angewachsen*," I said, meaning dirt that
> cannot be removed because it had grown
> on me.

Chapter 34

W e found the hospital; it was a primitive looking building, brown and dirty. My companion took me to the front desk and handed the nurse the doctor's slip. Gesturing to me, he said, "Take care of him; he needs help." With that he left.

I didn't know what the slip said about me, but the nurse didn't question it. She took a look at my emaciated state and it was enough. I was confused, scared and alone for the first time in an Austrian city. I thought they were all Nazis in this town.

I was put in a big room with other men and directed to get in a hospital bed with clean sheets. This was something new for me; I hadn't been in a bed like this for years. But I was frightened. I was even too afraid to talk to the other men in the room. All I could do was lie there self-conscious of my filthiness. Soon, the nurse brought some food to my bedside. After eating, I slept with one eye open, watching in case anyone would try to steal my clothes.

The next morning after breakfast, they gave me a hospital robe and I was taken to see the doctor. He examined me and asked some questions, then sent me for X-rays. They took some blood tests and then sent me back to bed without further explanation. The next day I was told to get dressed; I was being sent to a different hospital in Alt Ausee.

My new hospital was originally a resort hotel on Lake Traunsee, located in a lovely area, surrounded by rocky mountains. Used for the *Luftwaffe* (German air force) officers during the war, now it was a hospital for tuberculosis patients. I liked it at once and thought it was a nice place. However, when I arrived and saw all the German officers, I became frightened. I didn't dare tell them I was a Polish Jew.

I was given a nice room shared by three other young men, a Yugoslav partisan and two non-German people. Still, I was too afraid to tell anybody I was Jewish. The Yugoslav partisan was a little older than me and very smart. He didn't speak any German, but we could communicate somewhat. No one revealed much about themselves, where we had been during the war or what happened to us. Periodically, the nurses would come in the room and perform various tests on us.

Patients too sick to leave their beds were fed in their rooms, but the ambulatory patients took meals downstairs in a big dining room overlooking the lake. The food was served on china plates with real knives and forks. This was really something new, as I hadn't seen plates and silverware for years.

Most patients were dressed in their Air Force uniforms. I had mixed feelings. This was a nice place and I was treated well, but a Jew surrounded by German officers couldn't feel comfortable. When people asked who I was in polite conversation, I told them I was Polish. I used my real name, certainly not a Polish name, but nobody questioned it. I told them my parents were German and my father was a German from Austria.

The next day they sent me down for more X-rays, a medical examination, plus a slew of tests. The doctor was a friendly, former *Luftwaffe* officer. I sat on an examining table and he pulled apart my robe. I carefully hid my circumcision from view—my evidence of being a Jew—although he was mainly concerned with my chest area. After my examination, I was told I had had tuberculosis at some point because there was a TB scar on my upper left lung. He didn't know if it was active or not. He said that they were going to observe it for a few weeks and take periodic pictures to look for any changes. In the meantime, I was staying in the hospital, relaxing and enjoying it.

I had festering sores on my legs and feet, but the nurses took good care of them. Once, while the nurse was examining my feet, she noticed how filthy they were from dirt that hadn't been washed off in years.

She became irritated saying, "You have to take a hot bath and clean it off right now! You can't go back to bed dirty like that!"

I looked at my feet in guilty submission and said nothing. She took me to a room where there was a bath tub and left me there to get clean. I washed and scrubbed as hard as I could, but when she came back and looked at my feet she said in dissatisfaction, "They are just as dirty as they were before."

"I can't remove the dirt, its *angewachsen*," I said, meaning dirt that cannot be removed because it had grown on me.

Pointing her finger down at me, she said in a stern voice, "Never mind 'grown.' You clean it up or you will never get out of here." She handed me steel brushes, and in a threatening voice said, "You clean it up, and if you don't, I'll do it for you."

With that threat ringing in my ears, I worked on it scrupulously. She was formidable and I knew she would make good on her promises. I scrubbed and scrubbed until my skin was scratched in some places. She came back, took a quick look at them and said, "They are still dirty, but they are better than before." She let me go back to my room.

At least now I was finally rid of lice. It was a relief to sleep at night without them crawling on me. My hair began to grow, too, but I still had the *Lousestrasse* in the center.

I began to concentrate on getting as much food as possible. In addition to my three, good meals a day, I took the remaining food lying outside sick or dying patients' rooms. Each time I went to the bathroom, whether I had to use it or not, I saw food left out on trays. I couldn't comprehend throwing food away. Whether I was hungry or not, I had to eat it. From my point of view, it was almost like seeing money on the street and not picking it up. I would scoop up the pea paste with my hands and eat it. I did the same thing on the return trip to my room. I made several trips before the nurses took the food away completely. Gradually, I gained weight.

Every Monday, the nurses took me to be weighed and each time they told me how much I had gained. If I gained weight, I was so proud and pleased with myself. Gaining weight was a victory for me, proving that I had survived. In my room I had two hardwood chairs and a wood table. I never sat in the chairs because I had no meat, no cushion, just bones sticking out. As I started filling out, I could sit in those chairs somewhat comfortably. I hit a record fourteen pounds in one week. This was quite an achievement. After that record, gaining any less was a disappointment to me. My face began to fill out, but the left side was bigger than the right side. I was haywire somehow.

At the entrance to the hospital restaurant, there was a typewritten menu on display. One day, I noticed there was a mention of me: "There is a special ration of two ounces of milk for Jozef Kempler." Fresh milk was unheard of, but, because I needed the extra nutrition, they had made an unusual arrangement for me. The nurse gave me a small glass every day, but I couldn't drink it. Since early childhood, I gagged on milk and even if I was starving, I couldn't drink it. Each time the nurse brought it to me I traded it after she left.

Time was passing. I was gaining weight and tests showed my TB had not changed. The scar on my lungs was possibly from having TB in one of the camps, but it went away. However, I developed problems with a rapid heartbeat. The doctors couldn't slow it down. They gave me a fraction of a green-colored pill. I have no idea what it was, though I took it a few times a week. The doctors eventually stopped giving it to me after they saw that my heart, although rapid, was normal.

Now early August, the kid in the bed next to me read in the newspaper that the Americans dropped an atomic bomb on Hiroshima, Japan. I had never heard anything like this, but the damage described made an impact on me. Soon after the bomb fell, Japan surrendered and the war ended.

Meanwhile, the hospital notified some officials in town that they had a Polish survivor. One day I received a message to report to an office in Bad Ischl for repatriation to Poland. It was mandatory that I report. When I arrived at the office, I was terrified. In my opinion, the thought of going back to Poland was like being told to go back into the concentration camp.

I confessed, "I'm Jewish. Nobody is there for me. I have no one and I don't want to go back."

The man said, "By law, as a Pole you have to be repatriated. All Polish citizens have to go back."

"I'm not a citizen. I never was a Polish citizen," I countered. I walked out and went back to the hospital feeling free and relieved.

One day a friend of mine came to see me. He was scheduled to go on the immigration to Palestine with a program called the *Aliya Bet* or immigration B.

"I had to find you before I go," he said. "I couldn't leave until I confessed something to you."

My curiosity was aroused and he had my full attention.

"Do you remember that night you left your bread with me to watch for you while you were gone?" he said. I nodded dumbly as he continued. "And when you came back, I told you that I didn't know what happened to it, that it was just gone?"

"Yes, I remember," I said. In truth, I hadn't remembered the incident until he mentioned it. Waving him off I said, "It was a horrible thing, don't remind me."

Hesitating for a brief moment, he looked me square in the face and said, "Jozef, I was the one who stole the bread."

"It was you?" I felt betrayed; I thought he was my friend.

"I couldn't take the temptation," he said. "I was so hungry I ate it." His confession now out of the way, he became visibly relaxed, "I couldn't leave for Palestine until I told you the truth. Can you forgive me?"

I felt sorry for him. Stealing bread was such a deplorable crime and he had to go through much effort to find me to clear his conscience before he left. I thought he must have really gone through an ordeal.

"Of course, I forgive you." I understood the temptation he had faced. What I didn't understand was why he had to confess, or how his conscience worked, but it must have been really bothering him. I wouldn't have admitted it to anybody if I had done it. I guess he had a more sensitive conscience.

Soon after his visit, I was allowed to leave the hospital for a short period of time. This was the first time I had been outside. I decided to take a little walk around this pretty town and explore it.

I had no other clothing but my prison stripes. I was weak and unstable on my feet. I found a broken branch from a tree and used it to support myself. Slowly, I walked up a hilly street with a few houses on either side. I was panting hard and struggling to catch my breath. When I reached the top of the hill, I took a moment and looked ahead to the street down below where I spied two children, small boys about seven or eight years old. They were dressed in *lederhosen*, the typical Austrian fashion and playing a game. I stopped short in complete surprise. There are children alive in the world? How is this possible? Where did these children come from?

The boys, as if sensing me watching them, turned and appraised me in my prison garb clutching onto a tree branch for stability and huffing and puffing for breath. They shouted out at me, *"Geh weg du lousbube!"* "Go away you lousy boy!" They came running toward me as if to chase me away. I became ashamed, scared and surprised by their actions. I wondered how they had survived. I turned around and hobbled back to the hospital as fast as I could.

Every week or two, they sent some of the recovered Luftwaffe patients to Bad Ischl to be "de-Nazified." One day, I was told that with the next release of patients, which was set for the following week, I would be discharged from the hospital with them. I was surprised and disappointed by this news. I wasn't anxious to go back to Ebensee. Here I had my own bed with white sheets and plenty of food. One roommate had left leaving only two other people in the room. I didn't look forward to returning to the crowded room in Ebensee at Feuer Kogel.

I was given a pair of civilian pants, handed down from the hospital, a German *Luftwaffe* jacket and a pair of old leather shoes. I had no other belongings. My hair, once close-shaven with a bare looking strip down the middle, had grown back full and curly.

The time came for me to leave. I said good-bye to my two roommates and was loaded with a bunch of *Luftwaffe* officers onto a truck going to Bad Ausee. Once there, we boarded a train for the short trip to Bad Ischl. I followed the officers, knowing they knew where to go. We came to a building with a sign on the door, "*Entlassungzenter*," meaning Discharge Center. They tromped upstairs and I marched in like I was one of them. We entered a room full of German soldiers wearing various uniforms of rank and station.

As I sat in the waiting room, the soldiers were called in one by one for the "de-Nazification." Each one presented their papers at the desk. I didn't have any papers. I asked the man in charge what I should do. He said, "Wait. You'll be seen when your turn comes." After the soldiers went into the office they came out with happy faces. They carried money, train tickets and ration cards. Now they were free from any accusations of being called a Nazi. By late afternoon all the German officers had been seen. Now the man at the desk asked me for my papers.

"I have no papers; I wasn't a soldier," I told him.

"You can go," he said, waving me along. "You don't need to be de-Nazified." I hesitated, not knowing what to do. Seeing me still standing there he said, "Go now, you can go home. You're free."

That was it? That is all he had to say? I felt cheated and said, "Can I have tickets and money like the other people?"

"No, there is nothing for you." He continued to busy himself shuffling papers on his desk.

"How am I gonna get back? I have no money, nothing," I persisted.

After taking a deep breath he replied, "*Es tut mir leid. Ich kann nicths fur sie machen.*" "I'm sorry. I can't do anything for you." He sent me away empty-handed.

I felt lost, rejected by everybody. Somehow I made my own way to Ebensee, but it was difficult. When I arrived at Feuer Kogel, the ex-prisoners camp, it was evening. I noticed a lot of changes. There was a desk at the entrance with a woman sitting behind it.

When I approached her, she asked, "What can I do for you?"

"I'm from here. I was in the hospital and I came back. I'm one of the survivors," I said.

She looked at me closely. "Let me see your papers," she requested.

All I had was my identification card that had been issued when I was liberated months prior. I handed it to her.

"OK," she said, "Where is your release paper from the hospital."

"I never received release papers from the hospital," I said.

"Well," she said, "You can't come here. How do we know you didn't escape? We can't accept you here without papers."

I was beside myself, sick with worry and exhaustion. "What do I do?" I wailed. Austrians didn't recognize me; my own camp now didn't recognize me. "Every place I go, I'm not welcome. I'm lost," I cried. When I was in the concentration camp they told me everything they wanted me to do. Now it was a total reversal; I had to figure out how to function on my own. I didn't have any money or ration cards. I had nowhere to sleep. I continued to plead with her, "I can't go back; it's too late now."

Taking a look at my forlorn, misshapen face, she said, "I'll let you stay here tonight. Have you eaten?" I shook my head.

"No? OK, I'll give you something to eat, but you can't stay with the rest of the people. How do we know you aren't infected by some sort of disease?" she said.

She brought a small cot out to the hallway. Without a word, I sat down on it to eat some soup and bread.

The next morning someone handed me a round-trip train pass. I went all the way back to Alt Ausee to the hospital. I explained to the military people in charge that I hadn't been accepted back in my camp and why. After a long runaround, I was told, "We don't have standard papers for people like you." After seeing I wouldn't let up, they typed up a release document showing my medical condition. I made my way back to Ebensee, presented my paperwork and was admitted to the camp.

I was assigned to a large room with about fifteen other people. I didn't know anyone, but now I had a place to stay with my own bunk and I was provided a small monetary allowance. After exploring the building area, I realized I didn't recognize the place any longer. Feuer Kogel had transformed during my absence. Everyone was dressed in fancy clothing and they looked well fed. Some apparently had moved out and had apartments in town. Some didn't even bother to avail themselves of the food provided in the camp.

I developed friendships with some kids about my age. We were free to go anyplace we wanted to go. One kid told me there was a movie house in Gmunden. This city was the last stop in the death march before reaching Ebensee, I remembered. Now I was traveling there for entertainment. So some of us took a train and went to the movies to see a dumb comedy. Regardless, this was special to me because it was the first movie I had seen since leaving Krakow. Afterward, we went to a pub called a *kneipe*. The only beverage available at that time was beer, good, cheap and plentiful. I had sipped beer as a small child, but never had my own glass. This was the first time I had my own beer.

We had to leave if we wanted to make the train back to Ebensee, but my legs were so heavy I could barely walk. We laughed and stumbled toward the train station.

"The beer doesn't go to the head," someone said, "it goes to the legs!"

This was October, 1945. I was seventeen years old. Liberation was less than six months old and I had escaped a potentially dreadful death. For the first time, just from a movie and a few beers, I felt free.

The Altered I

Anita Laub

November 1945
17 years old

The two men faced each other. One said, "*Amchu*?" This was a secret word used by the Jews during the war to identify themselves to each other.

Chapter 35

After we became used to the fact that we had survived, the next big question arose, "Who else was left?" We asked the survivors whom we met, "What camp were you in?" or, "Did you know anyone by the name of …?" and, "My name (surname) is …; did you know anyone by that name?" Once we heard the names of the camps other survivors were in, we had a complete understanding of what they went through during the war. However, the conversation was never about our own family or their family. This was not only to protect our own emotions, but to protect the emotions of others, as well. Most of us didn't have families left after the war. Asking about their family would have been in poor taste and not a subject for polite conversation.

People were looking for any surviving members of their families, but in most cases they didn't find anybody. I knew my father was dead and assumed both Mamusia and Babcia were dead when I found out their ghetto had been liquidated in September, 1943, but I didn't know about Dolek or Dziunka. Later, I found out Renata had been sent away from Plaszow with many other women to Stutthof, in northern Germany. The SS took the female prisoners, all women as far as I know, to the seaport and loaded them onto two ships. When the ships were some distance out to sea, the SS sank them. Nobody survived.

One survivor I met said, "Oh yes, I knew your brother in Gusen; he's alive." But when I asked where Dolek was, he replied that he didn't have any idea where he was now. Whenever I ran into someone who had been in Gusen, I asked about Dolek Kempler. Another ex-prisoner told me he knew him but that he had died in Gusen of typhus. When we were separated that day in Mauthausen, I didn't know he went to Gusen, but now I had talked with two Gusen survivors who claimed to know him. I harbored no hope of finding him alive.

I also found some old family friends from Krakow, the Schiff's. They were on their way to Bindermichl, a displaced persons camp outside the town of Linz. They said if I needed a place to stay, I should look them up there.

These days, people were moving around a lot. Large transports were organized by the military authorities to send people back to their country of origin. This was easy to do if someone wanted to get back to his or her country. All you had to do was arrive at the assembly place and you would be sent back without question. There were many stories about enterprising characters, mostly Polish Jews, who traveled back and forth illegally between Austria and Poland smuggling things.

These characters had a route going from Poland to Austria through Czechoslovakia. When caught, they lied about where they were going. Still the Czech authorities managed to arrest some of them and put them in jail. I heard one such story. One ex-prisoner, who was arrested, claimed to be Greek, but was really a Polish Jew. The Czech authorities said, "We have another Greek in jail. Let's see if they can communicate." They brought the prisoner out and had the two men confront each other. They thought this would prove he wasn't who he said he was.

The two men faced each other. One said, "*Amchu?*" This was a secret word used by the Jews during the war to identify themselves to each other. *Amchu* in Hebrew literally means "of your nation."

When the Greek man heard this question, he smiled. Then in a clear, strong voice he affirmed, "*Amchu!*" Turning to the Czech authorities he said, "Yes, he's a Greek." Both were released.

I met a Jewish survivor who moved between Poland and Austria. I found out that he was traveling from Krakow. I wondered if by some chance he would have come across Dziunka and Jack. I introduced myself and asked him the usual question, "Do you know Dziunka Laub?"

"Your sister and her husband are in Krakow, definitely." He was so positive about it. He saw them just a few days before he left Krakow and he knew both of their names. I now had positive identification that my sister was alive and living in Krakow. I had always been very close to her. She was my only surviving family and I was anxious to leave right away and find her.

There was a transport to Poland leaving out of Linz. I left Ebensee without telling anybody what I was doing or where I was going. I carried an old, small, empty suitcase and left for Linz with no intention of ever going back to the Feuer Kogel camp. First, though, I traveled to Bindermichl, just outside of Linz, to see my friends the Schiffs. They lived in a big multi-storied structure where the refugees were housed. As a survivor, and with my release papers from Ebensee, I was allowed to register in the camp and get my rations. I moved in with the Schiff's into a tiny room of their apartment.

Later, toward evening time, I went to the bus station to inquire about transportation to Poland. Near the bus station was an open field. When I arrived, the field was completely filled with people living out doors. To me it was like a scene out of a horror movie. For days people had been waiting here for a train to Poland. They were sitting in groups huddled near open fires. I meandered among them and identified Polish couples and families with children, but I didn't see any Jews. These were resettling Poles desiring to go back to their homes, perhaps to locate their families or any others who might be waiting for them. These were not concentration camp people.

As a Jew, I was suspicious of Poles and didn't feel safe among them. I was determined not to go to Poland with this crowd. I felt discouraged and didn't know what I should do next. *Do I wait for a different transport? Maybe the Jewish traveler I spoke to was wrong about Dziunka. Maybe she wasn't in Poland after all, and if I go there, I will just be alone.*

Beginning in November, 1945, I resigned myself to stay with the Schiff's in Bindermichl. The displaced persons camp had friendly people and I made a friend or two. However, there was nothing structured or organized in this camp, and as a result, I had a lot of time on my hands. I took the bus to Linz a few times, but since the city had been bombed out there was little to do; I felt bored and restless. One day, while in camp, I found an old book titled, *How to Learn English.* I spent hours every day learning this new language.

While in Linz, I met another traveling survivor. I asked all the usual questions about Dziunka, and to my happy surprise, found out he had seen my sister. "Except," he said, "she is in Germany not Krakow. I know for sure she's in Germany; I just saw her a few days ago. She's in a camp, but I don't remember which one." Seeing my disappointment, he continued, "I'm going back to Germany. You write a letter, and I'll take it with me. When I see her, I'll give it to her."

There were a number of displaced persons camps in Germany. I simply addressed my letter to Judyta (Polish for Dziunka) Laub *Irgendwo Im Deutschland*, meaning Dziunka Laub Someplace in Germany. I gave it to him and he left. I wasn't sure what would happen.

About two weeks later, very early in the morning, I was still sleeping when *Pan* Schiff tiptoed into my room. He woke me up and whispered, "You should prepare yourself for a surprise." I was still sleepy and didn't know what he was talking about. Behind him through the open doorway, I could see a strange woman wearing bedraggled clothing with a blanket over her head. She burst suddenly into the room.

"Joziu!" she cried out. At once I recognized it was Dziunka. I bolted up from the bed in utter amazement. I was speechless for a while. She was crying and babbling for a long time. I sat back; I couldn't say anything. Finally I recovered my voice and we began to talk.

"How did you find me?" I asked her.

"A man was asking for Judyta Laub in Landsberg; he said he had a letter for her." Smiling at me now, she said, "He gave me your letter!"

I was stunned. The man actually delivered my letter to her as he said he would. Dziunka told me that he went to the *ver pflegungsamt,* a provision office where ration cards were issued to all residents of the camp and they have a complete list of names.

The survivor arrived at the provision office and he asked if there was anyone in the camp called Judyta Laub. One woman answered, "I'm Judyta Laub." He gave her the letter and told her the story of how he met me. She read the letter and almost fainted. She told him she wanted to travel to Linz immediately to collect me, but there was no official way of going from Germany to Austria. She couldn't acquire a pass since the American military didn't allow movement from one country to another.

Dziunka had a friend in Landsberg named Stapler, a man who was madly in love with her. He would do anything for her. Together, they inquired into how to get to Austria. They learned that the only way to get there was by crossing a big river bordering Germany and Austria. She took a risk, but she was anxious to see me, and decided to attempt it. Stapler wouldn't let her go alone and insisted he would accompany her. Together they traveled by train from Landsberg to a town near the river. Under the cover of night, they waded into the river and attempted to swim across.

Somehow, in the turbulent water, they were separated. Stapler couldn't get across and turned back toward shore and Germany. Dziunka succeeded in the crossing and made her way by train to Linz, then to Bindermichl. As she told me her tale, I concluded that finding me had been a miracle.

We had so much to catch up on. Dziunka told me Jack was still in Poland. I wanted to know how they survived the war. She told me when she was in the town of Tarnow during the final *Aktion* in the ghetto, a Polish family took them in and hid them. The family that risked their lives was called Banach. Jack taught music to the daughters. They knew Dziunka for only three months, but offered to hide her and Jack in their small city apartment. There were only two rooms, a bedroom where the family slept, and a kitchen that also doubled as a living room. In the bedroom was a large European-style wardrobe. Jack and Dziunka hid in that wardrobe by moving it slightly away from the wall during the day so Dziunka and Jack could stand. During the night the wardrobe was moved further away so they could lie down behind it, covered over with down comforters. During the day they had to remain quiet, for fear they would be found.

The price for hiding Jews was high; it meant a death sentence for everyone involved. Dziunka thought the war would end very soon, but as it turned out, they hid in the wardrobe for two years and three months. "Joziu," she said, "those people saved us, and I didn't really know who they were." She shook her head in disbelief, "They were just an old man and his family. He was always reading the Bible. They called themselves 'Searchers into the Holy Scriptures.' Jack and I thought he was crazy or something."

"I never heard of a group called by that name." I said, "I don't know who they are."

Now that she had found me, we both wanted to go back to Germany. Someone suggested we could go to Germany by train. We checked the schedule and the next day we got on the train heading west. Because it was packed with people, we had to stand. We arrived at a border town on the Austrian side. The train stopped for a long time. Two American military police came on board. They spoke German and questioned every single person one by one, inspecting everyone's papers. Then they came to Dziunka and me. We didn't have papers. We explained to them that we were going to Germany to a camp and we had just found each other. They didn't bother hearing the rest of our story. We didn't have papers, so they shuttled us off the train onto a military truck. They put a few more stragglers on the truck and then drove us to a building a little ways off.

Inside, the Americans were interrogating people one by one. When our turn came, they wanted to know not who we were, but where we were going. Dziunka said, "To Germany."

"Where are you coming from?"

"From Linz." she replied curtly.

"You can't go to Germany; you have to go back to Linz." The interrogator gave us a stern look, "Wait here until you are called."

Eventually they put us on a truck and drove us back to the train station, but by that time there were no trains going back to Linz. We had nothing to do but sit in the station. We talked to some people who knew how to get around. "If you want to go to Germany, you tell them 'I want to go to Austria.' They have no idea where you came from. People are traveling both ways and they are all questioned in that one big room. So, you tell them the opposite direction you want to go." Apparently, the situation was confusing even to the Americans. Nobody, it seemed, knew what was going on, and it was disorganized. Dziunka and I decided to follow the advice we were given. We were both exhausted from our ordeal. We found a large table in the station and soon both of us fell fast asleep on top of it.

The next morning the train going in the westward direction came. Again, it was crowded with people. We crammed in and some people made room for us. Striking up a conversation with one person, Dziunka told him that we were trying to get to Germany, but were told to tell the authorities we were going to Austria. Our fellow traveler said, "Yes, if you tell them you are going to Austria they'll send you to Germany; that is correct, but they will take you off the train to question you and you will have to go through the same procedure as last night." Dismayed, Dziunka and I looked at each other not knowing what do at this point. Would we ever make it across the border?

Another person began to advise us, "So here's what you do: When the Americans come to inspect again, go to the bathroom and lock the door. We'll tell them there's nobody in there."

"Do you think it could work?" I asked Dziunka.

"Well, we've got to try. Otherwise we'll never get to Landsberg," she said. The train left the station and a short time later it stopped at the same border town on the Austrian side. Just before it stopped, Dziunka and I made our way back to the toilet and locked the door. People crowded in tightly in front of the toilet door. Soon, we felt the train slow down and stop. We heard voices as the Americans were making their way through the car. When they came to our end of the car, they banged loudly on the toilet door.

"*Niemanda,*" someone said.

Convinced no one was in the toilet the Americans left and the train started up again. At Salzburg the train stopped. There was yelling from the outside, "Everybody off! The train doesn't go any further."

We didn't know where to go or what to do. We were directed to the refugee transient center. Upon arriving, we saw it was full of people in a big room with bunks. Apparently, all the people were waiting to go to Germany officially. Some people had waited for days for organized transports. We had to register and tell them where we were going. They assigned us to bunks. Neither one of us was prepared for this delay.

One of the refugees, an organizer, approached us. He told us we had to wait our turn to leave. Dziunka was an organizer herself and knew how to get things done. She had a bag with her, one she had carried all the way from Landsberg. In it she had a big pack of loose cigarettes. These were German cigarettes and very valuable.

Opening her bag she said, "What can we arrange? I have cigarettes; how about a hundred cigarettes. Will that get us out of here quickly?"

He took the bait. "I can arrange it," he said. He fixed it so we were moved ahead on the list and we boarded the next train to Germany.

The train was in bad shape; its windows were broken. We rode for several hours before arriving in the Munich train station where we would change trains for Landsberg. Upon arriving, I saw that the station had been bombed out, the structure above was twisted ruins. Passengers were desperate to get off the train: They were crowding all the doors. Because of the crush, we couldn't get off and were in danger of not getting to the ticket office in time to buy our tickets and make our connection. There was so much noise, screaming, shouting, pushing and shoving. Finally, we climbed out through one of the broken windows. We made our way to the ticket office and purchased tickets to Landsberg. In Kaufering, we changed trains again.

Finally, we arrived at our destination. We marched up the hill to the displaced persons camp in Landsberg, my new home.

Genia, Jozef and Pola Fogelman, Aug.29, 1946
in Prien am Chiemsee, Germany
5pm, Teaching English

The first time I truly sensed I was actually free was early in the winter of 1945.

Chapter 36

As we approached the displaced persons camp, I could see a fence around it and a guardhouse. We had to identify ourselves and show that Dziunka was a resident of Landsberg. Beyond the guardhouse, there were clusters of two- and three-story buildings used as a *kaserne,* or soldiers' dwellings. I followed Dziunka to block No. 18 and climbed the stairway to a long corridor. There were rooms on one side, and when I looked through the open doorways I saw they were filled with different families separated for privacy by hanging blankets. My heart dropped in disappointment at yet another unpleasant camp.

Dziunka led me to a door at the end of the corridor to room No. 91. She opened the door to a small room. There were two bunk beds with a small nightstand in between. My earlier disappointment evaporated into elation. This was a private room. Dziunka had a glass wardrobe on one side of the room. On the other side of the room was a connecting door to what I assumed was another room. On the nightstand was an electric hot plate. There was no heat source and it was a basic room, but I was happy to have it just to ourselves.

We went to eat in the large cafeteria where food was served once a day. After dinner, Dziunka took me to meet her friends and show me off. Dziunka knew how to operate in the world and I relied on her to show me what to do. I was now seventeen but I didn't know how to function in life any more than I had at thirteen. My knowledge was how to survive in a concentration camp and I was ill prepared for real life.

I started out the first few months—even the first couple of years after the war—as a relatively carefree person. I learned later that I was in remission from the trauma. For me, the idea of being alive and free was exhilarating. In those early days, I was always laughing and happy. Despite living in old, cold, crowded military quarters, it seemed that the young people around me felt the same way.

The first time I truly sensed I was actually free was early in the winter of 1945. One night, in particular, was extremely cold and miserable with sleet. Suddenly, I realized I didn't have to go outside. There was no one there to force me out. I was amazed by that discovery. Back in the concentration camps, I had no choice; the weather was the weather and I still had to go outside and work no matter what. Now, the thought materialized that I had a choice; that I was free to do what I wanted.

In Landsberg, Dziunka held a good position with many connections. She was working in an office preparing and filing the food registration cards. They were handed out to the newcomers in the camp, mostly Jewish survivors from various countries. Because of Dziunka's official position, we had excellent quarters and enough food to eat. We were beginning to have a "normal" life.

The Landsberg Displaced Persons Camp was well organized. Among other things, there were schools provided by the Organization for Rehabilitation and Training or ORT, an American organization. This organization was working throughout Germany in displaced persons camps offering free training to whoever wanted it. The training was in practical trades such as metal work and car repair. There was a radio course taught by two German men from town. One taught practical lab work, while the other taught theory. This course appealed to me, so I signed up for it. There were about twenty-five young men enrolled in the course. One young man named Leon Sperling became a close friend. He was several years older than me and brilliant. Working together created a friendly atmosphere. There was no competition, but rather we tried to help and encourage each other. We were all very eager to learn.

In addition to the radio course, three evenings a week, I attended a voluntary English class run by workers of UNRRA (United Nations Relief and Rehabilitation Association).

Of all the young people I came to know in Landsberg, I knew absolutely nothing about where they came from or what happened to their families during the war. As young people, our lives were very busy with activities, but we laughed and had big smiles on our faces. Nobody brought up the past or even wanted to talk about it. This struck me as odd later. Looking at the older people in the camp, I saw that many of them were miserable and downhearted.

Gradually, it turned into spring; the weather became milder and warmer. People were looking forward to getting out of the cramped buildings to enjoy the fresh spring air. A number of women now pushed around baby carriages with small children in tow. This became a very familiar sight in the displaced persons camp. People were eager to get married and start families again. I couldn't imagine how people could function normally and take care of children under such conditions. But starting a new family was considered a victory over Germany, which had attempted to wipe them out, especially the children. All the women appeared happy; the children were happy, healthy and well fed.

During this time, Jack remained in Krakow. He was in contact with us infrequently by mail. There was no regular mail service in those days, but we had to check regularly at the mail office to find out if any letters had arrived. All letters were opened and re-sealed with tape that read "Censored by American Authority." Because of the various channels that mail traveled from one country to another, it was unusual to receive correspondence. I didn't have a lot of confidence in the mail service system and I considered receiving a letter from Poland a real achievement for the mail service.

One day, to my surprise, we received a letter from Jack with good news for me. In his letter, he said he ran into my old friend Anita Laub and her family. They had survived the war. Jack wrote to say Anita was very happy to hear I was alive. She wanted me to know that she would write soon. I was excited by the news and couldn't wait for her letter to come.

When the anticipated letter from Anita arrived, she didn't say much about her experiences during the war, what happened to her family or how they had survived. She only wrote that her name had been put on a list, known as Schindler's list. She also wrote that she had gone to block No. 20 in Plaszow searching for me. Nobody knew what had happened to me, so they couldn't tell her where to find me. I realized this was tragic news. If she had found me, perhaps my name would have been on Schindler's list too and I would have avoided all the awful things I had experienced in the camps. We were both alive and all of that was behind us. I was delighted to renew our friendship. I wanted desperately to see her, but it was impossible. She was sixteen now and attending school in Krakow. I wrote her long letters and asked for a picture. She eventually sent one, although I was slightly disappointed because it was only a small, wallet-sized photo.

We kept up our correspondence, which gradually improved with time. She reminisced of our time before the war. She went on extensively about the games we used to play, the stories I used to write. She even re-membered the names of my heroes from the Karl May books I loved to collect and read. I was taken by surprise by all the things she remembered so vividly, things I liked and that were important to me.

The Altered I

Children House in Prien. The Strand Hotel

Early Spring 1946 - January 1947
17 to 18 years old

> This hotel was a different experience
> from my previous displaced persons
> camps. By comparison, I was living in
> complete luxury.

Chapter 37

There was a big bulletin board located near the camp office. On it peopled posted announcements concerning or affecting the inhabitants. Also, hundreds of slips of paper were posted by people looking for their families. In early spring of 1946, I saw an announcement on the bulletin board that I hoped would change the course of my life. Kids under the age of eighteen years old would have an opportunity of going to America. I signed up right away. I knew I was approaching the cut-off age, but when I came to Landsberg, somehow my birth month was recorded as October, not April. This must have happened when I was in the hospital in Alt Ausee and had to obtain my release papers in order to be readmitted to Feuer Kogel. I kept the secret to myself.

Soon, we received extensive instructions on how to proceed. On the assigned day, thirty or so kids assembled at the main office. I said my farewells to Dziunka, who was crying, but it was a happy sort of crying: "I'm so happy you will be going to America before me. I'll miss you terribly, though!"

"I'll write often," I said. "We'll be together soon. You'll see." I wiped the tears from my face, not wanting the other kids to see my emotions so plainly. We were loaded onto the back of a truck. There weren't any seats but we were too excited to sit. Most of the kids were orphans; my friends Genia and her sister, Pola, were there. I was attracted to

Genia, a friendly, light-complected, brown-haired girl. I was glad we could be together on this adventure. I waved good-bye to Dziunka as the truck drove away, bumping down the uneven road. I had no clue where we were heading. I didn't care. It was exhilarating to be on our way someplace new. After a few hours we arrived in Indeldorf, a small town in Germany. We drove past the township into the fields. There stood an ancient cloister where nuns had lived. I assumed they supervised it, but it was empty now in order to accommodate all the kids who were coming in from all over the countryside.

There seemed to be hundreds of kids scrambling off pickup trucks like ours. These were orphan kids, who, after the war, were stranded in Germany. UNRRA arranged to place them in various places throughout southern Germany with the purpose of arranging immigration to America for them. Unless they had family in America willing to take them in, some had to be placed in foster homes.

We were organized and led into a large room furnished as a dining room. Here, we waited for instructions and bed assignments. Since we had to register by nationality and religion, this process took a long time. Finally, I was assigned to a large room furnished with many small beds. Those of us from Landsberg were all Polish Jews, but there were some Jewish children from Hungary from various camps put in with us.

The countryside was pleasant. We were free and encouraged to go out in the fields nearby and occupy ourselves; however, we had to return at the prescribed hour for our meals. We enjoyed wonderful free time in the meantime. I wasn't familiar with many of the other kids from Landsberg. I usually stayed close to Genia. Often, we went off by ourselves into the fields where we lay on the grass in the warm sunshine and talked. I was preparing her for America by teaching her the bit of English I knew.

After about a week or two in Indeldorf, we were sent by train to the town of Prien Am Chiemsee. Prien is located a short distance from Munich and about three hours away from Landsberg. The pretty view distracted me and the trip passed quickly. After arriving in Prien we walked to a small, pleasant town down to the Chiemsee lake shore where we walked on a narrow winding road, alternating between woods and a beautiful lake view. I felt like I was on vacation. We arrived at a large, attractive building. We were led inside into a big dining room. There was a lady in charge wearing an UNRRA uniform. In a loud voice so all could hear, she welcomed us to the *Strandhotel*, the Beach Hotel. She introduced herself as Miss Walvis. She spoke in German but said she was Dutch. Clutched in her hand she had a list of all the kids. Thrown into the mix of Hungarians and Poles were a couple of French girls.

Miss Walvis assigned us to our rooms according to her list, girls on the second floor, boys on the third. Our rooms were all hotel-style rooms: rather small and narrow with two small beds. Once we saw our room, we went downstairs to get our table assignments and wait for dinner. We were each assigned to tables of four.

On the outside wall were glass windows and doors to maximize the lake view. One of the big glass doors in the room led out to a boardwalk to the lake. On one end of the room was the kitchen where several German men and women worked. There was a counter where we lined up, cafeteria-style, to be served. The food was homemade: simple, but good.

We were all young; the age among us ranged between fifteen and eighteen. The sunny weather was beautiful. The Chiemsee was a giant lake, pretty, blue and sparkling. Young people were running around playing on the beach. I wanted to go in the water, but it was too cold for swimming. Everybody was happy and laughing. We almost forgot our past. We had lively chats with each other, but no one exchanged real information about themselves. No matter how we felt inside, we didn't show it outwardly. To the casual observer, and to each other, we were nothing but a cheerful bunch of kids.

This hotel was a different experience from my previous displaced persons camps. By comparison, I was living in complete luxury. I didn't feel anxious to leave for America. There were no obligations; I could come and go as I pleased. I behaved as though I was a child of eleven not a young man of seventeen, fast approaching adulthood.

Instructions came for some of the kids to report to Munich to prepare for departure to America. They were required to undergo medical examinations, consulate investigations and other necessary preparations to qualify for emigration. This process took several weeks. Kids who were approved moved to Munich into a big staging area called *Funkaserne*, a former German military radio installation. There was a guarded fence and wall surrounding it. The only access was at the gate where a watchman stood guard. People stayed here until clearance was given to leave by train to Bremen. Once in Bremen, they again had to wait in a holding area until their scheduled ship to America arrived.

In the meantime, shortly after I had left for Prien, Jack joined

Dziunka in Landsberg. Their own papers for emigration were being processed and they were scheduled to sail to America soon.

During this time, a question from the consulate arose regarding my actual age. They were having trouble locating a birth certificate in Krakow, Poland for a Jozef Kempler and asked me to supply them with it. I wrote to the Jewish community in Krakow explaining my situation. I tried to unravel the confusion regarding my birth name. According to my family history, when my grandmother Knobloch married my grandfather Kempler, the marriage wasn't recognized as legitimate since it was a Jewish ceremony, and my father was, therefore, born with the surname Knobloch. I was also named Knobloch on my birth certificate. This was a confusing situation and not rectified until I was in the third grade when my name was changed to Kempler. I needed my birth certificate proving my age and my identity. My hopes for immigrating to America were hinged on getting it straightened out. I waited a long time without results. I wrote again and finally received an answer: They couldn't find any record of me. The only recourse I had was to go up before a rabbi with two witnesses. The rabbi could then issue a sworn statement about my name and birth date. I assembled the witnesses and the rabbi and it was done.

Despite the setbacks, my name came up to report for the exam in Munich. When I arrived at the consulate, it was crowded with people, all waiting to be processed. One of the American secretaries, who had been handing out papers, came out and asked if anybody there spoke English. I spoke up right away. She filled out multiple questionnaires about me and sent me off for the medical examination. I stripped naked and lined up with a group of other naked men to wait my turn. I was so nervous when it was my turn; my heart was beating hard and fast. Because I had so many setbacks and problems just getting to this point, I thought they were going to disqualify me. The examining doctor was friendly. He looked me over thoroughly and pronounced me "healthy as a fish." This was good. Afterward I went back to Prien, anxiously waiting for the next step.

I was instructed to report to a Catholic hospital in Munich. They took chest X-rays, and afterward I was instructed to return to the consulate a few days later for the results. When I returned, the secretary looked at my papers and coldly announced, "You have a spot on your lung; you can't go." I was struck numb. I was mortified that I would have to stay in Germany. Continuing, she said, "After three months you have to repeat the X-ray and see what the test results are. If you have active TB you can't go." I went back to Prien heartbroken and confused about my health. I didn't know what was wrong with me.

I decided to take matters into my own hands and found a doctor in Munich who offered X-rays. I walked into his office and explained to him that I wanted X-rays of my lungs. He obliged me and found a spot behind my left clavicle. The spot was difficult to see clearly, so he took another X-ray from a different angle but it was still difficult to see if the spot was active or not.

With new X-rays in hand, I marched confidently back to the consulate. I waited once again for my turn. I approached the secretary and said, "Maybe the X-rays weren't clearly visible when they took them; could the doctors examine it again with these new X-rays?"

"Outside X-rays are not acceptable," she said. "You have to wait three months." Again I was dismissed. With my hopes dashed, I went back to Prien to wait but I was very depressed. Would I ever get to America?

Dziunka soon informed me that she and Jack were approved and were leaving for Munich and Bremen. By now, it was mid-October 1946. My clerical error birthday of October 12th had passed. I was no longer qualified for the special youth quota. I had to say my good-byes to everybody at the *Strandhotel* and return to Landsberg. When I arrived back in Landsberg, I felt lost and forlorn.

Before she and Jack departed, Dziunka had arranged to pass her old room on to Stapler, who was now married. "They will be glad to give you a bed, Joziu, as a favor to me."

"Sure," I said, feeling slightly jealous. This was Dziunka and Jack's happy departure for America instead of mine. I couldn't help feeling abandoned. I believed I would never leave Germany.

Jack owned a nice German radio. When I came to visit them in Landsberg, he often had it tuned to a classical music station. He taught me how to understand music better and my long-lasting love for that style of music began. He left it with me and I spent a lot of time listening to it.

Many of my old crowd, including Genia and Pola, had already left Landsberg for America. The only friend I was enamored with now was Lena, a distant relative of Stapler. However, I avoided any real close attachment with her because girls in displaced persons camps, above all things, wanted to get married and have children.

Three months of waiting had passed. I returned to Munich and underwent another X-ray. When the results came in, the same, stern secretary said, "The X-rays are still unclear. We can't tell if your TB is active or not. You can't go. You have to wait three more months." My heart heavy, I returned to Landsberg.

Three months to the day, I rushed to the crowded consulate in Munich. After checking in with the American girl at the desk, I asked for my status. She checked through the files, flipping through until she found mine. She pulled it out, read it and announced coldly, "You are rejected." My blood froze.

"W-what happens now?"

"You have to wait three more months, have another x-ray and return here for the results," she said. This time I returned to Landsberg, sad and negative. What was wrong with me? Why won't they tell me? Do I have an active TB or something else? I felt fine. I wasn't coughing, but I had no way of finding out. I was forced to be patient.

In the meantime Dziunka and Jack had safely arrived in America. Dziunka wrote that she was working for a men's clothing store making alterations on garments. She and Jack shared one small room with a Jewish family in Brooklyn. She encouraged me not to give up hope, and that soon we would be together in a brand-new country.

Every few weeks Dziunka sent a carton of cigarettes. These had a fairly good black market value. I sold them to a man in our building for 200 marks per carton, which he in turn sold for several times that amount. I didn't quibble. From my cigarette sales I now had a small amount of money for movies and trips to Munich.

My food supply was well stocked. Dziunka managed to leave me three additional illegal ration cards. Once a week, I journeyed to the food supply warehouse and received four times the weekly ration of bread, cheese and eggs. I traded my extra rations with German women, the cleaning lady, a math teacher and some others who would do laundry or anything for bread. Later, I was caught and they took my extra ration cards from me but I didn't get into any serious trouble.

The Altered I

Landsberg D.P. Camp I.D.
Resident Card

The SS prisoner exclaimed, "I never did
anything wrong. I'm innocent!" he swore
up and down.

Chapter 38

While biding my time in Landsberg, I was called in to
the office building one day. Some Americans had requested to see me
because I was a registered survivor of Mauthausen. They showed me
photograph albums of SS men and wanted to know if I recognized
anyone. Looking at the photos I identified some men for the Americans. I learned that the Americans arrested hundreds of SS non-
commissioned officers who had served as guards or functionaries in
Mauthausen or other camps and were holding them in Dachau, a short
distance from Munich. The only way the Americans could determine
their guilt or innocence was to travel to displaced persons camps and
locate survivors from these concentration camps who could identify the
SS. If an ex-concentration camp prisoner recognized anyone, they were
to provide evidence during the preliminary procedures yet to be held.

In February 1947, I received an order from the U.S. military
informing me that I had to report on a certain date for the preliminary
procedures. On the set day, I took the train to Munich and then to Dachau and walked back into the former concentration camp. The camp
was guarded by American military police but with my orders in hand, I
was allowed to enter, state my name and endure the procedure of a
barrack assignment. I was assigned to the prosecution witness barracks.

Another barrack, situated behind barbed wire fencing and

guarded, was used to house the defense witnesses. These witnesses were Germans, probably mostly Nazis, who were called to defend their own. I realized then that, if we weren't kept separate, we would have killed each other.

On the prosecution witness side were two barracks with a mess hall, toilets and other buildings. Inside, there must have been more than 100 people. There were two levels of wooden bunks, each with good mattresses, sheets, and blankets. I had to remind myself that this was something different from the concentration camp days.

I didn't know anyone here but I was ready, as usual, to follow orders. In the evening we were called for supper. A surprise awaited us when we entered the mess barrack. We were met by the sight of a five-man orchestra, in the middle of the barrack, playing German melodies. Dinner tables spanned the length of one side of the barrack beneath the windows. The kitchen was on the other side of the room behind the wall. We were assigned, ten men to a table. Then the waiters, dressed in white uniforms, came out carrying plates of food. When they placed them down in front of us, I couldn't believe my eyes. This was food the likes of which I hadn't seen for many years, meat, potatoes and vegetables. Dessert was served with real American coffee or tea. It was a feast. We were served three incredible meals a day—different meals each day— while the orchestra kept us entertained with delightful music. I enjoyed my time here and, along with the others, began to relax.

Before I arrived, I didn't know what to expect during the proceedings. None of the prosecution witnesses talked much to each other at the table. There were different nationalities, but we all spoke German (the only language spoken in the concentration camps). After dinner, there was nothing else to do but sleep. We were given instructions to report to the dining room at 8 a.m. The people in charge assured us that they would wake us up at the prescribed hour. Back in the barrack the lights stayed on until 10 p.m., but I was knocked out tired after the first day and fell into a solid good night's sleep before the lights-out order.

The next day at 8 a.m., we set off toward the dining hall barrack. I sat at the same table as the night before. Soon, the waiters in the white uniforms brought out a fabulous American breakfast: real eggs, ham, bacon—the works! In the middle of the table I noticed a big bowl of canned peach halves. This presented something of a dilemma. We ate family-style and helped ourselves from the bowl. Of course everybody wanted to take as many peaches as they could, but we were careful not to take too many.

Still, each of us suspiciously eyed the others to check how much they were taking. Even though I was careful not to take too many, in my heart I wanted more. To my surprise, as soon as the bowl was empty, the waiters quickly brought out another full bowl of peach halves. This satisfied everyone. We had food in abundance. This was not like the former concentration camp days at all.

A few minutes before 9 a.m., some Americans, all fluent in German, came in. They told us to get ready to leave. They led us to another building, which I called the interrogation hall/barrack. The barrack had been converted into an auditorium with a lighted stage in front. The entire back of the hall was filled with benches where we were directed to sit.

Two American lieutenants instructed us on the interrogation procedure. They were going to bring one SS man out at a time, after which they were going to turn it over to us. If anybody recognized the man or identified him from the questioning and had something to offer, either good or bad, then he had the opportunity to question the prisoner himself. If there was anything to report, there was a special form available to fill out and submit to the Americans. The interrogations then began.

When the first prisoner was brought out, I was amazed at the difference in his appearance. Instead of the proud, crude member of the "master race," he now looked like a beaten, lost and pitiful soul. The lieutenant began questioning the man: "Name? What camps were you from? Where did you serve? Have you ever beaten any prisoner? Did you see any prisoner hit?" The formerly arrogant SS soldier looked completely humble now, his head hanging down. He wasn't even standing at attention. He looked utterly helpless and meek.

Repeating the question he said, "Did I ever beat a prisoner?"

"Of course, I didn't."

"Are you sure?" The lieutenant said.

"Well...maybe a slap."

The lieutenant asked him where he served. If the prisoner mentioned any place in Poland the lieutenant said, "I see. Since you didn't do anything here, we'll send you back to Poland."

All of a sudden, the SS prisoner remembered everything. He knew what would happen to him if he was sent to Poland. They made short shrift of SS in Poland and the German SS would do anything not to be sent there.

The prisoner said, "Yes, there were beatings here."

As the proceedings went on, I learned there were different questions for different people. For example, if the SS prisoner served in Austria or Germany, they couldn't be threatened with being sent to Poland. The U.S. officer may have asked, "What is the name of your widow?" This put the prisoner on the alert that his life was at stake and he'd best answer the questions. Sometimes a prisoner went unrecognized. Those prisoners were taken away and released.

Down in the front seats sat a bunch of big German fellows. They seemed to know more SS people than anybody else in the barrack. I never knew who they were but they were obviously *kapos* or other prisoner functionaries who somehow survived liberation and were now were being used by the Americans as expert eye witnesses. Often they were the first to recognize the former SS men.

The SS prisoner exclaimed, "I never did anything wrong. I'm innocent!" he swore up and down.

Lt. Kohn, one of the two questioning officers, had a secret signal. He bent down to light a cigarette and, while cupping his hands to protect the flame, he looked away briefly from the stage. In that moment one of the expert *kapo* witnesses jumped up on stage and punched the SS man in the stomach. The prisoner began talking. This of course was forbidden behavior but the American officer didn't "officially" see it happen. And since no one in authority saw it, it didn't happen.

Sometimes, during the interrogation, the big ex-*kapo* knew details about the SS man and confirmed them for the questioning officer. Sometimes an SS officer confessed because he didn't want to make it worse for himself by lying. I was still afraid of the *kapos* and never talked to them or even looked them directly in the eyes. They were tough and still very frightening.

This went on the whole day: One by one the prisoners came in, and hour after hour went by. We did have an hour break, at the dining barrack, for lunch with all the trimmings, relaxing to the soothing music of the German and Viennese waltzes performed by the quintet. After lunch, we went back to the interrogation barrack until dinner time. I didn't recognize anybody that day, but a number of others recognized some SS officers and filed reports.

After dinner, back at the barrack, we were more relaxed and wanted to know each other better. These people were rough, smoking, cursing and yelling. Some had alcohol; I considered most of them to be a bunch of rabble. However, there were two men in bunks to my left who were quiet and friendly. They laughed softly, not loud and boisterously, as the rest did. I was attracted to them because they were different. I decided to talk to them. To my amazement they were two Germans who identified themselves as Jehovah's Witnesses. I immediately told them my experience with Jehovah's Witnesses in Melk. The two of them said they were in various camps for years and finally wound up in Mauthausen.

This was the first time I spoke to real, live Jehovah's Witnesses without fear of punishment. The next day, after breakfast, we went to the interrogation barrack and I sat down on the bench next to them. From then on, we were inseparable. They were both older gentlemen, around fifty years of age or so. They told me they didn't volunteer for this, but after being shown the pictures and identifying some of the SS prisoners, they were ordered by the U.S. military to report to Dachau.

The Witness sitting next to me was the older of the two and I could see he was crippled. His left arm was hanging down limply, but he moved it slightly from the elbow down and he could move his fingers a little bit. The right arm seemed to be completely paralyzed: He couldn't lift it and it hung loosely from his frame. I didn't want to offend him and ask what had happened to him. I didn't know anything about Jehovah's Witnesses except they were persecuted; I wanted to ask them questions, but I kept silent. Some days later, the man with the paralyzed arm volunteered the information.

He told me that in the early days in the concentration camps, the SS attempted to break his integrity and to have him join the army. When he refused repeatedly, they tried different methods of inducement, hoping to break down his resolve. Still he refused. One brutal punishment was to hang him on a pole until he gave up or died. Other non-Jehovah's Witnesses were also hung on poles for various offenses, but they were hung by their wrists, tightened with rope, their arms straight up, which lasted approximately two hours. In the case of my new acquaintance and some other Witnesses, the SS hung him up, not by the wrists, but by hanging him by his fingertips with his arms twisted behind his back. Instead of hanging like this for two hours, he was kept hanging for most of the day. At some point he fainted. Thinking him dead, the *kapos* took him down. They left him lying on the ground for the corpse detail to pick him up the next morning.

His spiritual brothers (fellow Jehovah's Witnesses in the camp) knew what was happening to him and sneaked up in the dark, took him back to the barrack and took care of him. They hid him in the barrack and spoon-fed him because he couldn't move his hands or arms. Against all the odds, they revived him. I was told later that if someone was severely hurt, even if he could be revived, he would be killed by the SS because he was considered unfit for work. Nobody I knew had survived this kind of injury. My new Witness friend explained that after he recovered from the brink of death, almost all use of his arms was gone. His fellow brothers arranged for him to get a job in the camp as a painter because he could move only his left hand in an up-and-down motion. I don't know how they managed to care for him or hide him without being discovered or how he could work as a painter. He surely could never accomplish anything. But, because he had people taking care of him, he survived for years in this condition. I had to chuckle, he was a painter like me.

Soon after learning my friend's story, the Americans brought out an SS man who was recognized by my Witness friend. As Lt. Kohn was interrogating him, my friend turned and whispered to me, "This is the guy who hung me on the pole, who hurt and crippled me." Instantly I detested the SS man. Impatiently I sat through the questioning, burning with fury at his incredible cruelty. I couldn't wait until Lt. Kohn was finished with him so my friend could get up and testify against him. Sitting right next to me was the evidence of the SS man's crimes. I was almost shaking with excitement at what was coming. I glanced over at my friend. He appeared calm, sitting quietly, seemingly undisturbed.

Finally Lt. Kohn was finished and addressed the audience, "Does anybody recognize this man and have anything to say?" Normally, if there were no comments from the audience, he would be led away and most likely released. Anxiously, I waited for my friend to stand up and say something. However, there was no reply. No one stood up to accuse him. He was about to be taken away.

"Say something," I nudged my friend. "Now is the time; what are you waiting for?" I would have screamed if possible, I was so excited for him to get up and offer his testimony. I shook him by his powerless right arm, urging him to get up before it was too late, "Do it now! They're going to take him away. Do it before it's too late and you don't get your chance."

He turned and leaned his head close to mine, "I'm not going to testify. Vengeance belongs to Jehovah."

I was shocked into silence. I didn't know what to say. I sat there dumbfounded while they led the SS man away without any charges pressed against him. This really struck me. I saw someone who was living his faith. There was no gun to his head; he was under no obligation; he had the right to testify, and yet, he felt that his conscience, as he explained it to me, wouldn't allow him to do it.

"This was something in God's hands," he later said. "If God wanted to punish him, so be it, but I won't do it." This man was crippled for life and yet he wouldn't speak up.

While in the concentration camps their viewpoint was more understandable, but now they didn't have to prove anything anymore. His loyalty for Jehovah was bigger than his desire for vengeance. I couldn't understand this way of thinking, but my admiration for him increased immensely.

An SS non-commissioned officer was brought in. At first I did not recognize him by his name, Sergeant Pfieffer, but I recognized him by the description of his actions during the interrogation. Pfieffer was bragging about how he could save some stragglers from the death march from Melk to Ebensee by arranging for a truck to pick up those prisoners who could no longer walk. Prior to his interference, concentration camp prisoners who could no longer walk were shot on the road. He claimed he saved prisoners from death by shooting. After Lt. Kohn was finished with him, he addressed his questions to the audience. I didn't hesitate: I stood up and began taking my turn at questioning the prisoner. At first I confirmed his story, "It's true, there was a truck and many people got up in it." He nodded in agreement. He probably thought I was defending him. Some people in the audience began to react strongly to my statement. Then I said, "But how is it you saved them from certain death when they never arrived in the barracks at the camp?" He became flustered and hemmed and hawed, trying to think up some excuse.

"I took them to Ebensee," he said, "but I don't know what happened to them after that." He insisted he had saved them, but he couldn't confirm they were alive.

Rather than argue with him, Lt. Kohn said, "Just file the declaration sheet." And I did.

Each day I became friendlier with the two Jehovah's Witnesses, and I became steadily more impressed. Eventually, they began talking to me about their faith, not so much why they suffered, but they spoke about paradise on earth and other fantastic things. Even though I was familiar with the Bible, I didn't listen to them because I didn't want to believe or accept anything they had to say. God was still very remote from my mind. I felt that I didn't need a "crutch" and could do without God. They persisted in talking to me about living on earth forever in paradise. To me, these were utter fantasies, but I listened politely. They were so enthusiastic about their beliefs, I didn't want to offend them by saying I wasn't interested. I don't know whether they took my polite listening as acceptance or not, but they kept talking to me anyway

After three weeks in Dachau, now the beginning of March, I was called in before Lt. Kohn. He told me I was released from my duty. Before I left, I wanted to say good-bye to my Witness friends. They offered me a free book in German entitled, *The Creation*. I realized only later that this was a very generous gift: This book was a personal copy.

I returned to Landsberg and continued my vigil until I could take another chest X-ray.

In May 1947, one of my acquaintances working for the Americans in Dachau came to Landsberg searching for people who were in the Plaszow camp in Krakow. He rounded up six or seven of us and announced that while working in the Dachau POW camp, he recognized Amon Goeth, the former *kommandant* of Plaszow concentration camp, disguised as a *Wehrmacht,* noncommissioned officer, and using an alias.

My acquaintance, who I call Sam, arranged for the seven of us to go to Dachau. He set it up to have Goeth brought out to us so we could identify him to the Americans. Two days later, we went to Dachau as planned. We had to wait outside the gate until Sam arranged entrance for us. There was a military police officer standing guard in front of the gate. Sam, an older man, thought, perhaps the guard was Jewish. We always felt comfortable when we found a fellow Jew among the soldiers. Sam walked over to the MP and asked him the standard question, "*Amchu?*" We assumed everybody knew our secret code word that identified us as Jewish. The soldier looked at him and then looked down at his watch.

"It's a quarter 'till two," he said.

Sam returned and said, "He's not Jewish." A short time afterward, a soldier came through the gate and called us in. We went to an empty barrack, waited there until an officer came in a few minutes later with Goeth behind him.

This was strange. To see Amon Goeth in his glory was like seeing a superman. We were in fear of this man who had the power of life and death over us. At that time, he was truly part of the master race and we were nothing. Now to see him in the flesh, standing there wearing the *Wehrmacht* uniform, he looked forlorn, bedraggled, sort of lost and quiet. He was stooping with one knee crooked. I couldn't believe this was Amon Goeth, the master of Plaszow. How he had changed, this proud Nazi.

Back in Plaszow, the normal custom was for Goeth to be given a full report on the work done by any given work group. The man in charge would say, "So many Jews are here doing this and this."

Sam approached Goeth, stood at attention, and reported in Plaszow camp style, "Seven Jews reporting here to identify and denounce you." Goeth didn't blink an eye. He hung his head down and stood quietly.

"Do you recognize him?" the American officer asked us. "Is he who you say he is?"

Unanimously we said, "Absolutely, yes!" They took him away, and we were told to report to the office. We were each given sheets of paper and pencils and directed to write down what we knew about Amon Goeth. Then we appeared before an officer and each one of us swore what we wrote was true. The papers were signed and stamped by the officers. They thanked us for our information and sent us back.

Later on we heard Goeth was tried and hanged in Krakow. I had a part in it. I didn't feel that vengeance was wrong; for me it was just the right thing to do.

Malka Kempler (Mamusia)

May 1947 - November 1947
18 to 19 years old

I received all my meals in a large dining room. I recognized some people and gradually, I made new friends, too.

Chapter 39

Three months had passed, so I headed back to Munich to try to gain approval to go to America. I felt this was my last chance and I was scared stiff. At the consulate, I went through the whole process again, and then waited in line for the same American woman to tell me my test results.

When she had my file in front of her, she looked at the papers and in the same cold tone of voice I had come to dread said, "You are accepted." I was speechless.

"What do you mean?" I asked.

"You can go to America." Then she handed me papers with directions for the procedure. I had other medical exams to take to make sure I didn't catch anything before my sail date. I was told to report to the *funkaserne* in Munich.

I was, however, allowed to leave Munich on a pass and went to Landsberg to visit the Staplers, Lena and other friends to say my good-byes. Back in Landsberg, there was a man I considered a "smooth operator." He collected wall-size museum paintings. When he found out I was leaving for America, he had a proposition to make. He informed me that paintings were allowed to be brought into the States without duty.

"If you take the painting with you and deliver it to my brother in New York, I'll pack up your radio for your journey," he said. My only belongings were my suitcase and radio. Strangely, I agreed to his request.

I was in *funkaserne* two months prior to leaving for Bremen and my ship. This giant camp housed not only Jewish survivors, but many people from other countries waiting to immigrate to America. Life in *funkaserne* was different from any of the other places I had been. The grounds, consisting of several multi-storied buildings, were surrounded by walls with strict security. Once inside, I couldn't leave without a pass.

I was assigned to a large room with many bunks. Also, I was assigned a cleaning duty one day each week. I received all my meals in a large dining room. I recognized some people and gradually, I made new friends, too.

My ship wasn't scheduled for departure yet, so I was allowed to go to Landsberg on a pass, though I had to return once a week for my cleaning duty. I was on call in case I was needed to return to Munich.

Finally, I received my schedule for departure. Although it was several weeks away, I learned the name of the ship was Marine Flasher. I also received emigration papers from the consulate. They were delivered in a large, mysterious envelope.

I was very curious about the contents and what they said, however, I didn't want anyone to know I broke the seal so I crumpled it up to make it look abused in some way and managed to open just a small corner of the envelope. Laboriously I worked out some of the papers. One line caught my attention. It said, "Due to a previous TB, he might not be able to make a living in the United States." I understood this, but it scared me. The idea of leaving for another country with some doubt lingering of not being able to make a living was frightening to me. I considered everything to be a threat. Carefully, I put the contents back together. I would deal with whatever came.

When the notice for departure came, I was more than ready to leave for the port city of Bremen. We were put on a crowded train and traveled two days and one night. I had no luggage to speak of, just my toiletries and papers. The wall-sized painting, my single suitcase, and radio had long since been taken to the port where they were stored until the ship docked.

Once in Bremen, we were taken to a large building, a former military installation now used as a transitory camp. There were thousands of people here, all waiting for their designated ships. I was used to this type of camp by now, not luxury living, but I had a place to sleep and was fed sufficiently.

Soon after arriving, those leaving who would be departing on Marine Flasher were assembled and separated, men from women. We were informed Marine Flasher would depart Bremen in the middle of November, which was two weeks away. This was a transit place, with little to do, so most people left the grounds to go into town not too far away.

Before long, I was notified to remain in the camp since, shortly, Marine Flasher would be arriving in Bremenhaven. At this time, I underwent some medical tests. My history with medical tests invoked a slight fear that after coming this far, I still might not make it to America. Thankfully, I passed these tests. Then, to simplify the boarding process, we were shown the layout of where we were going to be bunking on the ship.

Once in Bremenhaven, we were divided men from women. This was a troop ship with several thousand people quartered together, but the women were on a different level of the ship and had their own bathroom facilities. Everyone received $10 U.S. onboard spending money. We were given assigned bedding numbers and our rooming location onboard. They had it well organized and moved us right along.

I found my way to my assigned bunk located in a big hall with three tiers of bunks set close to each other. I pounced on the middle bunk and quickly discovered that I could only lie flat and lift my head a little, but I was going to America so it didn't matter.

Once I found my bunk and figured out the sleeping arrangements, I went on deck to watch our departure and wave good-bye to the Germany I hated. All of us on deck were laughing, happy to leave, yet, underlying my happy exterior, I felt uncertain about my future in America. After all these months, I couldn't imagine I was finally going to America. I would be with my sister, I'd see Genia and Pola again and my other friends from Prien and Landsberg. Suddenly, at the moment of departure, a tremendous sense of freedom washed over me and my fears subsided.

The port was behind me and soon the ship was in the North Sea.

We ate in shifts, so at my assigned time, I went down to the dining room. While eating, the boat began to rock and sway, but this was great fun to me.

The air was too cold to enjoy being on deck, so I went to my bunk and fell into a deep sleep.

The next morning, we were in the English Channel. The water was rough and the boat began to bounce. Everybody was sick and went on deck despite the frigid temperature. Dinner time was the only time anyone went below deck, though the boat was rocking so much that all the dishes were sliding off the long, metal banquet tables. Most passengers were getting seasick and didn't want to go down to the sleeping quarters. A group of us went down just to take blankets off the bunks, but then we crowded back up on deck. There were a number of deck chairs, but not enough for everyone, so most of us wrapped ourselves in the blankets, huddled close together for warmth and slept wherever we could find a spot.

By the next day the rocking grew even worse. I, along with many others, didn't have an appetite. Some were bent over the railing vomiting. I couldn't watch or I would get sick too, but there was no getting away from it. I overheard one passenger, speaking in Yiddish, cursing Christopher Columbus for discovering America.

Eventually, I was overtaken too. I developed an acute headache and became sick and nauseous. There was not one place to go on board that wasn't swaying. I couldn't take the discomfort anymore, so I headed to my bunk and lay down. The hall reeked of body odor and ship fuel. The smell made me feel worse. A few times I had to climb down and go to the toilet where, to my disgust, I kept throwing up. The next day, I felt a little better and decided to go to the bathroom and shave. Without warning, I vomited so violently I got a nosebleed. As soon as the bleeding stopped, I was no longer stricken with seasickness. Even though the boat rocked over much of the North Atlantic, I didn't get sick again. I began to enjoy the mountain-like waves and the swaying of the ship.

Movies were shown in the evening and the trip became fun with happy camaraderie. I liked being on deck so much that I slept there for the rest of the journey. The weather gradually warmed, people recovered from their seasickness, appetites returned and the journey became pleasant.

After eleven days at sea, I saw a long chain of yellow lights in the distance. I became excited knowing we were nearing our destination. This was America. Somehow, it was different from what I expected. I thought there would be multicolored lights and skyscrapers, but all I saw was the low long chain of lights at the water level.

The ship approached closer to shore, stopped and dropped anchor. We didn't know where we were, but one crew member told us this was Long Island, New York. We stood at the railing and watched from a distance. All I could see were car lights moving quickly along a road of some type.

I had mixed emotions. I was excited at the prospect of a new country and a new life, but I was nervous about what would happen next. People were talking about their plans once they arrived in New York. Many already had arrangements with their American relatives. Others said they were going to hotels for temporary lodging. The air was full of speculations and excitement. I knew I was going to live with a family in Brooklyn, but that night, in my bunk once more, I was restless. As soon as I felt the engines starting up, I rushed to the deck to observe our arrival into New York. Gradually, buildings appeared in the distance. The Statue of Liberty was a familiar, welcome sight to all of us, and I could see downtown New York. I recognized the Empire State Building. Germany now seemed far in the past, unreal even.

As the ship moved into the Hudson River, I saw pier after pier and many boats tied to their docks. Eventually, we were pulled by a tugboat and parked at a dock.

The disembarkation procedures began in the morning and took a long time, as there were various officials who wanted to see my papers, but in the late afternoon, I walked down the gangway onto shore. Next, I faced going through customs. I saw at a distance the big crate with the giant wall-size painting in it. Surrounding it were at least four or five customs officers. They had already broken open a corner to peer inside. Next to the crate was my radio and tiny suitcase. As I approached them to claim my belongings the officers launched into a barrage of questions.

"What's inside this crate?" one officer asked.

"I carried this for a friend," I said.

"Who's your friend?" they wanted to know.

"He'll be out here," I said. "He can tell you." The brother of the "smooth operator" back in Landsberg was waiting outside of customs.

"Don't you know what this is?" an officer said, pointing at the crate.

"Talk to him," I insisted, pointing outside of customs. "Whatever you do, it's not my business." With that they let me go with my radio and suitcase. I went outside and there was Dziunka and Jack waiting right at the exit gate. Dziunka was crying with joy, but I was too busy looking at all the new sights around me.

I met the man who was waiting on the painting from his brother. His name was Mr. G. He was grateful to me for bringing the crate to New York and said he would take care of the package. He owned a ski school in New York and worked there as a ski instructor. He promised to take me skiing, but I had never skied before and didn't have a clue how to go about it. Dziunka thanked him for his generous offer. Dziunka, Jack and I left him and walked out of the harbor to the 8th Avenue subway, where we took a train to Brooklyn. Coming out of the subway station, I saw for the first time my new home in America.

The Altered I

302

Part III

A New Life

"Woe to him, when the day of his dreams finally came, found it to be so different from all that he had longed for!" —Viktor Frankl

Radio School Landsberg
Front Row, 5th From Left ,Jozef laughing

Late 1947
19 years old

> **That morning the phone rang and, to my surprise, it was for me. Mrs. Mandel said it was Jack.**

Chapter 40

We arrived at a nice residential street in Brooklyn. We walked up a pretty, tree-lined sidewalk to East 17th Street in Flatbush and arrived at No. 1938. The Mandel's and their two giant sons greeted us at the door and showed us inside. Dziunka, now referred to as Judy in America, and Jack occupied a tiny room with one small bed. There were seven adults living in a cramped, two-bedroom home with a puny bathroom. I slept on the floor in the bedroom, which doubled as an office, with the two Mandel boys, who slept on foldout beds.

Early that evening Jack, Judy and I went out to celebrate my arrival. We went by subway to Church Avenue where there was a big, crowded Jewish delicatessen. Jack suggested I go to the counter and order anything I wanted. As I looked over the offerings, I was completely overwhelmed by the amount and variety of food items. I didn't know what anything was, as I never saw anything like it before in my life. However, I obeyed instructions, and ordered the only food item I recognized and the only one I could ask for in English: two kosher frankfurters with mustard. This was my first meal of my choosing in a free country.

The next morning after everyone else left for work, I was left alone with Mrs. Helen Mandel. She was a very big lady, who not only carried her weight literally, but she was the head of the house. Nothing got by her. There was just one phone in the house on which we could receive calls, but, if we wanted to make calls, we had to put a nickel in a glass jar, placed by Mrs. Mandel herself, beside the phone.

That morning the phone rang and, to my surprise, it was for me. Mrs. Mandel said it was Jack. He wanted me to meet him at a local cafeteria called a Horn and Hardart. I had never heard of it, nor did I know how to get there. Mrs. Mandel gave me directions, and I was out the door, quickly learning the subway system. I climbed the stairs out of the subway station and found myself in a big square, bustling with people coming in and out of shops and filling the sidewalks. All around me was noise and confusion from the blaring horns of the cars to the blazing, billboard lights. I scanned some shops, located the cafeteria and went inside.

I found Jack sitting at a table waiting for me. He directed me to the automatic self-service food dispenser. This was the first time I ever saw anything like this. I put a nickel in and slid open a slot, similar to mail slots, and pulled out a piece of apple pie. I joined Jack at a table where we talked for a while and drank coffee.

"I haven't been working," he said. "I'm looking for a job as a musician but it's difficult to find one. I have to be in a musician's union and that's almost impossible to get into." His demeanor was glum. I could tell he was depressed about his situation. He was a professionally trained musician who didn't want to work at side jobs; he wanted to play music. "I'm gonna have to give it up; it's a hard thing to accept, but if I'm gonna get a job I have no choice. I'm forced to do it." I didn't know what to say. Judy supported the two of them with her good job altering men's clothing. I could tell that Jack's jobless state was becoming a strain on both of them.

After our pie and coffee, we went by subway train to see Judy in Brooklyn. She was planning to buy me a new suit. I was wearing all the hand-me-down clothing from Landsberg. Besides being way out of fashion, Judy told me, "They're dirty and stinking."

She introduced me properly to her co-workers. Then there was a flurry of activity as she began handing me different suits to try on. Finally, she found just the right one, a beautiful blue, three-piece suit. Next, I was outfitted with a white shirt and a big, broad necktie bearing palm trees. This was the first white shirt I had ever owned. Buttons went all the way down the front. I had never seen that before. Nor had I owned a tie either, so one of the store employees helped tie it in a knot. I looked in the mirror and I couldn't believe the transformation. I touched my curly mop of blond hair, which was in dire need of a trim, but the outfit looked great.

I walked out of the store wearing my first brand-new suit. We walked two doors down to a shoe store where Judy bought a pair of men's dress shoes to go with the suit. When we walked out of the store, I felt like a million bucks. We went back to the Mandel's house beaming.

I began to feel comfortable in my new city. However, I still had instances of fear. One night while walking down 34th Street in Manhattan, I encountered two police officers walking toward me. I grew afraid when I saw their uniforms and I didn't know what to do. There was too much traffic to cross the street, so I steeled myself and walked straight ahead, eyes forward, my heart pounding like a drum. They passed right on by me without incident.

Judy and Jack were not getting along. Despite what he had said in our conversation, Jack stubbornly refused to do any kind of work that didn't involve playing music. He practiced violin, saxophone and clarinet and chain-smoked cigarettes all day long. He spent his days sitting in coffee houses visiting with his old friend from Germany by the name of Schreut. Jack had expensive habits and Judy, as the sole provider, had to supply his needs. Things became worse between them and they were divorced by the end of the year. Judy and I eventually left the Mandels' home and rented an apartment of our own.

Miss Walvis- Harriet Walvis, 1946
Location: Prien Germany

June 1948 - February 1953
20 to 25 years old

> **"You're in IA classification. That means you'll be one of the first ones to be drafted. This is a way to avoid it. Are you in?"**

Chapter 41

In 1948, President Truman announced a new draft law that would go into effect in June. My old friend, Leon Sperling, from the radio school in Landsberg came to see me about it one night.

"The draft law goes into effect at midnight but whoever is a member of the reserves or National Guard by midnight will be exempt from the draft. That's what I'm going to do," he said.

He seemed more knowledgeable than me about the ways of the world. My mind was preoccupied with high fidelity sound systems.

"I don't know; I don't feel like going. What am I going to be involved in?"

"You're in IA classification. That means you'll be one of the first ones to be drafted. This is a way to avoid it. Are you in?"

He convinced me to join. Together we went to the armory on 61st Street in Manhattan and signed up in the National Guard. Every Thursday, I went for training and once a year we were sent for a two week military training in Maneuvers at Camp Smith in New York. I was a formal member of the 142nd anti-aircraft battalion which was part of the 42nd infantry division, known as the Rainbow Division. Since Leon and I both had radio training, we were in the communications unit.

We were the only new adult volunteers to join. The others were American teenagers with whom I couldn't communicate and didn't understand. Leon became my closest friend. He was serious and hardworking. In college he was very studious. He was critical of me and took it upon himself to mold me. While riding the subway from Thursday night National Guard training, he saw I was reading a Reader's Digest. "Why are you reading such junk?" he said." You're flippant and not serious about your future. Just look at your life. It's the same routine day after day and month after month." He gave me suggestions on what I should be reading, but I ignored him and continued reading what I found interesting.

I had no idea how Leon supported himself financially. I knew he lived alone but I didn't ask him too many personal questions. Although Leon and I were both Holocaust survivors, we didn't talk about the war or our experiences. It wasn't considered good etiquette.

On a warm Sunday in June, 1950, while on my way to Brighton Beach for the day, I passed a newsstand where a group of people gathered over newspaper headlines announcing the outbreak of the Korean War. There was a conflict between North Korea and South Korea. When I went to the armory for weekly training, we were advised that we should prepare to be called in for active duty. This scared me. I didn't realize the National Guard could be in the war. I looked at the National Guard as a sort of home army.

As Leon had accused, I fell into my old routines, prepared to go to war but not responding to it emotionally. There were rumors that The Rainbow Division of the National Guard, my division, was going to be mobilized for Korea. I was receiving draft notices for selective service every three months and I had to prove I was still in the National Guard. Some survivors were drafted and lost their lives. I knew one survivor who was proud to go to war. He said he wanted to do it for America, and in fact, he was highly decorated for his tour in the Korean War but that wasn't what I wanted.

In 1952, I was preparing to qualify for American citizenship. I was called into the naturalization office to appear with two witnesses before a judge. I took along two guys from my company and dressed in my National Guard uniform. By this time, I had three chevrons indicating I was now a sergeant. After answering a few questions the judge granted me citizenship but I had to wait several weeks before swearing in and receiving my citizenship papers.

About this time, I befriended a kid in my company of the National Guard by the name of Joe Dreifuss. He attached himself to me as his guide and instructor. He was very eager to learn, but naïve. He had a sister named Marion. He wanted me to meet her. One day, I took him up on it. I went to her house in the projects in upper Manhattan. Marion was a nice, pretty girl. Her father, Adolf, was an old German-Jew and her mother, Alice, was a mousy little lady. They both questioned me thoroughly. When I told them I was a Polish Jew from Krakow, their eyebrows raised up. There was an old animosity between German Jews and Jews from the East. Before they let us go on our date, they wanted to know some things.

"What are your intentions?" Adolf asked.

I was dumbfounded. This was only our first date.

"Strictly honorable, sir," I said.

"No, no," he said, shaking his head. "What are your intentions; where are you going to take my daughter?" Finally understanding his meaning, I told him where we were going and he let us go.

I liked Marion. We went out a few times to the movies or the boardwalk on Coney Island and talked a lot.

One day she opened up to me and told me her story. She came from a well-to-do family living in a town in Germany called Aachen. The Nazis had given permission for one thousand small children to be sent away to England on a *Kinder* (children) transport. Marion was six or seven when her parents sent her away on this transport. After all the children arrived in England, they were immediately assigned to English foster homes in the country. She was the only child assigned to a Christian family, called the Stanbridge's, in Coventry. Marion wasn't from a religious family, but she knew she was Jewish and felt a conflict. Her new foster parents were good to her and gradually she began to look upon the W's as her real parents. In the beginning she wrote to her parents, but they eventually lost contact. Over time, her Jewish parents became a distant memory.

She went to school and learned English. Soon she became more English than German. During Marion's story, I didn't dare ask questions; she volunteered the information and admitted that the new adjustments were difficult for her.

One night, she escaped some of the worst bombing that took place in Coventry. She was in her bed with her beloved German shepherd dog when heavy bombing began. A bomb fell directly on her house. The ceiling of her room collapsed on her bed. At the very last second, her dog jumped on the bed and covered her body with his. He saved her life but sacrificed his. Her only injury was a shattered elbow, fixed with metal pins. She healed normally and had full use of her arm.

Since hearing her story, I developed a love/hate relationship with German shepherd dogs. In Germany, belonging to the cruel Nazis, were the killer German Shepherds from the concentration camps, and I hated them. Now, I had come to learn of the self-sacrificing German shepherd who saved Marion's life.

Marion's parents eventually made their way to the United States. They contacted Marion's foster parents in England and brought her over to New York. Marion confided in me that she had a hard time leaving her foster parents to go live with strangers.

Our relationship was growing closer and Marion hinted at marriage. I was hesitant and scared. In the past I avoided close relationships but I agreed to marry her. Marion warned me that her parents were suspicious of me. They wanted her to marry someone rich, a professional who could support her in style. Adolf was terribly afraid of poverty. He worried that all the bad things that had happened to him in the past would happen again.

Adolf was an unpleasant dictator and Marion didn't dare tell him we were getting married knowing how he truly felt about the matter. She confided in Alice, her mother, who also wasn't pleased about it and resisted the idea initially, but gave in and helped plan the wedding when she realized we were determined to get married.

I wasn't allowed to visit Marion at the apartment anymore because Adolf didn't want me around. Our relationship had worsened. We resorted to planning the wedding in secret. We found an apartment in the Bronx, which was to Marion's liking. All I cared about was having a suitable location for my corner hi-fi system. I moved into our apartment just before we were married. Marion didn't bring anything over yet because she was still keeping the marriage a secret from her father. Alice arranged for a rabbi in Manhattan to marry us. As an atheist, at this point, I wasn't happy about the rabbi, but it was what Alice and Marion wanted so I went along with it as the dutiful groom, obeying instructions.

On February 22, 1953, we were married. The wedding was a tiny affair with the rabbi's wife and Alice as the only witnesses. Afterward Alice took us to a little restaurant for tea and dessert by way of a celebration and then she left us alone.

That evening, we attended the Metropolitan Opera. It was the only time we went to the opera together. The opera was my way of offering Marion the best. We spent our wedding night in a hotel near Central Park.

Two days later, news reached Adolf that Marion and I had been married. He was furious and forbid us from entering his house. We managed to visit Alice when Adolf was away at work, but this didn't happen often. I remained on friendly terms with Marion's brother Joe, who I saw every week at National Guard training.

We settled into a good married life. I taught Marion to like music and every Saturday evening we listened to the NBC Symphony Orchestra, conducted by Arturo Toscanini. We had music all the time.

I advanced in the National Guard and was now a Sergeant 1st Class. The chances of going to Korea were now much smaller. Life became peaceful and comfortable.

12 "B" Street Apt. Krakow, Poland -Taken in 80s

1954 -1955
26 to 27 years old

> **On May 11, 1955, Marion delivered a**
> **healthy little girl who we named Susie.**
> **Marion felt good and happy.**

Chapter 42

In October 1954, Marion discovered she was pregnant. She didn't feel well, which we attributed to the pregnancy, but then she developed swelling in her lymph nodes. We went to the family doctor, Dr. Weiner, and he became worried, though he didn't want to diagnose it right away. I thought perhaps it was because it wasn't his field of expertise. Together with my mother-in-law, Alice, we went to see Dr. Carver, a top endocrinologist. He took a biopsy and talked to Dr. Weiner and my mother-in-law; however, Marion and I were in the dark. Finally, they informed us that Marion needed radiation therapy. He recommended a radiologist who applied injections to her neck at $75 per treatment.

On our second visit to Dr. Carver, he mentioned to me that Marion had Hodgkin's disease. I had never heard of it and asked him dumbly, "How long does it take to cure it?"

He took a long, grave look at me and said, "We don't dare to speak of a cure." Because this was serious, I kept it a secret from Marion. I didn't want her to be upset. She was only 22 years old, and she had to undergo two more radiation treatments.

Things were tight for us financially, and the treatments were expensive.

"We have to stop the treatment; I can't afford it anymore," I told the radiologist.

"She'll need at least two more treatments," he said. "I can let you pay it off a few dollars a week if that helps, but she really needs this treatment." It seemed like a suitable solution, and I wanted to do whatever I could for Marion, so I agreed to the terms.

Marion quit her job, and by 1955, I was thankful that her health had stabilized somewhat and the swelling had gone down. To the relief of both of us, she advanced normally in her pregnancy.

After seven years in the National Guard, I wanted out, but I was still draft age and couldn't quit. Between caring for a sick pregnant wife, and increased responsibilities at home and work, I really wanted to leave. I had taken a new job in electronics at a company called American Measuring Instruments and was now head of an important project involving a military contract for the Navy. My boss, Jerry Zauderer wrote a letter indicating I couldn't go on leave for the upcoming two weeks training because the project was behind schedule. It was sufficient and I was released from the National Guard.

Despite Marion's illness, I wasn't allowed into her parents' house. Adolf was angrier than ever with me. Now, Marion was sick, but instead of having a rich husband who could get her the best medical care, she had a husband who was too poor to take care of her properly.

On May 11, 1955, Marion delivered a healthy little girl who we named Susie. Marion felt good and happy. Two days later her health took a serious downward turn with her temperature reaching 104 degrees. The resident doctor told me this was a flare-up of the Hodgkin's. The maternity hospital couldn't care for her properly so she was transferred to the Frances Delafield Hospital, a cancer research center at the Columbia-Presbyterian Medical Center. The hospital was ideally located in our neighborhood. I thought it was a fine hospital, clean and modern, and I had high hopes of a full recovery for Marion.

In the meantime, Susie could not remain in the hospital where she was born and I couldn't take her home with me. Alice and I found an orphanage in Far Rockaway on Long Island. Marion's brother, Joe Dreifuss, had a car. He offered to drive me to the orphanage, saving me from traveling by subway and train with a newborn infant. On the way, Joe had the radio tuned to a classical music station. When "Carmina Burnana" by Karl Orff came on, I became absorbed in it, forgetting about my problems with Marion and the baby. I was on my way to an unknown orphanage to give up my newborn daughter. Instead of becoming morose, I was transported by the music to another place and time. Music was a tranquilizer for me.

When we arrived, I went in to see the woman who owned the orphanage. She had already been informed about Susie and our situation. We haggled over the cost of keeping Susie and finally settled on $75 per month. This was a major concession for me, but I had no choice. I didn't know how to care for an infant and I knew they did, so I left her there.

I visited Marion in the hospital every night after work. Her fever was still high despite being administered medications and numerous blood transfusions. She was so sick she didn't even ask about Susie. I needed someone I could talk to about it. Judy had now married again. Her husband was named Andy Billys, formerly Bialystock. He had survived the war on Ukrainian papers. She was now living in Colorado. She was the only one I could confide my thoughts. I wrote her often describing my situation.

Finally, Marion's fever broke. She had lost a lot of weight and couldn't walk on her own. She remained in the hospital for several weeks recovering at a slow pace. The doctors and nurses were very friendly to her. Marion was a sweet girl and everybody loved her. Eventually, they allowed me to take her home, but they warned me that this sickness can be fraught with frequent remissions and relapses and she would have to go back for periodic blood work. They assured me there would always be a bed ready for her at Delafield. As the doctors warned me, Marion had frequent relapses. Along with blood transfusions, the doctors gave her experimental drugs, but these only made her sicker.

When Marion was strong enough, I told her where Susie was. She was satisfied that I had found a place for her, but she was anxious to see her. My custom was to go to the orphanage once every week or two. When I would arrive, I was shown to her crib. She sat there looking at me without any expression on her little face. I smiled at her and tickled her but she wouldn't smile or respond to my goofy sounds. "She never smiles," a nurse told me. Susie was like a stranger to me and I knew she didn't know me.

The orphanage was full of little kids, but only a few nurses. One nurse said, "We have a procedure of picking up each child once a day for fifteen minutes. This gives them some feelings of love." Apparently, for Susie, it wasn't enough. She wouldn't respond to any of it. She was numb as I had been while in the concentration camps. I couldn't take the sadness of it and I never stayed for long. I asked the head nurse if I could bring Marion to see the baby, and she said, "Certainly," then left me.

When Marion was stronger, her brother Joe, Alice and I drove to the orphanage to see Susie. Marion was too weak to pick up the baby but she wanted to have a picture of Susie. The nurse brought Susie outside into the sunshine where Marion posed for a picture. Marion held her for just a minute or so because she had so little strength. I felt heartbroken to see her struggling to hold the baby; it was as if she was holding a doll, not her daughter. That was the last time she held Susie. We cut the visit short because Marion didn't feel well and drove back to town without talking much. I didn't know what to say.

Marion was becoming sicker. Although she was getting treatment and she had been released to come home, it was for shorter and shorter stays. Then one day, I had to take her back to the hospital because she had a serious infection, a perforated bowel and other serious conditions. She went into a coma lasting several days. When she came out of the coma, the hospital wouldn't release her.

.

Jozef & Genia- Rowing on Maxl
Rowing on Lake Chiemsee

1956 - March 1958
27 to 29 years old

"This stuff is interesting, but it's too incredible. I can't believe it," I said.

Chapter 43

One Sunday morning in 1956, the doorbell rang. No one usually came to the house on Sunday mornings. I went to the door and opened it. Standing there before me was a heavyset black woman. Upon seeing my inquisitive face, she began to talk to me. I wasn't really paying attention to her words, but I grasped she was saying something about the Bible. She spoke with a thick, southern accent and I had trouble understanding what she was saying at first. After a few minutes, she asked, "Do you have a Bible?" I did actually. The Bible belonged to Marion, one she had been given from her English foster parents. Sometime during the past few months I had picked it up, skimming through the pages; I was intrigued. Never before had I seen the complete Christian Bible. Marion and I had attempted to read it together, but gave up. We laughed our heads off because of all the "begets."

I went to the bookshelf where I had stashed it, pulled it down and brought it to the door. The woman wasn't aggressive, but she sure was assertive: "Open up the Bible. Read this scripture." I followed her instructions. I had no idea who she was or what she wanted from me, but I was too polite to tell her to leave. Finally, from her bag she pulled out a red-colored, hardbound book entitled, *This Means Everlasting Life*. She offered to sell it to me for fifty cents. I bought it for two reasons, first, I wanted to get rid of her and second, in my opinion, any book of this quality was certainly worth fifty cents regardless of the subject. I gave her the money and she left. I put the book on the shelf and forgot all about it.

Much of the time, I was alone on weekends. My only escape from reality was in music. During the weekdays I worked, ran errands and visited Marion's bedside in the hospital. She was now very sick, weak and losing weight. There was a bottle of blood almost always hanging by her bedside. She slept a lot and often, while she slept, I spent the time sitting in the waiting room.

The day Marion learned of her disease, I felt sick with worry because it was my fault. No one, including myself, could stand the idea of telling her why she was so sick. I was wheeling her downstairs for some tests and neglected to see a tank attached to the chair with her name on it and "Hodgkin's disease" written in bold print. Before I could hide the tank from view, she read it. I was scared of what her reaction would be, but she looked at me with a sad smile and said, "Now I know what I have." She knew Hodgkin's disease was a serious illness, but instead of being upset she reassured me, saying, "I'm glad to know what I have. I'd rather know what it is than be sick without knowing what is happening to me." I was relieved she wasn't mad at me for keeping it a secret. I was proud of her willing attitude with all the doctor's tests and her quiet submission to the nurses, who poked so many needles into her delicate skin.

On Sunday, about two weeks later, the large, black woman came back again. This time, a white man accompanied her. They were well-dressed and polite but as soon as I opened the door, she asked me whether they could come in. I had no idea what they wanted, but I wanted to be courteous, so I complied and ushered them inside.

Once seated, the lady asked me, "Do you have the book I left with you?" I thought she wanted it back and the fifty cents must have been a lending fee. I brought it out and she began to babble on and on about the book and the Bible and all kinds of things. I had no mind or patience to hear any of it. Then the man pulled out a Bible. The lady kept talking about Jesus Christ. I came to the conclusion that they were some religious group, so I mentioned I was Jewish. That didn't faze them at all. They started talking about Moses and David. I was totally confused about what their intentions were. Finally, the lady pulled a magazine from her bag and handed it to me. I could see "The Watchtower" printed across the top. Then they proceeded to pull out two more copies of the same magazine, one each for their own use. The woman instructed me: "Turn to the first page." Pointing to the page, she continued, "See there, it shows a list of publishers from various countries."

"What are publishers and what do they publish? Are they in the business of publishing books and selling them?" I couldn't understand what these people were doing in my house. When I could take it no more, I asked outright, "What kind of religion are you?" For the first time, they fell dead silent and appeared visibly nervous.

With great hesitation, the man said, "We are Jehovah's Witnesses." Because I was Jewish, they told me later, they expected to be kicked out of my apartment once they identified themselves to me as Jehovah's Witnesses.

To their surprise, as soon as I heard "Jehovah's Witness," instead of scowling, my face brightened into a big smile. I exclaimed, "Jehovah's Witnesses! I didn't know you were in this country." I had lived in America for almost nine years and I was totally taken aback by this discovery. This was the first time I had come into contact with Jehovah's Witnesses since being in the concentration camps. I had believed that the Witnesses were some form of Germany-based religious sect. I didn't know they were also in the United States. I wanted to know who they were, so introductions were made. The lady's name was Minnie Easley and the man was Joe Farinacci

I took over the talking now and outlined my past. I told them how I had seen and heard about Jehovah's Witnesses in the concentration camps and how I admired them for their stand. I told them about the outstanding loyalty they demonstrated and how it encouraged all of us in the camps. But, I still didn't know who Jehovah's Witnesses were. I asked, "Are you Jewish because you use the name Jehovah?" I peppered them with questions. I wasn't really interested in their religion, but I wanted and insisted upon knowing what it was that gave them their strength and loyalty. To my way of thinking, this was what made them different from everybody else.

Minnie and Joe pulled out their Bibles and started to chatter on about integrity, dedication, Satan's persecution and all kinds of stuff. I couldn't understand what it all meant. At this point, none of it began to answer my questions. They continued to talk about faith, but faith didn't mean anything to me. I couldn't identify with faith. They used words like "love" and "loyalty." I became frustrated with their answers. I really wanted to know what kind of religion it was that gave its members the kind of strength they demonstrated in the camps. I'd never seen this kind of strength before. In the concentration camps, there were individuals belonging to other religions, but the Jehovah's Witnesses were there because they were part of a religious group that Hitler couldn't tolerate.

In frustration, I asked Minnie and Joe, "How could they do it; where did it come from?" They couldn't explain it to my satisfaction. They handed me some booklets and left, with Minnie promising to return with more information.

The prospect of learning more about these people excited me. I skimmed through the book, but it seemed to be boring stuff. The booklets were more interesting because they summed up the Jehovah's Witnesses' beliefs in just a few pages. Some of their beliefs, as described in the booklet, seemed to be sheer fantasy, and I wondered how anyone could accept such nonsense.

The following Sunday, as promised, Minnie came back. This time, she brought a whole bunch of booklets, including a little brochure about creation versus evolution.

"This stuff is interesting, but it's too incredible. I can't believe it," I said.

"What is published in these books is in the Bible," Minnie explained, "You have to look up the scriptures to see it for yourself." Pointing to the book, she continued, "What is written in this book conforms to what the Bible says." Then she showed me how to look up the scriptures.

The first scripture we read together was from Isaiah 1:18, and it made a big impression on me, "Come now let us reason together, says Jehovah." This verse struck me as extraordinary because my contention was that religion was a matter of faith. A person has it, or they don't. I was convinced I could not reason my way to faith. The two concepts seemed mutually exclusive.

She left more booklets with me, and I began to read them and look up the scriptures in my Bible. Indeed, everything the literature stated was in the Bible. But, I doubted whether the Bible was true. These Jehovah's Witness people quoted the Bible accurately, but that didn't mean the Bible was 100 percent true. However, the things spoken of in the Bible were wonderful promises, and I began to wish that those promises were true. But my background and experiences blocked my ability to see the love and benevolence of God. How could I trust the God of the Bible? I had prayed to him in my childhood and early on in the war, but he let bad things happen. Praying to God didn't make sense to me.

Also, the idea of accepting Jesus Christ stuck like a bone in my throat. To Jewish people, the idea that Jesus was the Messiah wasn't possible. The saying among the Jews was that Jesus was a *Mumser*, a bastard. If there was a Messiah, it was not Jesus. There were more Jews killed in his name than in any other name, so how could it possibly be considered? Nonetheless, I was curious about these people and their religion, so I kept reading the material Minnie left with me, along with my Bible.

After a while, the Jehovah's Witnesses' explanations combined with the teachings from the Bible began to fit into place. To my amazement, my old Jewish training, joined with what the Jehovah's Witnesses presented, fit perfectly together like a jigsaw puzzle. I considered becoming Jewish again, but not one of Jehovah's Witnesses. The thought of becoming a Jehovah's Witness was like jumping from the frying pan into the fire. I had been persecuted for being a Jew and the Jehovah's Witnesses had been persecuted in Germany and were not viewed favorably in this country. If I wanted to pick a religion, this would certainly be the last one I'd pick!

In the midst of it all, I had a sick wife to take care of and a child sitting unloved in an orphanage. What was I going to do with Susie? I was pulled in so many different directions. But, Minnie kept coming back to see me.

One Sunday, Minnie and I sat down to discuss a book entitled, *Life Everlasting*. This became our pattern. Still, my original question kept surfacing, and Minnie couldn't answer it. She could only answer with the scriptures. This didn't satisfy me. I was stubborn, and I wondered if there was something in my subconscious resisting this new knowledge. Also, I was a strong believer in evolution. The book Minnie had left me to read on that subject was effective because it didn't require that I have faith in the Bible. This book was more scientific in its approach, which appealed to me.

Another Sunday, there was a terrific storm outside. I didn't want to have to go outside for anything, not even to the hospital to see Marion. I thought Minnie wouldn't come on a day like this, but there was an unexpected knock at the door. Who could it be in weather like this, standing at my door soaking wet, but Minnie? She had walked more than twenty blocks in the storm. This made more of an impression on me than all her books and pamphlets would ever make. Now I understood what dedication meant.

I related this dedication to my time in the concentration camps. I was forced outside in bad weather. But now, in America, no one was forcing me out, I could stay home when there was nasty weather. But Minnie still went out in her ministry even though the weather conditions were bad. From that moment on, I saw her through different eyes. This poor, uneducated woman was really intent on helping me. She called herself a "pioneer"—someone who dedicates many hours in voluntary ministry work. She did this apparently for love of God and the people she contacted.

From that day forward, I read everything Minnie gave me and my knowledge increased. As the words in the Bible were proven true, by leaps and bounds, even my scant faith began to increase. I derived a certain comfort from the Bible, which was what I needed during this critical time in my life.

Marion was declining rapidly. The doctors warned me that she wouldn't survive much longer, but I still didn't truly believe what they said. She had hepatitis and other complications due to the blood transfusions. Most of the time she was only semi-conscious. I never knew what to say to her, but I thought she could benefit if I told her some of the new things I was learning from my Bible study. I began to tell her about the scriptural promises of living forever in paradise.

Kneeling down close to her, I whispered, "Soon you will close your eyes and when you open them again, you will be new and healthy in paradise on earth." I believed those words. I had confidence that what I read in the Bible was true. However, I didn't trust Jehovah with all of my heart, and I couldn't pray to him yet.

On April 11, 1956, I received a call stating that Marion was in critical condition. When I arrived at the hospital, my mother-in-law, Alice, was the only one from the family there. Marion was unconscious and breathing hard. Nurses and doctors bustled around her bed. The doctor administered injections into her heart with a long needle. Alice sent me away to the waiting area. She didn't think I was needed in Marion's room.

As soon as I removed myself from the situation, self-denial took over. All of the trauma and emergency of the situation disappeared from my mind. When the war started, I had escaped stressful situations by absorbing myself with other thoughts, ignoring reality.

Alice came running into the waiting room and said, "Joe, come quickly!" When I came to Marion's bedside, I saw that her face was green and yellow. The doctor was pounding her chest with his fist, but there was no response. She lay still and quiet. Marion was dead. It was 11:45 p.m. The nurse drew a curtain around Marion's bed and left me and Alice alone with her.

Alice turned to me right away, "The doctor is likely to come and ask you for permission to do an autopsy, you have to tell him no, claim your religion forbids that." She knew me well enough that if asked, I could not say no.

Shortly thereafter, one of the doctors came in. "We used all kinds of experimental drugs on her," he said. "And it's very important to check the effects these drugs had. We can learn how to treat others with similar conditions. Will you consent to an autopsy?"

In accordance with Alice's instructions I told him no and referenced my religious objections. He tried to persuade me, but I refused. I left the hospital and made my way home, where I fell asleep. Early the next morning, there was a knock on the door, and a man handed me a telegram from the hospital announcing in bold print, "Marion Kempler died yesterday." I reacted like a robot. The day was a blur. Later, I received a call from Alice informing me that the funeral was scheduled for the next day. She told me the address and the time and hung up. The next morning I got dressed and walked to the funeral home. There was a crowd of people already there, many of whom I didn't know, except for one married couple with whom Marion and I had been friends. When they saw me, they rushed to my side.

Marion was in an open casket in the next room. I went by myself to look at her. She was made up with makeup and had pink, full cheeks— perhaps they were stuffed with something to make her emaciated face appear more normal looking. She looked beautiful to me and at peace. I felt so proud just looking at her.

I ran back into the other room searching for my friends. When I found them, I grabbed each by the arm, "Come look at Marion!" They were crying and one woman was hesitant, but I insisted. In an unusually cheerful voice, I said, "You have to see her." Together we went into the other room. Gesturing to Marion, I said, "Just look how beautiful she is!" I didn't weep; if anything, I was at peace.

The casket was loaded into a hearse and a few cars followed it to a New Jersey cemetery. I was riding in the car with my father-in-law, Adolf Dreifuss. I hadn't seen him since before Marion and I were married, but we had nothing to say to each other. There were several other men in the car with us. Adolf was laughing and telling stories the entire trip to the cemetery. This was crazy behavior, but survivors, including myself, behaved abnormally. We arrived at the cemetery and they brought the coffin before the open grave. The Rabbi said the prayer.

Alice leaned over to me and whispered, "Give the rabbi $45 before he leaves." She also informed me that the annual upkeep and maintenance of the grave was my obligation. They lowered the coffin into the ground, and I was handed a shovel to throw in the first ceremonial shovel-full of dirt. I poured soil over the coffin, but instead of handing the shovel over, I kept shoveling. There was an uncomfortable stirring among the funeral guests, but I wouldn't stop.

"It's enough," someone said.

"No, it's the least I can do." I kept shoveling dirt until somebody forcibly took the shovel away from me.

Afterward, I went home, undressed and put some music on. The date of Marion's funeral was Friday the 13th. I was superstitious and felt this was the worst day they could have picked for the funeral. I felt empty inside, mentally exhausted, confused and lost. I didn't know what I should do next. The only escape I knew was to turn on sad music.

According to Jewish custom, I spent the next seven days at home in mourning. Judy was on her way from Denver to spend this week with me.

One of my co-workers came by my apartment. He handed me an envelope with $13.75 inside. Apparently when they learned of my wife's passing, they took a collection at work. I had encouraging visits from friends, and once Judy arrived, I began to feel like myself again. I realized that my life was now easier, yet I had a daughter who needed my attention. Susie was still in the orphanage. I needed to do something about her, but I had no money to take care of her properly. I took Judy to the orphanage to see her. This was the first time she had ever seen her niece. She picked Susie up and held her close. Looking at me she said, "You shouldn't leave Susie here. Let me take her to Denver; I'll raise her as my own child."

I couldn't make an important decision like that right away. I stalled for time, and we returned to my apartment. Some days later, the Dreifuss' came to my apartment for a visit. My former in-laws were also concerned about Susie. When I told them I was thinking of letting her go to Denver to have a home with my sister and her husband, they became upset with me, particularly Adolf. Unexpectedly, he went into a strange stupor and had to lie down.

"Go to him. Pacify him. Just tell him that you are considering leaving Susie here," Alice said.

Overhearing our conversation, he jumped up and tore into me and his wife, "If Marion had married a rich man instead of you, there would be a decent home for Susie with a nurse to care for her!" Talking with them was difficult and when they left, I was totally confused. Judy insisted on taking Susie, but my in-laws wouldn't allow me to do that. They wanted me to take care of her myself, but I couldn't commit. Someone suggested I see a psychiatrist for help in coming to a decision, which I did.

The psychiatrist asked, "What would you like do? What is your preference?"

I didn't want to answer her. I felt guilty because what I really wanted to do was give Susie up for adoption. So I decided not to see the psychiatrist again. I avoided both my in-laws and making any kind of decision on the matter.

Soon, I received a phone call from the woman in charge at the orphanage: "This is my business Mr. Kempler. I know the best thing for that little girl is for you to give her up. You can't take care of her, so please listen to me. This is the best solution."

I didn't want to hear this. I couldn't give up my child to a stranger. I knew Judy wanted her, but I had a hard time with that. I didn't know what my responsibility was. I had researched orphanages and knew firsthand how the children were brought up. The nurses took turns holding a different child for only a few minutes and I knew this wasn't enough love. I resolved to let Judy raise Susie, who was now about eleven months old. Without informing the Dreifuss', I made the flight arrangements to Denver and informed Judy of our estimated time of arrival. As soon as Judy got Susie home, she and her husband, Andy, bathed her. Neither of them had any experience with babies and they were arguing nervously about the best way to do it. I knew even less than they did, so I let them take care of things.

When I returned to New York, I informed my in-laws that Susie was now in Denver with Judy. They were very angry and we severed all ties. I felt I had made the right decision and tried to convince myself that Susie was better off with Judy and Andy. I would still be in her life but now she had two fathers, rather than having none at all. Eventually, Susie was officially adopted by Judy.

I resumed my Bible study with Minnie and began attending

meetings at the Kingdom Hall. When I first attended, I expected to hear a preacher with loud, church-like sermons, but the speaker had a normal, pleasant tone and proved every point he made with the Bible. Minnie sat next to me beaming with pride, as she helped me locate all the scriptures. I was very impressed with the meeting and decided I would go again.

I began to make friends among the people in the congregation. Several of them were Bethelites, meaning they lived at the world headquarters of Jehovah's Witnesses in Brooklyn, New York and attended this congregation. I could tell from the way they spoke that they had extensive Bible knowledge. I began to ask them the questions, the ones that Minnie couldn't answer to my satisfaction, and they supplied the answers I needed.

I began to understand how a God, who is supposed to be loving and all-powerful, could permit the Holocaust to happen. Often I had wondered, What was his role? How could he do that? Why did he leave us to die like that? What did we do wrong? No rabbi could answer these questions. Nobody else could answer them for me, except the Jehovah's Witnesses. They did it with the Bible, without speculations and theories.

I had one problem. This religion was based on love for God and love for neighbor. I did not have any such feelings. I did not have the sense of love — this was an emotion that was missing in me. But, I kept attending the meetings and gradually, the logic of the teachings really made sense. I could better understand how the Witnesses endured the persecution in the concentration camps.

The Jehovah's Witnesses held to the teaching of the resurrection. This hope was a very real thing to them and nothing could take it away. Jehovah's Witnesses trusted God implicitly and felt he was always with them, no matter where they were or what happened to them.

Their relationship with God was real, close and personal. But I questioned the relationship. What if something happens? Is God going to let me down again like he let me down before? I did not feel the joy that the other Jehovah's Witnesses felt. I felt separated and disjointed and I had difficulty trusting God. However, because of all that I had learned, I decided to become one of Jehovah's Witnesses, but my dedication became an intellectual choice, not an emotional one. I believed the teachings and could explain them, but it was in my head, not deep in my heart where it should have also been.

Part of being one of Jehovah's Witnesses involves going out preaching to others. I went door-to-door, and soon I acquired a list of people who showed some initial interest in the Bible's message. Primarily, I called on Jewish people. They were plentiful in my neighborhood. Some even became good friends. Others gave me a hard time, but all of them were interesting.

I knocked at one door and a woman answered, "I'm Jewish and not interested in what you have to say."

"I'm Jewish too." She gave me a strange look, but invited me to come into her home. She directed me to take a seat across from her and indicated that I should speak. I began by telling her that I was a Jewish Holocaust survivor.

"I'm a psychiatrist," she said. "I want to know when you first began hating the Jews."

"I never hated the Jews," I said, a little surprised at her question. "I'm more of a Jew now than I was before."

"You're lying. Why would you switch over to the other side unless you hated who you were? You are afraid of being a Jew." She had many questions, and I tried to give scriptural answers. Finally, she ended our conversation with, "I really don't have time right now to discuss this."

"Can I come back another time to continue our conversation at a more convenient time for you?" I asked.

"You're welcome to come, but I charge $80 an hour." That was the end of that visit.

I became quite regular in the ministry work, going door-to-door at least once a week. I met many people, some nice and some not so polite. I was still inexperienced and had much to learn about tact. When I encountered a nasty person at the door, I threatened them. Sometimes I gave in to pride, as in the time I went door-to door with a Circuit Overseer. We were visiting at a Jewish home, I was speaking, and afterward the Circuit Overseer informed me that I hadn't used the scripture correctly and showed me how I should have presented it. I responded haughtily that we had been at a Jewish home and the way I did it was the proper way to handle the situation. He remained quiet. He was more experienced than I and was trying to help me learn how to preach properly at the door. I was tactless and realized I still had more to learn, but I was serious about becoming a Jehovah's Witness.

I had problems stemming from the Holocaust and as a result still dealt with emotional immaturity, but I prayed about it, and decided to be baptized as a symbol of my dedication to God. So, at the next opportunity, in March 1958, I was baptized as one of Jehovah's Witnesses.

Susan

1947 - 1974
19 to 46 years old

During 1954, while in the National
Guard, because I was developing my
knowledge in communications, I
became the battalion expert.

Chapter 44

Since my arrival in America, I had tried to have a normal life. I was called a "greenhorn," a newcomer. I tried to make friends, but received little understanding from my new American acquaintances. I found that most American Jews didn't want to know about what I had been through during the war. Usually, whenever I started to talk about the war, they patted me on the back and said, "You're in America now; the past is behind you. We know how you feel because we had problems here, too." Or, "Our sugar and gas were rationed, so we had a hard time." And, "Well, that's all behind you now, you can forget about it. You're in a golden country; don't talk about it." The Americans I met tried to be kind, but they completely misunderstood my background. After a while, I didn't speak of the Holocaust. As a result, for many years, the subject was never mentioned among fellow survivors or by our new countrymen.

I wanted to find work so, right away after arriving in America, I registered with AJDC (American Joint Distribution Communities) the group that had brought me to America. They asked me if I had any profession and I told them that I had radio training. They gave me a gift of $50 and a card for the radio union. I waited for several hours at the radio union until an appropriate job was announced. Once in a while, a woman would come out and announce openings and specify what kinds of jobs were available. People jumped up at once and applied but I didn't understand what the jobs involved. After a couple days, I was still unemployed. Then I took a chance on a job as an assembler. When that job was announced and no one applied for it, I jumped up right away and applied. I didn't know what an assembler was, but I applied for it anyway. I was sent to Jewel Radio on East 21st Street. I was assigned to a socket-riveting machine.

My idea was to work as fast as possible, so my boss wouldn't find fault with me. When I thought about this kind of work, I realized I hated it. When I was a kid reading about how Americans worked, I imagined it was on an assembly line like this and I figured this was the way I was going to survive in America. However, after about two weeks as an assembler, I was taken off the line and given a job soldering radio components to switches, but I was too slow for this type of work. Two days later, I was put to work placing finished radios into packages. At the end of this week, I was fired and found myself amongst the ranks of the unemployed. The next day, I went back to the radio union, and they found me a job at Fisher Radio Corporation on Bleecker Street.

Fisher Radio was in the business of making fancy radio consoles. I was welcomed by a friendly supervisor and assigned to soldering rotary switches on radios. Technology was advancing and people were informed that television was soon to come out. As a result, consumers stopped buying Fisher Radios, which were becoming obsolete and expensive. By Christmas 1947, I was once again unemployed.

Fellow ex-workmates gave me pointers on how to look through the classified ads of the newspaper. I started to look for jobs, but usually the employer wanted someone with a high school education, which I didn't have. Mr. Mandel offered to get me a job in the maintenance department at Weiss and Klau, a Venetian blind company. I was hired and worked there as a grease monkey for the next four years. The maintenance shop where I worked was run by three German men. From my point of view, they were like Nazis, bossy, unfriendly and demanding. One of the electricians I worked with was impatient and harsh when I didn't understand his instructions. He would slap me across the face when I did something to displease him. My reaction was the same as when my German boss in the labor camp of Rakowice slapped me — I kept quiet.

A chance encounter with two deaf men changed the focus of my career path. Music was often played throughout the factory floor. One day, a lively march was playing. I was caught up in it and began waving my hands around as if I was conducting the orchestra. I failed to notice two deaf men signing back and forth to each other. While in the locker room, the taller, friendlier of the two handed me a note. He wrote: "We didn't expect you to make fun of our sign language." I felt a stab of regret and wrote back: "No, no. I would never do that! I was conducting music. I like music."

The next day, the man who handed me the note brought me three pages cut out from Reader's Digest Magazine. The subject was on some new sound equipment being released soon. The subject of high fidelity sound fascinated me and I became absorbed in learning all I could about this new equipment.

While in the National Guard, Leon Sperling and I were assigned to "communication, radio and telephone." Our job was to install radios in half-tracks (vehicles with regular wheels on the front for steering and caterpillar tracks on the back), string up telephone wires all over camp and hook up phones. Gradually, with this experience, I advanced in radio technology.

Over the next four years, every day, I scanned the newspaper for jobs in electronics. Early in 1952, I wrote to American Measuring Instruments Corporation and applied for a job. AMIC was looking for an electronic tester for radiosondes, small instruments with radio transmitting capabilities. A radiosonde was attached to a large balloon and sent up into the air to measure air temperature, pressure and humidity. I was put on a two-week trial. After determining that I had the necessary skill for the job, I was hired full time. I was very pleased to leave my job at Weiss and Klau and find work in the electronics field. Eventually, I was made assistant foreman making complete cable assemblies for underwater military devices.

During 1954, while in the National Guard, because I was developing my knowledge in communications, I became the battalion expert. I taught classes to the battalion on how to use the M-209 converter (a code converter) and other new communications equipment.

Later that year, AMIC sent me to Washington, D.C., to study a manual for a special video recorder for the Navy aircraft carriers. My boss wanted me to find out what the project involved before they bid on the contract. Based on my report, AMIC decided to bid on the contract. They won it and put me in charge as project engineer. This was new territory for me. I wasn't an engineer. I worked on the complex project full-time. I bought books on mathematics and audio, and other materials related to the project. This was a forerunner of the video recorder, still some years away in development. The design for the special recorder used four rotating heads, three-inch-wide paper magnetic tape, 1,200 feet long, and could record two, twenty-four hour programs on one tape. In the meantime, I learned how to write a technical manual, and a monthly report to the U.S. Department of Defense.

In 1956, AMIC declared bankruptcy. This news shocked me. In the meantime, I had finished the first model of the video recorder and was submitting it to the electronics division of the Brooklyn Navy yard for approval testing. After two submissions, the Navy approved the model. Back at AMIC, we were beginning to schedule the recorder for production. I contacted Audio Devices, Inc., a manufacturer of magnetic tape, for a bid on the type of tape we needed; however, they had never made this kind of tape before. As the order was for about 10,000 tapes, Audio Devices was anxious to work with me. After, five years, my time with AMIC had drawn to a close. AMIC was sold to another company. This new company cut down on personnel. I was made chief engineer of the recording project, but I spent limited time on it and eventually the company closed down operations.

I looked over newspapers once again. I went on several interviews. Audio Devices was interested in giving me a job with higher pay than AMIC, but that involved transferring to Connecticut, where their headquarters were located. The people at Audio Devices invited me to inspect the facilities and meet the employees. They were some of the friendliest, kindest people I had ever met. After thinking it through, I took the job with Audio Devices and started on April 1, 1957.

At first, I commuted to Connecticut from New York, but this became difficult, as the trains were often delayed which made me late for my meetings at the Kingdom Hall of Jehovah's Witnesses. I bought my first car, a Dodge Rambler, passed my driver's license test and hoped this would make commuting easier. Often, there was traffic to contend with and finding suitable parking was challenging. Ultimately, I realized I would have to move to Connecticut. So, in May 1960, I found a room to rent in a two-story private home and moved.

My move to Connecticut was fortuitous. There, I met my second wife, Virginia, at the Kingdom Hall of Jehovah's Witnesses. Often, we went out, door-to-door , preaching together. She became a good friend and tried to help me with my issues from the Holocaust. She listened carefully and sympathetically. We courted and were married November 9,

1963.

In 1965, we increased our family when Philip David was born and again in 1967 with the birth of Paul.

About 1970, Audio Devices was bought by Capitol Records. Gradually, management and the sales department were moved to California. I was informed that the company would be better served if I were in California. Begrudgingly, I complied, and in the fall of 1974, I moved my family to Los Angeles. We located a Kingdom Hall and began attending meetings with the Eagle Rock congregation of Jehovah's Witnesses. We spent the next twenty-four years in sunny California, enjoying outdoor living.

Left: Jack Laub
Right: Dziunka (Judy) Laub

1996-2006
68 to 78 years old

In 1996, Jehovah's Witnesses produced a
video documentary entitled, *Jehovah's
Witnesses Stand Firm Against Nazi
Assault.*

Chapter 45

When I dedicated my life as one of Jehovah's Witnesses, I set out to learn as much as I could about the history of the German group of Jehovah's Witnesses imprisoned in the concentration camps. From my personal research I learned that in 1933, the Jehovah's Witnesses in Germany were a small group of about twenty-five thousand members. When the Nazi's came to power, Jehovah's Witnesses were the first ones imprisoned in concentrations camps. Persecution of Jehovah's Witnesses intensified and some ten thousand were arrested. Of these, approximately two thousand five hundred to five thousand died in concentration camps or prisons. More than two hundred were tried by the German War Court and executed for refusing military service. Despite extreme persecution, their death rate in the camps was the lowest of any other group. Jehovah's Witnesses were the first ones to publish articles on the German government's plans involving the concentration camps. Stored in the archives at the United States Holocaust Memorial Museum in Washington, D.C. are publications written about Germany by the Jehovah's Witnesses.

As a result of my personal experiences during the Holocaust and my unique relationship with Jehovah's Witnesses, I was privileged to be a part of various educational projects about Jehovah's Witnesses and the Holocaust. In 1996, I received a telephone call from a young journalist, Joel Engardio, who was working for one of the television weekly news programs. He was preparing a program about Jehovah's Witnesses and was interested in my story. I spent about five hours on the telephone talking with him and answering his questions. Several weeks later he called to inform me that management had canceled the program but he liked the information I had given him and used it for another project. Some of the information I had given him was incorporated in his article "Jehovah's Witnesses' Untold Story of Resistance to Nazis." Although I was not interred in the Ravensbruck concentration camp in Germany, the focus of the article, Joel used some of my story in the introduction and conclusion to the article, which *The Christian Science Monitor* ran on the front page.

In 1996, Jehovah's Witnesses produced a video documentary titled, *Jehovah's Witnesses Stand Firm Against Nazi Assault.* Through first-person interviews, the video told the story of the Jehovah's Witnesses' experiences in Germany during the Nazi regime. The documentary garnered interest from various universities and won an Aurora gold award for the History Documentary category in 1998. Due to the increasing interest, there was a demand to orchestrate what were called "Stand Firm" presentations. Expert speakers on the subject of the Holocaust were invited to speak to other educators at colleges and universities.

In 1998, Jehovah's Witnesses in San Diego, California, were planning a Stand Firm presentation to be conducted at San Diego State University at 6:30 p.m., Thursday, October 8, 1998. The purpose of the Stand Firm program was to present information important to historians, sociologists and educators in the community. The guest speakers were professors and educators who were experts, some having written books about the Jehovah's Witnesses under Nazi persecution. Along with some Jehovah's Witness survivors, I received an invitation to speak as an eyewitness about the courageous stand Jehovah's Witnesses made under Nazi attack. The presentation was successful and the first of many presentations I would be invited to give around the world.

The Stand Firm presentations had wide appeal. I was invited to give a presentation at Stanford University in California. There was open seating and many people wanted to attend. To accommodate all the people, several noon and evening programs were scheduled. The Stanford presentation had added publicity as the programs were covered by the press. Local Witnesses organized the event and worked long and hard preparing for the program. They worked for several days preparing food, invitations, signs and posters advertising the event. Copies of the video,

Jehovah's Witnesses Stand Firm Against Nazi Assault, were on hand from the branch office of Jehovah's Witnesses in New York for distribution.

While traveling for these various seminars, I happened to meet a number of Jehovah's Witness survivors. My reaction to the Holocaust was so negative that I wanted to talk to the Witnesses who were there and went through it, yet came out of the concentration camps with stronger faith and a positive attitude. Every time I met a Witness I asked: "How could you come out of the camps unbroken? You are no different from me; what is the secret?"

The common answer was, "faith and loyalty," which I didn't understand when I first learned what Jehovah's Witnesses believed. Beyond that they felt they were supporting something very important, which rose above all other matters, namely God's name and His reputation. They could withstand anything simply because they had the strength from God, and they proved it. One such woman I met was kept in solitary confinement for three years. She seemed, to me, to have suffered no emotional damage because she had joy in her face and her eyes sparkled when I spoke with her.

I asked her, "How is it that you weren't damaged? Weren't you lonely?"

She looked astounded and responded adamantly, "Lonely! No, God was with me all the time!"

This is what they meant by strong faith. Even at age 70, I was still trying to grasp how they did it. What puzzled me the most was the strong conviction many of them retained even after spending as long as twelve years in the camps. I was imprisoned for some three years and came out utterly broken and transformed, while they still appeared whole.

After the war ended, some Jehovah's Witnesses were arrested for subversion and spent many more years in prison, as in the case of Rudolf Graichen, a German Witness brother, who later moved to Texas. We met at a Stand Firm presentation at Trinity University in San Antonio, Texas. After being released from a German prison in Stollberg on May 9, 1945, Rudy was arrested in September 1950 by the *Stasi,* who accused him of being a spy for the American government. He spent five more years in one of the worst *Stasi* prisons in Brandenburg, East Germany. Yet, he is full of joy and his smile never leaves his face. He is not bitter, broken or damaged.

I said to him, "Rudy, how did you do it?"

He said, "The scripture says God will never let us go beyond what we can take." His answer wouldn't make sense to someone unless they experienced that saving power first hand.

In 2000, at the Stand Firm seminars in Japan, Dr. Michael Berenbaum, a leading expert on the Holocaust, said people living in the concentration camps were classified in two categories: martyrs and victims. Victims had no choice; martyrs had a choice. The Witnesses were the ones who had the choice to go into the camps, rather than renounce their religion and escape imprisonment. Dr. Berenbaum said that this was the only group that qualified as martyrs of the Holocaust.

As for Jews like me, we were the victims and didn't know what wrong we committed. Some Jewish people said we were being punished by God because of something we did not do correctly. Others said it was something else, but nobody had the answer. Not knowing why the Holocaust happened is a huge frustration and difficult to comprehend, especially for survivors. Some Jewish survivors I know abandoned the idea of God altogether. So when I meet joyful, undamaged, healthy and happy non-Jewish survivors, there has to be some reason for their success.

In my opinion, there is a lack of love in the world. Love has become an impractical word and, as in the concentration camps, has very little meaning. The selfishness we see in societies around the world today is parallel to that in the camps—maybe not at the same critical level, but the way the world is in general, some may wonder which direction it is headed. As far as I am concerned, God has the answers. Whatever is happening now on the world scene has been predicted in the Bible. This is incredible and wonderful, because the prophecies in the Bible show we are at the end of the line. This system will be replaced by a world in which people live as true brothers and sisters, where people won't oppress each other and never learn war anymore. People will never get sick or die. This is God's purpose for mankind.

I was also invited to Israel. In cooperation with the branch office of Jehovah's Witnesses in Tel Aviv, the event was to take place in Jerusalem. Initially, there were serious problems finding a suitable location. In Israel, Jehovah's Witnesses, especially those who formerly subscribed to the Jewish faith, were considered dangerous by the ultra-orthodox Jews who looked at anyone converted from the Jewish faith as subject to everlasting destruction. The ultra-orthodox view the proselytizing of Jehovah's Witnesses as a direct threat to convert all Jews to the Jehovah's Witnesses faith. Some view this as a means to eliminate Jews — a continuation of the Nazis' work. As a result, Jehovah's Witnesses were considered worse than murderers and were persecuted by the ultra-orthodox. Licensing for restaurants and public places was controlled by some members of this group, who also had ties to the *Knesset*, the Israeli parliament. Some business owners feared the loss of their licenses if they allowed Jehovah's Witnesses to rent from them and worried about the threat of mobbing. Due to the nature of the program, there was difficulty renting a venue. Jehovah's Witnesses, formerly converted from Judaism, had already witnessed attacks by ultra-orthodox Jews on their homes and on the branch office in Tel Aviv. The atmosphere was disconcerting, and my wife, Virginia, learning some of these stories, was afraid we might be killed. Due to the connections of a spiritual brother who was a travel agent, the program was held at a world-class hotel, the King David in Jerusalem. He assured us that there would not be any trouble at this hotel.

The exhibition was held in two rooms. One, open to the public, was filled with photos and other documentation of the history of Jehovah's Witnesses. The second room, accessed by invitation only, was used for the Stand Firm presentation. Before the program began, we noticed some ultra-orthodox Jews come in. I was concerned there might be trouble, but they looked at the exhibition in the first room and walked leisurely out without incident.

During the actual presentation, there were speakers from Yad Vashem, the Holocaust Museum in Jerusalem. Also, guest speakers gave their eyewitness accounts from the perspective of both Jews and Jehovah's Witnesses. Overall, the program was successful and reached many people with its positive message of endurance under trial.

Next on our itinerary was Haifa. The purpose of the program was to demonstrate that we were fellow sufferers with the Jews. One brother had possession of a Yiddish newspaper originally published in Danzig in 1939. The article had originally been sent to a Jewish newspaper in New York and reprinted with commentary. The brother translated the New York article into Hebrew. The point of the article was how Jehovah's Witnesses behaved humanely toward Jews in the community before the war started. When the Nazis came into power, Jews were not allowed to shop for food or other necessities. Certain Jehovah's Witness women brought food to the Jews. The article ended by stating, "Let's look to these people, as we are fighting a common enemy." We distributed this article to the people of Haifa hoping to raise awareness, and it was well received.

As the years passed, I started a cycle of speaking engagements in schools and universities throughout the United States and Canada. I told the students and educators my personal experiences, followed by a question-and-answer session. The students in each school were instructed to write questions or a comment about what they had learned. Each time the response was the same - overwhelming appreciation. They were respectful and silent while I spoke, even shushing other children acting up during the presentation. They really wanted to hear what I had to say. They had many questions and wrote many letters of thanks and appreciation, which I cherish. I felt very privileged to be a part of that incredible experience.

I liked speaking to the youth at the universities because I feel young people are in trouble today, often because of peer pressure. They make the wrong decisions, often based on conformism. The Study Guide for the video *Jehovah's Witnesses Stand Firm against Nazi Assault,* published by Jehovah's Witnesses, states: "Every young person today could face similar dilemmas in his life." Then it asks these important questions: "When do I go along with others, and when do I stand up for what I believe in? Is it possible to maintain conviction in the face of threat of serious harm? Is it worth it? Does the law of conscience and human decency ever overrule national law? If so, then when?"

The Stand Firm seminars showed it was possible to make the right decisions based on the law of one's conscience, even though the decision was difficult. We live at a time when there is little compassion being shown. There is so much hatred in the world. Young people need to know it is possible to do the right thing under any conditions.

In 2002, Joel Engardio, the young journalist, called to ask if I would be interested in participating in a video program sponsored by PBS that he was producing and I said I was. The documentary film, *Knocking,* dealt with three important issues related to Jehovah's Witnesses: their stand regarding medical decisions involving blood transfusions, civil liberties, and neutrality (primarily Jehovah's Witnesses standing up to the Nazis). I was not one of Jehovah's Witnesses during my time in the concentration camps, but I was an eyewitness to their admirable conduct.

Together with my wife, two sons, daughter, and one of her sons, we began the interview process of making the film. Then, we were videotaped visiting many of the places in Poland that were important in my life, including my childhood home in Krakow, the village of Nieznanowice, the labor camp in Rakowice, and the concentration camp Auschwitz. Then we traveled to Mauthausen, Ebensee and Melk, visiting those former concentration camps in Austria.

Knocking was well received and won many awards. I enjoyed the privilege of attending the premiere and other screenings, where question-and answer-sessions took place, as well. I especially enjoy the privilege of using my personal history as a way of reaching people with the Bible's message of hope for the world.

My Family, My Journey

"As my family and I slowly departed the train from Dworzec Glowney train station, I knew this this time in Poland would be different from the many other times I've visited." This time I came back to Krakow with my children including my daughter, Susie, my two sons, David and Paul and my grandson Andrew, Susie's oldest boy. I wanted to show them this place, my home, where it all began for me. In many ways, it was the beginning of death for me. I wanted to show them how I became the man I am today, the events in life that shaped me and transformed me from a precocious Jewish boy with all the opportunities and advantages before him to ultimately becoming none of those things I had at first imagined myself to be. Instead I became a shattered young man without hope of betterment. A person without trust of fellowman, without hope in God, a god-hater it might be said of me. Then miraculously I discovered a new kind of hope in the most unlikely of places, a concentration camp. It was in that place, devoid of all hope that I encountered an unusual brand of people that would later, much later in life, re-define my entire life and belief system. With my newly found perspective of life changed I had been told on numerous occasions that I was a traitor, that I was using religion as a crutch. And the most absurd thing of all, I was asked when I first started hating Jews.

The Journey

I want to share life, to explain myself to them. I want to take them on this journey to see my home where I spent my early childhood, to see the village my family lived in when we were ordered to leave Krakow. Finally, I want to walk together through each of the camps I was interred in.

Now I can fully explain why I made the choices I made and how I came to be here with this terrific, loving family. I have expectations of sharing my life experiences with my family and re-connecting with them on a level I have never before reached.

I hope the outcome of this trip together will make up for the many lost years. But how can an entire lifetime of confusion and dealing with an emotionless father make up for anything? It is a high standard to reach, but I feel I have to try.

Our Lives Together

I don't think I taught my children much, especially about me, what things I used to like to do as a child or about my parents and siblings. They only knew some of the stories, some of the things that happened to me. The main things they knew about were that I and my older sister survived the Holocaust and the rest of our family didn't. I didn't teach them as a father would teach his children, like how to play football, soccer or how to fish.

Except for one time, we never played catch in the yard. I remember my son said "Come on Dad, let's toss the Frisbee." We went outside and threw it back and forth a few times and that was about the extent of it. How surprised they will be to know that I loved sports, I loved to play games. In fact I was very competitive. How surprised they will be when I show them the grassy field I once played soccer on and tell them how happy and carefree I once was. The things we did do together as a family were things like any ordinary family in America. There were camping trips and excursions to Disneyland, even luxury cruises, but I never talked to them about myself. I was with them physically, but mentally very far away.

My sons would often shout out to get my attention "Earth to Father, come back to Earth!" or "This is Earth calling, is anyone there?" My oldest son said I didn't speak eight words to him before he moved out of the house and that it was still hard to connect with me and have a conversation. As my boys grew older, they left me behind emotionally, they became my seniors and it was impossible to talk to them.

Often I live in my own reality. I have a lack of closeness and I avoid intimacy. It was a life-saving mechanism during the war; without it, no one could survive. The problem surfaced when that safety mechanism didn't turn off even after the war. As a child survivor that part of my personality formed in my brain and became part of the norm. It became my way of dealing with things.

As a Survivor

I continue to be a survivor; it never quits. The numbness, the detachment the disassociation becomes the life I have to live with. Like a cripple I have to live with it. When I come together with my family and my children, I cannot relate to them as a father normally relates to his children.

My wife would often remark how difficult it was to be with me when my boys had performances in school. It was such a challenge for me to be there, I would become some sort of a zombie sitting there with eyes glazed over and an expression on my face, as if there were a vacancy sign blinking across my forehead. I was so totally disconnected from everyone around me and from what was going on right in front of me. I would disappear into my own world, not even seeing what Paul and David were doing.

As a boy I was active in school plays, recitals, and special school programs. Sitting there in the school auditorium watching all these young people I was so jealous! Jealous of them, not only because I was restricted from school from the fifth grade on, but because these children were active in school and performing. The kids were having a good time doing all the things I used to do and the memory of it was killing me. I have so many regrets on that level; regrets of all that I missed.

Some ask me, "Were there hugs and kisses while your children were growing up? " Sure, but the embraces were not warm. The closer the person is the more I avoid intimacy. The fear of losing my family is my way of self-protection but it is dangerous because it keeps us isolated from each other. My wife and children suffer the most. I don't want to hurt them with my stories, or make them feel sad for me. I also can't talk about it for the fear of being misunderstood. Even survivors don't speak to one another about their experiences. If somebody said "I was in this camp." that was enough, there was no need to talk. The feeling of not being understood is a very pervasive one. It is important for us to be understood and it is better not to say anything than to be misunderstood by what we say. I cannot draw them close to me, I want the opposite but it doesn't happen.

My Children, My Grandchild

It was impossible for me to live vicariously through my children, I didn't want that. What I wanted was to have that time back, even though I couldn't have it back, I was missing it terribly. I did not want to sit in a school auditorium with feelings of guilt or remorse.

I did not realize how much Susie, David and Paul suffered because they could understand what kind of father I was. The distance is there, we all sense it, and we are all powerless against it.

My sons had more of my personal attention than my daughter. She was raised in a different household with a different father figure. I am sure she noticed the differences between her two fathers, and this oftentimes must have frustrated her. She could never be close to me and I didn't have any kind of clue how to be a normal father for her. Over the years, I was in and out of her life and we could never build on a consistent sort of relationship. My grandchildren have suffered from this also. Andrew is not as close to me as he is to other people he is not even related to. He fondly calls them Aunt, Uncle or Cousin. He says, "I feel like their family, in terms of talking to them, about almost anything then I do about my direct family here. I wanted to go on this trip, but it is still strange for me." He says that it is partly the distance and partly that he doesn't hear my personal stories, "It is really weird; I hear him talk and I know history but I still can't "connect" with him somehow."

So it would seem that regardless if my children lived with me or apart from me the remoteness was experienced by all of them.

Happy to Have My Family

If I had not survived the Holocaust my children wouldn't be alive. That simple fact remains. I was one of the fortunate ones and I cannot account for it. To me, to be given a family is a special treasure, life is a gift. So many others were cut off and never had children, never had grandchildren. I have a family a wife, children, and grandchildren. Dwelling on the past, destroying myself mentally, doesn't do me any good.

My hope is that we will get closer, to communicate together so they will know what I went through so they can understand better and they can forgive me. They tell me there is nothing to forgive, this is just how I am, how I have always been, they've adjusted to it, and no matter how many trips to Poland we take our problems will not be suddenly solved.

Paul says how he has adjusted to living with me, how it is me who hasn't adjusted. He says, "All my life I have been hearing how you want to change things, feel things. You keep saying, 'maybe later it will come, maybe later' I'm hoping it will come. But you know what? At this point I don't believe it will come, it's not going to happen anymore, so I'm accepting that."

His words seem hard to accept when I want to change so badly, when I have changed already. He tells me, "If you lost your leg on a land mine in a battle field somewhere instead of losing your emotional side in the concentration camps, I wouldn't expect you to be able to run with the

349

Olympic athletes, that just wouldn't happen. None of us expects you to have emotions, and you shouldn't be so hard on yourself." What I lost wasn't a leg. It was something else and it is gone; I can't find it. My children accept it. They adjust to the fact that it is missing, and like the athlete who lost their leg, I should put my lack of emotion aside and learn to walk without my emotional side.

I want all of us to reach a better place in our relationship. They tell me they love me, they are willing to go on this journey and come to some kind of understanding. This a good thing to start with, because I can't accept myself the way I am. I continue looking for avenues to do it better.

Family photo-Front & center Jozef
Left To Right: Szaj, Babcia, Mamusia (Malka), Hanka
Back row Left to Right: Shmil, Icek

Epilogue

Joseph Kempler's early years can be likened to a funnel – wide open at the top, gradually sloping into a narrow tunnel that closes in ever tighter until there is but a small opening at the bottom. In the beginning, he had many different possibilities available to him; there were no restrictions. Due to the circumstances of the war, achieving his personal goals became impossible. As he slipped down the slope of the funnel, Joseph's life became more constricted. He found himself in situations where he had to adapt in order to survive. Eventually, he abandoned emotions that got in the way of his survival, and became numb. Gradually, Joseph was squeezed almost to the brink of death. Then, like a miracle, he experienced liberation from Ebensee in 1945, but he barely survived. The funnel opened up, and Joseph was again free to make his own choices in life. After the war his love of trains greatly diminished. While he preferred traveling by train to get from one place to another, the magic the locomotive held for him had evaporated. When Joseph came to America, he wanted to take advantage of the many opportunities that presented themselves. He didn't even want to deny himself food that would ordinarily be restricted by Jewish religious beliefs, such as shellfish or pork. Lacking the emotions he had abandoned during the war negatively affected every relationship he had, especially in the roles of husband and father. Later on, as certain psychological problems came to the surface, Joseph tried to learn why he behaved the way he did, and spent nearly fifty years seeking counsel from books on psychology, psychologists and doctors, but still, he struggled to heal himself. Joseph has said over and over that he wants to feel things emotionally; that he wants to change things within himself. He is continuing to work toward the goal of making those changes in order to bring his family closer emotionally, but for Joseph, it has been a long and frustrating journey. He now has to contend with increasing health problems that get in the way of his goals.

Nearly every time he related his experiences in the schools, the question was brought up, "Do you still hate the Germans?" He would say,

"I don't hate them. I cannot hate them." As with the feeling of love, negative feelings such as hate are also gone. As an example of this, he will tell the story of how he was in Germany on business, and was sitting by himself in a restaurant drinking a beer, taking in the scenery. At a nearby table he noticed a group of old Germans, who were having a good time. They reminded him of Nazis. In his imagination, he saw them as arrogant Nazis enjoying themselves, acting as if they hadn't destroyed families and lives. In this fantasy, he tried to hate them. "There they are right on top again, as if nothing had ever happened. I wanted to hate them for what they did to me, but even looking right at good examples of ex-Nazis, I couldn't hate them. I couldn't even conjure up negative feelings for the people who hurt me personally, so how could I hate these strangers?" Joseph would say.

Joseph always had a relationship with his daughter, Susie. She knew he was her real father, but they were not as close as they could have been. There were deep issues that Susie hadn't been able to talk about with Joseph. Why had he given her up for adoption? Why didn't he take care of her? How could he shirk his duty as a father? Even though father and daughter managed a good relationship, there were certain issues better left untouched due to their delicate nature. Joseph always felt that the documentary *Knocking* was instrumental in opening doors between him and Susie. There were more opportunities to speak openly about things they had kept hidden in their hearts for so many years. Through *Knocking*, Joseph was able to discuss the impact the Holocaust had on his life, as well as on the lives of his family. Although the family has accepted Joseph the way he is, he can't accept himself.

Susie is married to Jeff Grant, and they are both active in their Jewish community. She was exposed to the teachings of Jehovah's Witnesses, but chose Judaism. Their two sons, Andrew and Brian, were raised with Jewish traditions. Joseph's sons, David and Paul, are dedicated Jehovah's Witnesses. Joseph is proud, of his children and grand-children. In his own words Joseph has said: "Even though my children have damage, caused by me, they have turned out to be wonderful people. They are much better than I am or can be. All my children are true blessings. My wife and children have been very supportive of me, and I feel privileged and blessed to have such a family in my life.

The Altered I

354

Appendix

Historic Note on Kazimierz

The Kazimierz was founded by Kazimierz the Great, a Polish king during the 14th century. Jews had lived in Poland before the reign of King Kazimierz, even so, he allowed them to settle in Poland in great numbers. Although his crown and title meant little to his neighbors, who called him King of Krakow, he gained respect from his Jewish citizens when he protected them as people of the king. Late in the year 1334, he reconfirmed privileges that were granted to Jewish Poles in 1264 by Boleslaw V the Chaste.

Children were being kidnapped and forced to undergo Christian baptism, but King Kazimierz prohibited this treatment under penalty of death. He instilled a heavy punishment for the destruction of Jewish cemeteries. The Nazis undid this historical precedent once Germany conquered Krakow in 1939.

Nuremburg Law

The Nuremberg Laws were passed in Nazi Germany. The first law, The Law for the Protection of German Blood and German Honor, prohibited marriage, or extramarital intercourse, between Jews and Germans, and the employment of German females under the age of 45 in Jewish households. The second law, The Reich Citizenship Law deprived persons of their German citizenship. This introduced a distinction between Reich citizens and nationals. People who descended from four German grandparents were of German blood and considered Reich citizens. If someone descended from three or four Jewish grandparents, they were not classified as a Reich citizen, but as a "Jew." A person with one or two Jewish grandparents was called a *Mischling*, meaning "mixed blood." They were not considered a Reich citizen and were denied the common citizenship rights of Germany.

Jehovah's Witness Articles

From ushmm.org website [excerpt]: "The International Society of Jehovah's Witnesses fully and publicly supported the efforts of its brethren in Germany. At an International Convention in Lucerne, Switzerland in September 1936 Witness delegates from all over the world passed a resolution severely condemning the Nazi regime. The international organization also produced literature denouncing Nazi persecution of Jews, Communists, and Social Democrats, criticizing the remilitarization of Germany and the Nazification of its schools and universities, and attacking the Nazi assault on organized religion.

Holocaust Program in Israel

While in Israel, Professor Lawrence L. Langer, professor of English emeritus at Simmons College in Boston, Massachusetts, started an unusual Holocaust program. He showed videos of some of his case studies. In the late 1970s, Yale University conducted and archived interviews of Holocaust survivors. Professor Langer then wrote a book based on these interviews. I read it and was totally absorbed. The book mentions one case study in particular, a man described only as Leon S. Leon S. told Professor Langer some terrible experiences he had. I was especially moved by his story.

As I watched the video program, I saw to my absolute surprise, the man called Leon S. It was my very good friend Leon Sperling. I had been with Leon in the displaced persons' camp in Landsberg, the radio school, and through emigration to America. Then we spent seven years together in the National Guard. As a rule, survivors don't mention their personal stories, so I had never known about any of his personal Holocaust experiences. To discover this about my friend after so many years was really something!

Judaism

This is a brief overview of the beliefs and practices of Judaism as well as those of Jehovah's Witnesses. It is not the intent of the author to compare one religion over another. This summary is solely for the purpose of showing Joseph Kempler's point of view as a follower of Judaism but who later became one of Jehovah's Witnesses.

This overview should not be viewed as a detailed description of Judaism. For further insight into Judaism, a thorough study of the beliefs and traditions is recommended.

Jew – The name is derived from Judah, a son of Jacob and one of the twelve tribes of Israel. Eventually the term was applied to all Israelites, not just descendants of Judah.

Judaism – As a religion it is practiced in the State of Israel, United States, Europe and the Diaspora (dispersion around the world). Man is created in God's image and his purpose for life is to obey God, obey the law and atone for sin. Man was created with a free will, but must exercise that free will to practice good things and be good to others.

Synagogue – A place of worship.

The various Divisions, or branches of Judaism, called movements are:

Orthodox Judaism – Accept *Tanakh* (TNK, acronym for *Torah*, Hebrew for Law, *Nevi'im*, Hebrew for Prophets, and *Ketuvim*, Hebrew for Writings) as inspired Scripture.

Reform Judaism –Discarded traditions and rituals such as circumcision, laws on diet, purity, and dress. In modern times the movement has returned to a more traditional approach.

Conservative Judaism – Conserve the Jewish traditions while embracing modern culture. Jewish holidays, dietary laws, Sabbath and life-cycle events are observed. Accept the *Torah* (first five books of the Jewish Bible) is from God. Men and women are allowed to sit together during worship and women may become rabbis.

Hasidic – Ultra-Orthodox. The focus is on the emotional aspect of worship rather than the execution of religious education and ritual. The manner of the worship, how it is felt, is more important than the meaning of the worship. The Hasidic movement is influenced by the Kabbalah movement. Hasidic Jews can be recognized by their Eastern European style of mainly black clothing, of the eighteenth and nineteenth centuries. They wear conspicuous hats, robes, and other garments associated with being ultra-orthodox.

Kabbalah – The mystical side of Judaism. In simple terms there is a force, or "Upper Force" in which all individual souls were split from. These souls need to unify with that force. Kabbalah is the map to that knowledge of unification with the force.

God – YHWH, the Tetragrammaton, replaced with Adonai, rendered Lord. A common pronunciation of YHWH is Yahweh. According to *The Jewish Book of Why*, second printing 1981, Alfred J. Kolatch writes: "But what is God's name? The biblical reference to God as *Yehova* (Jehovah), spelled out with the Hebrew characters *yad*, *hay*, *vav*, *hay*, is generally considered the 'authentic' name of God, a name never to be pronounced."

Star of David – An emblem used as identification with the Jewish people. Literally means "Shield of David" but has a clouded origin and probably is not connected at all with King David of the Bible. Used as an ornament, or article of jewelry.

There are three garments of biblical origin associated with Judaism:

Tallit – Prayer shawl (Numbers 15:37-41).

Tefilin – Phylacteries (Exodus 13:1-10; 13:11-16; Deuteronomy 6:4-9; 11:13-21)

Mezuzah – A case hung on the doorframes of Jewish homes. Inside the case is a scroll with a passage from Deuteronomy 6:9.

Jewish Sacred Texts:

Tanakh – Three divisions of the Hebrew Bible (Law, writings, and prophets)

Torah – The first five books of Moses (or Pentateuch)

Talmud – Oral Torah, comprises *Mishnah* (text) and *Gemara* (commentary)

Midrash – Stories, sermons and parables explaining the *Talmud*

Mishnah – Written recording of Oral Torah, "repeating"

Responsa – "Queries and replies" thousands of volumes of answers to specific questions. The Responsa are composed by rabbis who have been asked a specific question, and include a full description of the situation, references to the applicable Talmudic passages, the rabbi's answer, and the reasoning behind his opinion.

The Septuagint – Greek translation of Hebrew Bible

Zohar – Kabbalah, mystical branch of Judaism

The Ten Commandments:

You shall not worship other Gods

You shall not worship graven images

You shall not take name of the Lord in vain

Remember the Sabbath day and keep it holy

Honor your father and your mother

You shall not murder

You shall not commit adultery

You shall not steal

You shall not give false witness against your neighbor

You shall not covet…anything that is your neighbors

The 13 Articles of Faith – written by twelfth century philosopher Moses ben Maimon, called Maimonides:

God exists

God is one and unique

God is incorporeal

God is eternal

Prayer is to God only

The prophets spoke truth

Moses was the Greatest of the prophets

The written and the oral law were given to Moses

There will be no other Torah

God knows the thoughts and deeds of men

God will reward the good and punish the wicked

The Messiah will come

The dead will be resurrected

The Messianic Age – This is when the Messiah comes. Ezekiel 36:16 points to when he will come. Righteous dead will be resurrected. Wicked will not resurrected. This will be a time of peace. There will be a restoration of the land and organization of Israel. The Messiah will adhere to Jewish law (Isaiah 11:2-5).The Messiah will be a righteous judge (Jeremiah 33:15).The Messiah will be a great military leader. (Isaiah 55:4; Daniel 9:25; Psalms 2:6; Genesis 49:10). There is a difference of opinion concerning the conditions of the world when the Messiah arrives: the Messiah will come when the world is especially good or, the Messiah will come when the world is especially evil. The Messiah will come after a period of war and suffering. When the Messiah comes there will be peace among the nations (Isaiah 2:4; Micah 4:3).When the Messiah comes there will be perfect harmony between man and nature (Isaiah 11:6-9). Jews will return from exile to Israel (Isa 11:11, 12).There will be universal acceptance of the Jewish God and Jewish religion (Isaiah 2:3; 11:10; 66:23; Micah 4:2-3; Ezekiel 37:24). There will be no sin, no evil. All Israel will obey commandments (Zephaniah 3:13; Ezekiel 37:24). The Temple will be reinstated (Ezekiel 37: 26-27). World to come is physical world after the Messiah has come and God has judged the living and the dead. The righteous are resurrected to life.

On the subject of the afterlife, the beliefs vary on Heaven, Hell and a resurrection. Much of the focus is on daily activity in this world.

Heaven – *Gan Eden*, which is Hebrew for Garden of Eden. This is the place where the righteous dwell. There is some argument whether this is a place for souls after death or resurrected people to life in the "world to come."

Hell – *Gehinnom*, or *Gehenna*, A place of punishment for unrighteous Jews, Jeremiah 7:31; 2 Kings 23:10. At the end of twelve months, punishment of the wicked one is finished and they can enter *Gan Eden*, if they have repented, or they are eternally destroyed if their sin doesn't merit forgiveness.

Life-cycle Events – the rituals conducted for the various facets of everyday life including birth, becoming a man or woman, marriage, death, and mourning.

Sabbath – This is a sacred Day of Rest (Deuteronomy 5:12-15; Exodus 31:16-17).

Holidays:

Passover – Celebration of the exodus of the Israelites from bondage in Egypt (Exodus 23:15; 12:1-34).

Lag b'Omer – Scholars Day.

Shavuot – Fest of Weeks, Festival of First fruits (Numbers 28:26; Exodus 34:22).

Shiva Asar b'Tammuz – Commemorates the day Jerusalem's walls were breached by King Nebuchadnezzar of Babylon, in the sixth century B.C.E.

Tisha B'Av – Mourning for the first destruction of the Temple in Jerusalem by Babylonians in the sixth century B.C.E

Rosh Hashanah – Jewish New Year, recognized as a Day of Awe (Leviticus 23). This is a return to God.

Fast of Gedaliah – A Jewish official appointed by King Nebuchadnezzar of Babylon, in the sixth century B.C.E. He was assassinated by some Jews who remained in Jerusalem after the Temple was destroyed by King Nebuchadnezzar. He is now mourned as a hero.

Yom Kippur – Day of Atonement (Leviticus 16:29, 30; 23:27).

Sukkot – Called the Festival of Booths (Leviticus 23:42, 43). This is the first day of the festival.

Hoshana Rabbah – Seventh day of *Sukkot*.

Simchat Torah – Conclusion, derived from gathering, or assembly. This is the last day of the reading of the Pentateuch, and the Festival of Rejoicing This festival is observed as part of *Shemini Atzeret*, the eighth day of *Sukkot* (Leviticus 23:36).

Chanukah – Rededication of Temple in 165 B.C.E after it was made into a pagan shrine by King Antiochus IV of Syria.

Asara b'Tevet – Commemorates the beginning of the siege of Jerusalem by the Babylonians around the sixth century B.C.E.

Chamisha Asar b'Shevat – In modern Israel this is known as Arbor Day. It is the celebration of the new year of tree growth.

Fast of Esther – Jews fasted to lend support to Queen Esther who did not have permission to enter in before the King of Persia, Ahasuerus. This was punishable by death.

Purim – Feast of Lots, *Purim* is derived from a word meaning "lots". This feast commemorates deliverance of the Jews of Persia by Esther and her cousin Mordecai; see the Bible book of Esther.

Shushan Purim – Celebration of *Purim* on the fifteenth day of the month of Adar. This is the day after *Purim* because the Jews of Shushan lived in a walled city.

Jehovah's Witnesses

This is a brief overview of the beliefs of Jehovah's Witnesses. It should not be considered as a detailed account of their teachings. For more information about Jehovah's Witnesses a thorough study of their beliefs is recommended.

Jehovah's Witnesses believe the entire Bible is the inspired word of God comprised of Hebrew, Aramaic and Greek Scriptures. (2 Timothy 3:16, 17; Romans 15:4).

God – Worship one God, Jehovah (Exodus 6:3). (See Douay Version Footnote on Ex. 6:3)

Jehovah – Widely recognized as God's name, YHWH, also known as the Tetragrammaton. (Job 37:23; Revelation 4:11). He is God Almighty. His four qualities are love, justice, wisdom, and power.

Jesus Christ – God's son (Acts 4:12; 10:43; Colossians 1:15:17; John 17:3).

Holy Spirit – God's invisible active force, used to create all things, also translated as spirit or ru'ach in Hebrew. This spirit is energy from God projected and exerted on people or things to accomplish his will. By use of this spirit we are directed or guided in a recommended course of life (Genesis 1: 1, 2; Revelation 4:11; Psalms 104:30; John 20:22; 1 Corinthians 12:4-11; Jeremiah 10:23).

Kingdom – Mankind's only solution. It is a real government in heaven over the earth (2 Timothy 4:18; Psalms 11:4; Daniel 2:44).

Armageddon – This is God's war against the unrighteous to end wickedness on the earth (2 Thessalonians 1:6-9; Psalms 37:38).

Heaven – 144,000 will go to heaven to share rulership with Jesus Christ. They rule as kings as priests over the earth and its subjects

(Revelation 14:1; Revelation 5:9, 10).

Earth – God's original purpose for the earth will be fulfilled, and the earth will be completely populated by worshipers of Jehovah. Humans "out of all nations, and tribes and people and tongues" (Revelation 7:9) will have the opportunity to live forever in human perfection on a paradise earth. Included are the ones who come out of the great tribulation and those who are resurrected from the dead. (Revelation 21:3-5; 7:9, 14; Genesis 1:28; 2:8-15).

Last Days – The time of the end of this system of things. The time we are living now since 1914 (Matthew 24:3, 14, 34; 2 Timothy3:1-5; 1 John 2:17).

Death – Mankind suffers death due to inherited sin. The dead are not conscience of anything. Man is a soul, not given one. At death the soul dies (Genesis 3:17, 19; Romans 5:12; Ecclesiastes 9:5, 10; Ezekiel 18:4).

Resurrection – Anastasis, Greek word for resurrection, literal meaning "a standing up again" and refers to a rising up from death. According to God's will the person, who has been existing only in God's memory, is restored to life in either a human body or a spirit body. After resurrection the individual retains their personality and memories as when he/she died. There will be a resurrection of both the righteous and the unrighteous. Unrighteous resurrected ones are given the opportunity to prove themselves righteous before God. All will have the opportunity to live forever on earth in human perfection. Only 144,000 individuals are resurrected to heavenly life. These ones share rulership in heaven with Jesus Christ who is God's appointed king (1 Corinthians 15: 40, 42, 44, 49; Revelation 20:4b, 5, 13; Revelation 21:3-5; John 5:28, 29).

Jehovah's Witnesses – They believe the line of witnesses of Jehovah reaches back to Abel, Adam and Eve's son. Modern day Jehovah's Witnesses had their start in the United States in the 1870s. These were known as Bible Students until 1931, when they adopted the name Jehovah's Witnesses. "Jehovah's Witnesses beliefs and practices are a restoration of first century Christianity," Reasoning from the Scriptures, page 203 par. 3, published by Watchtower Bible & Tract Society of New York, 1989.

Kingdom Hall – Place of worship.

Memorial (Lord's Evening Meal) – This is the only notable celebration that Jehovah's Witnesses observe. It is the commemoration of the death of Jesus Christ on a torture stake. It takes place on Nisan 14, of the Jewish calendar that was common in the first century ("the beginning of the month of Nisan was the sunset after the new moon nearest the spring equinox became visible over Jerusalem. Fourteen days later is Nisan 14," Reasoning from the Scriptures, page 269 par. 2, published by Watchtower Bible & Tract Society of New York, 1989). Only those of the "little flock" or part of the 144,000 partake of the unleavened bread and wine (Luke 12:3; 22:19; 1 Corinthians 11:26; Hebrews 9:15).

Jehovah's Witnesses are politically neutral. They have given their allegiance to God's government. Jehovah's Witnesses do not go to war, vote, run for political office, or preach nationalism. Instead they teach that God is love and we must love each other.

Sources

The Jewish Book of Why by Alfred J. Kolatch, 1981, Jonathan David Publishers, Inc.

Mankind's Search for God, 1990, published by Watchtower Bible and Tract Society of New York, Chapter 9, page 205-234, 1990.

Reasoning from the Scriptures, 1989, Watchtower Bible and Tract Society of Jehovah's Witnesses, page 199-200, subheading "What Beliefs of Jehovah's Witnesses set them apart from other religions?" points 1-10.

Bible sources:

The Holy Scriptures According to the Masoretic Text, published by The Jewish Publication Society of America, Exodus 6:3 "My name YHWH, footnote: the ineffable name read Adonai, which means Lord.

New American Standard Bible, Text Edition, 1901, 1977, World Bible Publishers, Exodus 6:3 YHWH Adonai rendered Lord. Exodus 3:14, footnote reads: "related to the name of God, YHWH rendered Lord which is derived from the verb HAYAH, to be.

New World Translation of the Holy Scriptures, 1984, published by Watchtower Bible and Tract Society of New York, Inc.

The Living Bible, 1971, Tyndale House Publishers

Website sources:

www.drbo.org/chapter/02006.htm, Douay-Rheims Catholic Bible

www.religionfacts.com/judaism/beliefs.htm, 2004-2013,Tracy R. Rich, Judaism 101, George Robinson, Essential Judaism, 2000, Pocket Books

www.religionfacts.com/judaism/beliefs/afterlife.htm, 2004-2013, by Rabbi Amy Scheinerman, Is There Life after Death?

www.judaism.about.com/od/judaismbasics/a/Afterlife-In-Judaism-Jewish-Beliefs.htm, Ariela Pelaia.

http://www.religionfacts.com/judaism/texts/responsa.htm

www.jewishvirtuallibrary.org/jsource/judaism/The-Origins-of-Reform_Judaism.html

Notes

[1]The Jewish Passover celebration commemorates the Exodus, the deliverance of ancient Hebrews from slavery in Egypt.

[2]"Henry Rosner, a violinist, and his brother Poldek, an accordionist, entertained Amon Goeth, commandant of Plaszow, and his frequent guest Oscar Schindler at numerous dinner parties. Oscar Schindler's fondness for the Rosner compelled him to add the entire Rosner family to his famous list of 1,100 workers saved from death camps. Source: www.oskarschindler.com

[3]See appendix: Nuremburg Law.

[4]Disney historian J.B. Kaufman at the Walt Disney Family Museum confirms that a dubbed version of *Snow White and the Seven Dwarfs* opened in the city of Warsaw in October 1938 and played for six weeks. Mr. Kaufman said, "I don't think it's too much of a stretch to speculate that the film made it to Krakow by 1940 — in fact, I'd be surprised if it wasn't shown there long before that."

[5]Carbide is acetylene, which when mixed with calcium carbide and water produces a gas that can be burned. These lamps were often used by miners.

[6]Some Jews would say later that these arches were in the shape of tombstones pointing to a grim future for the Jews penned in behind them.

[7]Auschwitz and Belzez were extermination camps where people were killed by poison gas.

[8]The Plaszow (Pwa' shuf) labor camp was beginning to be made ready for Jewish prisoners during this time. Plaszow was built in the area of two Jewish cemeteries located on Jerozolimska and Abrahama streets. The Nazis chose to destroy Jewish gravesites and rob them of their tombstones. The broken slabs were used to pave the entranceway to Plaszow camp. Source: www.holocaustresearch.org

[9]One SS man named Hujar was particularly cruel. It was under his instructions that all parents were to take their children under the age of 14 to a *kinderheim*, a children's home. He told the parents that while they were at work in the camp, their children would be safe under German care; however, all children in *kinderheim* were shot and killed, and any of the parents who stayed behind with them suffered the same fate. To save bullets, the children were lined up, one behind the other, and shot with a single gunshot, the bullet passing through all of them at one time.

[10]Source: www.deathcamps.org/occupation/plaszow.html

[11]Plaszow was intended as a penal labor camp under the jurisdiction of local SS men in the general government. However, it began to look suitable as a stage for deporting Jews east, since it had easy access to the railway located just outside the camp. Amon Goeth would become its infamous commandant. Since it was not a concentration camp, Goeth did not have to report directly to Berlin; as such, the camp was completely under his jurisdiction, and he had no one to answer to for his actions.

[12]Before being taken to the Plaszow forced labor camp, Diana Reiter had worked for the Krakow district building department.

[13]Oskar Schindler, a German industrialist, was made famous in Steven Spielberg's movie *Schindler's List*. Schindler relocated to Krakow, Poland, where he acquired an enamelware factory through a Court of Commercial Claims. He is credited with saving the lives of twelve hundred Jews.

[14]Soon after the war, I found out why our train bypassed Auschwitz. Apparently, they were having a capacity problem due to the large number of Hungarian Jews the Nazis were gassing and burning. Hungarian Jews were being taken out of Hungary by the tens of thousands and sent to Auschwitz for immediate extermination. Evidently, the gas chambers and crematoriums were operating at full speed. Nazis were killing about 12,000 people a day and turned our train away saying to our SS guards, "We have no place for you. We have all these Hungarian Jews to take care of!" This was another reprieve. My life was saved because something went wrong according to their plan. One wrong decision, one wrong move, or one wrong situation, I would have been dead.

[15]Years later I read a book by Viktor Frankl, an Austrian psychiatrist and neurologist, who had been interred in Nazi concentration camps. Once, when someone was asleep in the barrack and was having a nightmare, he wanted to shake them awake. But another prisoner stopped him, and said, "No, leave him be. No nightmare can be as bad as the reality. Let him sleep."

[16]"Classification System in Nazi Concentration Camps: Criminals marked with green inverted triangles, political prisoners; red, 'asocials' (including Roma, nonconformists, vagrants, and other groups) with black or—in the case of Roma in some camps—brown triangles. Homosexuals were identified with pink triangles and Jehovah's Witnesses with purple ones." Source: www.ushmm.org

[17] Wernher von Braun was a member of the Nazi party, who started his career as *Untersturmfurer*, second lieutenant, and was promoted three times by Himmler. The last and third time was to SS Sturmbanfurer, Wehrmacht Major. He surrendered on May 2, 1945, to an American private, who happened to be riding a bicycle when he found von Braun. The U.S. Army recognized what a catch he was, and after the war he was hired by the U.S. Army to build rockets for them. His ultimate dream was to use these rockets for space exploration

and eventually he ran NASA's Marshall Space Flight Center. He became a hero rather than a criminal because the Americans needed him.

[18]Despite the Nazis best efforts, the Witnesses were able to share their faith with others and made converts right in the camps. I came to know some of them years later. I learned that some of the Nazis assigned to guarding Jehovah's Witnesses heard the things they were speaking of and began to share their beliefs. These ex-Nazis were stripped of their ranks and thrown right in the camp with the Witnesses. These most unusual stories gave people a reason for living. They highlight the message of hope and encouragement that the Witnesses provided.

[19]Many years later, while wandering around the Holocaust Museum in Washington, D.C., I came across an interesting brochure specifically about the Jehovah's Witnesses. In that brochure, a statement is made from Rudolph Hoess, the commandant of Auschwitz. He is quoted as saying Heinrich Himmler admired the Witnesses so much he didn't want to kill them off, but instead he wanted to switch them to his side. He often used the Witnesses as an example to SS troops. He said if people had the same loyalty to Hitler that the Witnesses had for Jehovah, the future of the third Reich would be assured. *Source: United State Holocaust Memorial Museum brochure on Jehovah's Witnesses pg. 13 and 14.*

[20]I found out later this day happened to be the day Franklin D. Roosevelt died, a Thursday. Somehow we always knew the dates even though we never had calendars.

[21]Unbeknownst to me, Ebensee did not have a gas chamber.

[22]I left before I saw my former work group lift the train out, but I believe they couldn't accomplish the job and buried it in the crater.

[23]In Melk, some people became so addicted to cigarettes they traded their bread ration for them. As a result, they starved and eventually died from their addiction.

[24]This is a subject that is very hard to find written about anywhere. People don't talk about it. There is a statue located in the cemetery at the mass gravesite of people in Ebensee who died after the war. It is a naked man lying on his side with part of his buttock cut off. This statue was put up by Ebensee survivors and proves that cannibalism existed in Ebensee.

[25]Years later, I was in the Holocaust Museum in Washington, D.C. I had permission to be in the archives for several days. There was a special exhibit in the museum called "Liberation." A big poster displayed a famous liberation scene from Ebensee. There were a bunch of people wearing striped shirts, standing at the fence, and none of them are wearing pants. I asked the archive

director, "Do you know why these people have no pants?" He said he didn't. I then proceeded to tell him the story about why they weren't wearing trousers.

[26]I was traveling in Indonesia many years later and saw some beggar women with some terribly sick-looking babies. Passersby were giving them money. I later found out that these women rented the sick babies in order to play on the compassion of others. Whatever they made, they took a percentage as a commission to the parents. This was the same concept used when the organized group from the camp took me along with them. They wanted to elicit sympathy from the farmers.

[27]Before 1948, Israel was called Palestine.

[28]I found out later that they were Jehovah's Witnesses. "Searchers into the Holy Scriptures" is a Polish name meaning Bible Students. They risked their lives hiding Dziunka and Jack because they valued life and had no prejudices. They didn't do it for money; they wanted nothing in return. They hid them because it was the right thing to do.

[29]When I eventually came to America I learned that a report got back to President Truman about the bad conditions in displaced persons camps in Europe. The president sent the dean of the University of Pennsylvania, Earl G. Harrison, to investigate the conditions in Germany. Harrison reported: "The conditions have not changed. The people still live as if they are in the concentration camps. The Americans are guarding them now instead of the Germans. The Germans are walking around free, and these people are sitting behind barbed wire." Truman ordered Eisenhower to straighten things out in Germany. Things began to improve but the first six months living inside a displaced persons camp was difficult.

[30]According to statistics I saw later, the birth rate in displaced persons camps at that time was the highest in the world.

[31]*Wehrmacht*, meaning defense forces, coordinated the efforts of the German army (*heer*), navy (*kriegsmarine*) and air force (*luftwaffe*).

[32]Years later Professor Victoria Hertling of the University of Nevada, Reno, was in Warsaw researching a book she was writing about Plaszow. She found the record of Goeth's trial and made a copy for me. In the copy was an excerpt from the testimonial I wrote that day in Dachau. I quote Goeth asking: "*Willst du nicht oder kanst du nicht.*" meaning "Can't you do it, or won't you do it?" He asked this of a helpless prisoner not working to his satisfaction. Goeth frequently stopped people when he didn't like something he saw. There was no satisfactory answer to his question, and it always ended with the shooting death of the prisoner.

33Webster's Encyclopedic Unabridged Dictionary of the English Language defines begets (noun, plural) as genealogical lists especially those found in the Old Testament.

34A Kingdom Hall is where Jehovah's Witnesses meet for worship.

35A Circuit Overseer is an elder who has leadership responsibilities over a number of Christian congregations in an assigned territory.

36United States Holocaust Memorial Museum brochure entitled, *Jehovah's Witnesses.*

37See Appendix: Jehovah's Witness Article.

38Invited were several survivors, including Max and Simone Leibster, who lived in France. We became acquainted and talked for a while. Simone said, "What camps were you in?" The last one I mentioned was Ebensee. She looked at me in shock and exclaimed, "Ebensee!" She turned pale. Grabbing my arm, she took me aside to a private spot. She seemed to have a hard time speaking, but finally said, "Is it true that there was cannibalism in Ebensee?"

"Yes," I said. Then Simone went on to relate her father's story. He told her there were Russians in the camp scavenging the dead bodies for meat. Then, they began sneaking into the barracks cutting away flesh from the living. Simone said her father was afraid to fall asleep, terrified of what the Russians would do to him. At first when Simone's father returned home from Ebensee he didn't talk about his experiences, but after a while he began opening up and told her there was cannibalism in Ebensee. She didn't believe him; she thought he was out of his mind. Now, after all these years, she heard it from me, and she finally believed it.

39*Stasi* is the abbreviation for the German word *staatssicherheit* meaning state security. The *Stasi* were the East German secret police.

40Prior to World War II, Danzig was a free city-state that bordered Poland on the Baltic Sea. The Nazis took it over, and after the war, it came under Polish control.

41*Knocking* won Best Documentary, Jury Award, 2006 USA Film Festival (Dallas).

42http://www.jewishvirtuallibrary.org/jsource/Holocaust/nurlaws.html

43Some oral testimony is taken from The Mauthausen Survivor Documentation Project archives.

To find more of your favorite titles and authors, go to
www.lrpnv.com